The Smithsonian Guides to Natural America
SOUTHERN NEW ENGLAND

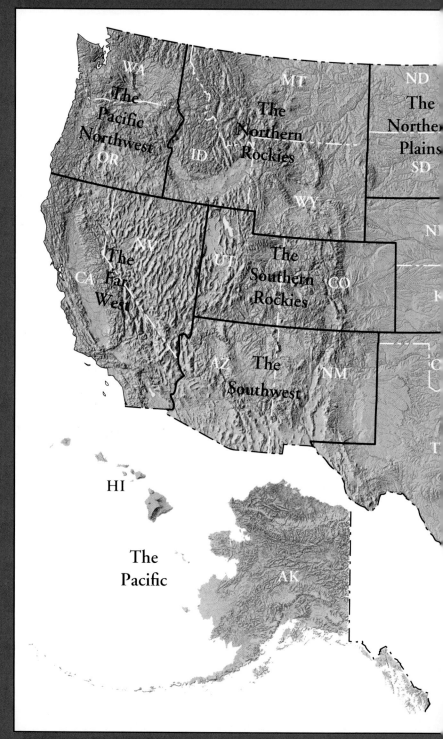

WA

The
Pacific
Northwest

OR

MT

The
Northern
Rockies

WY

ND

The
Norther
Plains

SD

N

NV

The
Far
West

CA

UT

The
Southern
Rockies

CO

K

AZ

The
Southwest

NM

C

HI

The
Pacific

AK

T

Northern
New
England

ME

VT

NH

Mass

Conn

The
Mid-Atlantic
States

NY

Southern
New
England

PA

OH

MD

The
Great
Lakes

MI

IN

WV

VA

The
Atlantic
Coast

MN

WI

IA

IL

KY

The
Heartland

MO

Central
Appalachia

TN

NC

The
South
Central
States

AR

MS

AL

GA

SC

The
Southeast

LA

FL

SOUTHERN NEW ENGLAND
MASSACHUSETTS – CONNECTICUT
RHODE ISLAND

THE SMITHSONIAN GUIDES TO NATURAL AMERICA

SOUTHERN NEW ENGLAND

MASSACHUSETTS, CONNECTICUT, AND RHODE ISLAND

TEXT
Robert Finch

PHOTOGRAPHY
Jonathan Wallen

PREFACE
Thomas E. Lovejoy

SMITHSONIAN BOOKS • WASHINGTON, D.C.
RANDOM HOUSE • NEW YORK, N.Y.

Front cover: Crane Beach, Ipswich, Massachusetts
Half-title page: Wild turkey, Felix Neck Wildlife Sanctuary, Martha's Vineyard
Frontispiece: Berkshire Mountains near Shelburne, Massachusetts
Back cover: Tiger swallowtail; showy lady's slipper; peregrine falcon

THE SMITHSONIAN INSTITUTION
SECRETARY I. Michael Heyman
COUNSELOR TO THE SECRETARY FOR BIODIVERSITY
AND ENVIRONMENTAL AFFAIRS Thomas E. Lovejoy
ACTING DIRECTOR, SMITHSONIAN INSTITUTION PRESS Daniel H. Goodwin

SMITHSONIAN BOOKS
ACTING EDITOR IN CHIEF Alexis Doster III
MARKETING MANAGER Susan E. Romatowski

THE SMITHSONIAN GUIDES TO NATURAL AMERICA
SERIES EDITOR Sandra Wilmot
MANAGING EDITOR Ellen Scordato
PHOTO EDITOR Mary Jenkins
ART DIRECTOR Mervyn Clay
ASSISTANT PHOTO EDITOR Ferris Cook
ASSISTANT PHOTO EDITOR Rebecca Williams
ASSISTANT EDITOR Seth Ginsberg
COPY EDITORS Helen Dunn, Karen Hammonds
FACT CHECKER Jean Cotterell
PRODUCTION DIRECTOR Katherine Rosenbloom

Library of Congress Cataloging-in-Publication Data
Finch, Robert.
    The Smithsonian guides to natural America. Southern New England—
Massachusetts, Connecticut, and Rhode Island/ text, Robert Finch;
photography, Jonathan Wallen; preface, Thomas E. Lovejoy
        p. cm.
    Includes bibliographical references and index.
    ISBN 0-679-76475-5 (pbk.)
    1. Natural history—Connecticut—Guidebooks. 2. Natural history—
Rhode Island—Guidebooks. 3. Natural history—Massachusetts
—Guidebooks. 4. Connecticut—Guidebooks. 5. Rhode Island
—Guidebooks. 6. Massachusetts—Guidebooks. I. Wallen, Jonathan.
II. Title.
QH104.5.N4F46 1996   95-26053
508.74—dc20   CIP

Manufactured in the United States of America
98765432

How to Use This Book

The SMITHSONIAN GUIDES TO NATURAL AMERICA explore and celebrate the preserved and protected natural areas of this country that are open for the public to use and enjoy. From world-famous national parks to tiny local preserves, the places featured in these guides offer a splendid panoply of this nation's natural wonders.

Divided by state and region, this book offers suggested itineraries for travelers, briefly describing the high points of each preserve, refuge, park, or wilderness area along the way. Each site was chosen for a specific reason: Some are noted for their botanical, zoological, or geological significance, others simply for their exceptional scenic beauty.

Information pertaining to the area as a whole can be found in the introductory sections to the book and to each chapter. In addition, specialized maps at the beginning of each book and chapter highlight an area's geography and geological features as well as pinpoint the specific locales that the author describes.

For quick reference, places of interest are set in **boldface** type; those set in **boldface** followed by the symbol ❖ are listed in the Site Guide at the back of the book. (This feature begins on page 259, just before the index.) Here noteworthy sites are listed alphabetically by state, and each entry provides practical information that visitors need: telephone numbers, mailing addresses, and specific services available.

Addresses and telephone numbers of national, state, and local agencies and organizations are also listed. Also in appendices are a glossary of pertinent scientific terms and designations used to describe natural areas; the author's recommendations for further reading (both nonfiction and fiction); and a list of sources that can aid travelers planning a guided visit.

The words and images of these guides are meant to help both the active naturalist and the armchair traveler to appreciate more fully the environmental diversity and natural splendor of this country. To ensure a successful visit, always contact a site in advance to obtain detailed maps, updated information on hours and fees, and current weather conditions. Many areas maintain a fragile ecological balance. Remember that their continued vitality depends in part on responsible visitors who tread the land lightly.

CONTENTS

HOW TO USE THIS BOOK   vii

PREFACE by Thomas E. Lovejoy   xii

INTRODUCTION   2

PART I MASSACHUSETTS   18

ONE   Southeastern Massachusetts:
        The Legacy of the Ice   20

TWO   Eastern Massachusetts:
        Urban Wilds and Rocky Shores   60

THREE   Central Massachusetts: The Plateau
        and the Connecticut River Valley   88

FOUR   Western Massachusetts:
        The Berkshire Hills and Marble Valleys   114

Part II CONNECTICUT   148

   Five Western Connecticut: The Metacomet
         Ridge and Western Highlands   150

    Six Eastern Connecticut: The River,
         Eastern Shore, and Highlands   184

Part III RHODE ISLAND   208

  Seven Rhode Island:
         The Ocean State   210

         Further Reading   252

         Glossary   254

         Land Management Resources   256

         Nature Travel   258

         Site Guide   259

         Index   274

PREFACE

The long history of human impact on the landscape of southern New England belies the richness of its natural history. The region provided endless wonderment for me when, as a youth, I cut my naturalist's teeth. Here one can find *Opuntia,* or prickly-pear cactus, on traprock ridges; a remarkable marine mollusk, *Crepidula,* which can change its sex; an extraordinary zoological discovery, the primitive arthropod *Hutchinsoniella,* in the sediments of Long Island Sound; or a carnivorous aquatic plant, the Goose Pond bladderwort.

The imprint of glacial periods is strong. Massachusetts, Connecticut, and Rhode Island are dotted with the lakes and ponds left by glaciers, including Linsley Pond (now Linsley Lake) near Branford, Connecticut, where so much early research on the ecology of freshwater was conducted, and Long Pond in Plymouth, Massachusetts, a much-loved family retreat. Glacial drumlins form islands in Boston Harbor, and terminal moraines where glaciers spilled their rocky, sandy burden today form islands such as Nantucket and Martha's Vineyard. Most famous of all is the glacial erratic or boulder known as Plymouth Rock, a piece of which sits on a red plush pillow in the Smithsonian's Arts and Industries Building as part of the re-creation of the 1876 Centennial exhibition.

Older geological features of the region include steplike traprock ridges such as the two that frame New Haven, Connecticut, one of which Dutch mariner Adriaen Block named Roodeborg or "Red Hill" in 1614. Dinosaur footprints, apparently so fresh one seems to have just missed the dinosaurs themselves, are abundant in some spots in the Connecticut Valley.

Southern New England is also a part of natural America where much can be appreciated on a small scale. In the Berkshires of Massachusetts, the 277-acre Bartholomew's Cobble includes such a variety of

---

PRECEDING PAGES: *As if tumbled from a giant's beanbag, granite boulders brought by glaciers line the base of Block Island's Mohegan Bluffs.*

alkaline and acid habitat that roughly 700 species of plants occur including an astonishing 53 species of ferns and 500 species of wildflowers.

This region boasts extensive coastline, and despite the loss of nearly half its wetlands, many natural areas remain. Most famous of course are Cape Cod in Massachusetts and Rhode Island's Narragansett Bay, but much of the shore, even that long used for harbors and other facilities, is home to abundant wildlife. On Monomoy Island off the Cape's southeastern tip a profusion of sandpipers and other shorebirds skitter along the waterline in a perpetual dance with the movement of waves and tides.

Although the nation's smallest state, Rhode Island has plenty of natural attractions. In addition to its impressive bay, the state's borders encompass Great Swamp (a terrific spot for bird-watching); Little Compton and neighboring islands; and Block Island, one of the few places where the American burying beetle survives and home too for the Block Island vole.

Southern New England undeniably has been heavily used and marked by people. Extensive deforestation for agriculture and timber has had the largest impact, but quite significant as well was the pre-colonial Native American management of the landscape, so brilliantly analyzed by historian William Cronon in *Changes in the Land*. The current return of New England forests is one of the great land-use stories of natural America, but it is important to realize that the return does not mean full recovery. The American elms that so bewitched Charles Dickens on a visit to southern New England are mostly gone, as is the American chestnut, a keystone food source for much of the region's wildlife. Efforts continue to find disease-resistant forms of these species, and the remains of one such experiment with chestnuts by Arthur Harmount Graves can still be seen by those who know how to find their way to the right spot in the White Memorial Foundation in Litchfield, Connecticut. On Martha's Vineyard, the last heath hen was recorded in 1932. However, wood duck populations have recovered in an effort in which the Smithsonian's eighth secretary, S. Dillon Ripley,

---

OVERLEAF: *Bounding over its rocky bed, the Cold River rushes through Mohawk Trail State Forest, one of the wildest places in Massachusetts.*

participated, and wild turkey now roam again in less-populous areas. Atlantic salmon once again swim up the Connecticut River, in an area chosen by the Nature Conservancy as one of its Last Great Places in the Western Hemisphere. Populations of ospreys have recovered from the effects of DDT and other pesticides and are abundant once more in places such as Great Island, off Cape Cod, Massachusetts, where I had a chance to play a small part in the recovery effort.

Southern New England has been a region that has greatly influenced how Americans think about natural America. It has been home to great nature writers such as Henry Beston, who wrote *The Outermost House,* and Edwin Way Teale. The Gifford Pinchot Sycamore in Simsbury, Connecticut, commemorates the man who created the nation's first forestry school and is largely responsible for the creation of the United States Forest Service itself. Towering over all is Henry David Thoreau, whose Walden Pond in Concord, Massachusetts, lies not far from Longfellow's rude bridge that arched the flood. Today, in Old Lyme, Connecticut, Roger Tory Peterson, whose field guides and bird paintings did so much to enhance access to natural America, lives, paints, and writes.

The joy and challenge of southern New England is that there is so much nature from which to choose: The Litchfield Hills and the Cathedral Pines; the Myles Standish Forest and the Plymouth redbelly turtle, which was a perpetual pleasure for an older cousin of mine with herpetological leanings; the tidewater arrowhead and Torrey's bulrush in the wetlands of the Connecticut River; the yellow lady's slippers at Lime Rock Preserve. Whatever wonders you choose to investigate, Robert Finch's text and Jonathan Wallen's photographs will lead you to many more.

—Thomas E. Lovejoy
Counselor to the Secretary for
Biodiversity and Environmental Affairs,
SMITHSONIAN INSTITUTION

LEFT: *A sunlit woodland trail beckons visitors to explore the 4,000-acre White Memorial Foundation, a quiet private preserve that includes the largest old-growth stand of hemlock and white pine in Connecticut.*

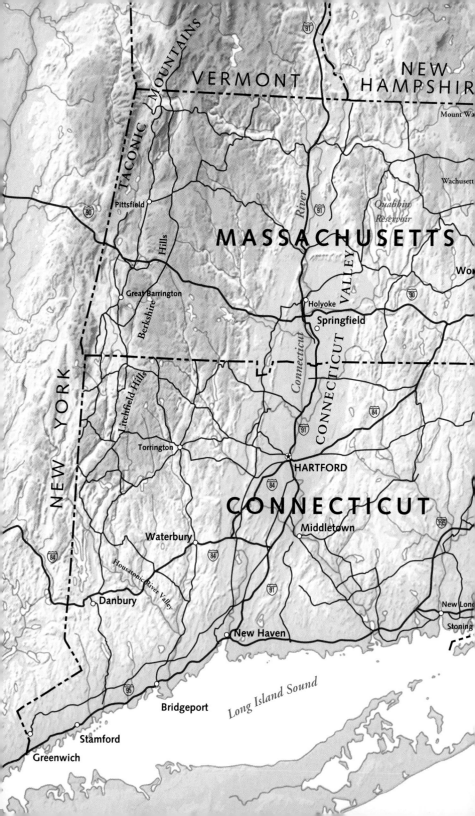

SOUTHERN
NEW ENGLAND

25   0   25 Miles

25   0   25 Kilometers

INTRODUCTION

INTRODUCTION:
SOUTHERN NEW ENGLAND

In the late autumn of 1620, when a sea-weary band of English Pilgrims entered Cape Cod Bay and made their first landfall in Provincetown Harbor, their future governor, William Bradford, described the scene before them as "a hideous and desolate wilderness, full of wild beasts and wild men." A few weeks later, settled across the bay in Plymouth, the new arrivals began to take a second look. They soon discovered that the rugged southeastern coast of Massachusetts was clearly inhabited—and far from untamed. Cornfields, fish weirs, longhouses, and other structures dotted the landscape. The surrounding forests reflected careful agricultural and game management. For centuries the Wampanoag nation had prospered here, like their predecessors millennia earlier. In the end, the Pilgrims owed their survival to the skill and benevolence of the resident "wild men."

Today, few people would mistake any part of southern New England for a "wilderness." Indeed, its history reveals a thoroughness and intensity of human use probably unmatched by any other area of the country. Working hard to scratch a living from the region's stony soil, the first European farmers cleared pastures and fields, built innumerable stone walls, and burned 30 or 40 cords of hardwood each winter to keep warm. The colonists cut virgin timber to build their farms, their towns, and their ships. By the mid-nineteenth century, nearly 90 percent of the landscape was deforested—an ecological transformation that, in proportion, outstrips the current destruction of tropical rain forests.

The Industrial Revolution in the United States also began in southern New England when the first textile factories were established in Lowell, Massachusetts, in the 1820s. All over the region rivers were dammed and canals built to provide power to the mills and a means to ship the manufactured product. Railroads quickly transformed the landscape; the celebrated Hoosac Tunnel (1875), for instance, was blasted through the mountains of western Massachusetts to connect Boston and Albany. On the

---

PRECEDING PAGES: *From the Mount Greylock Visitor Center in Lanesborough, Massachusetts, the gentle summit of Potter Mountain materializes through a purple haze above a meadow of goldenrod and milkweed.*

coast, nearly half the region's wetlands and marshes were filled, dredged, or otherwise altered to create harbors, waterways, and facilities for the growing fishing and shipping industries, turning Boston, Providence, New Haven, and other coastal cities into booming metropolises. In this century, a complex network of highways and interstates have been constructed to accommodate an increasingly mobile population.

Today, to the motorist traveling I-95 from New York to Boston, the region sometimes seems one uninterrupted strip of decaying industrial areas and sprawling suburban subdivisions. But, as in the case of the Pilgrims, first impressions can be deceiving. On closer inspection—off the main arteries—southern New England possesses a rich natural heritage, one that should be appreciated for what it is rather than what it is not.

Nature in southern New England is different from nature in other areas of the country. There are few vast tracts or spectacular vistas and no national forests or national parks; the largest expanse of publicly owned land is a reservoir. The characteristic "natural area" of the region is a 300-acre sanctuary owned by a private or municipal conservation organization, not a 3-million-acre federal wilderness area. Here natural beauty rests in thousands of exquisite details, quietly preserved in small places.

Visitors quickly discover that hardly a square mile of the southern New England landscape has not been substantially altered by human activity. In the middle of a dense woodland, hikers find foundations of old mills and houses or the crumbling remnants of long-abandoned dams and stone walls. A major natural area may well lie next to a busy highway or within sight of an urban skyline; some even have power lines or railroad tracks running through them.

Today's communities of plants and wildlife too are often the result of interactions between humans and nature. For instance, about 22 percent of New England's original flora—especially indigenous wildflowers and grasses—has been supplanted by introduced aliens, which have naturalized themselves even in "wild" settings. And more than in other regions, many original animal species—wolves, caribou, wolverines, mountain lions, walruses—were driven or hunted out long ago.

Still, southern New England's landscape is not so much "used" or secondhand as historical, incorporating human as well as natural history. That combination of histories is not necessarily regrettable, nor does it diminish the nature of the region. As William Cronon observes in *Changes in the Land,* "Our project must be to locate a nature which is within rather than without history, for only by so doing can we find human communities which are inside rather than outside nature."

The region's basic landforms are the result of ancient, complex forces that long predate the presence of human beings. Encompassing some of the oldest and youngest geologic formations on the continent, southern New England possesses one of the world's most violent geologic histories. Here for more than half a billion years, the large, constantly shifting portions of

the earth's crust known as continental plates have collided repeatedly. The force of these impacts threw up massive mountain ranges, which over eons eroded down to nearly level plateaus, only to be uplifted again by the next continental collision. This repeated crushing of the plates formed the north-south orientation of the region's major mountain ranges and river valleys, which in turn determined much of its settlement history and even today's traffic patterns.

Above: *Once common in the region, eastern bluebirds are now much rarer because of increased competition from starlings and English sparrows.*

Right: *Wet meadows in Massachusetts's Berkshire Hills provide some of the region's most colorful autumn foliage.*

The second of these continental collisions, about 380 million years ago, raised the great northern Appalachian Range, mountains that may once have towered as high as the Andes. Today's modest Berkshire and Litchfield hills and the Taconic Range are the worn-down roots of these ancient ranges. Today no peak in the region reaches 4,000 feet, and the average is only 2,000 feet. Although people often associate granite with New England, that igneous rock is relatively scarce in southern New England, generally appearing east of the Connecticut River—in the Blue Hills near Boston, western Rhode Island, and on the rock-bound coast of Cape Ann. Most of southern New England's hills are composed of schist and gneiss, resistant, metamorphic rocks with a layered texture, resembling the pages of a book when seen end-on. The hills were formed when mudstone and sandstone, respectively, were heated and pressed deep in the crust of the earth, then raised during the mountain-building periods. Folded, uplifted, thrust sideways, tilted, warped, twisted, in places even flipped entirely over, these hills' long, tortured history is apparent in many of the region's road cuts.

Between the mountain-building epochs, inland seas covered the area for eons, and the thick layers of sedimentary rock—sandstone, shale, limestone—that accumulated were often thousands of feet deep. Running south through the Berkshires in western Massachusetts and Connecticut, the Housatonic River valley contains such large deposits of marble, a metamorphic form of limestone, that it is often called the Marble Valley.

Some 200 million years ago the continental plates were ripped apart, forming several rift valleys in the region. By far the largest—known as the Great Crack—is the Connecticut Valley, a 100-mile lowland that splits the region in half from north to south, forming the bed of New England's largest river, the Connecticut. Intense volcanic activity followed. Three times molten magma forced its way up through the valley's thick sandstone layers. Eventually the lava hardened into a crystalline rock called basalt. As a result of the Great Crack, the eastern edge of the valley slipped, or faulted, dropping thousands of feet and tilting the entire lowland from west to east. Subsequent erosion then removed the softer sandstone and exposed the hard basalt, which today forms a prominent series of "traprock" ridges—with steep westward-facing cliffs and gentle easterly slopes—that run from New Haven to Holyoke.

Major tectonic activity in southern New England ceased about 150 million years ago. Although not unknown, earthquakes are rare and usually mild, and there are no active volcanoes. Erosion continued to wear down the western and eastern hills, and today only a few peaks, such as

Wachusett Mountain and Mount Watatic, rise above the nearly even plateau of eastern Massachusetts.

About three million years ago vast ice sheets began to move south from central Canada, periodically blanketing the region in ice up to a mile thick. The advances and retreats of these massive glaciers transformed the terrain and created the distinctive landscape that is southern New England today. Often progressing only inches per year, the glaciers flowed south like giant bulldozers, leveling the remnants of the ancient Appalachians and transforming sharp V-shaped gorges into the U-shaped valleys that currently characterize the area. As mountaintops were scoured off, thousands of boulders known as glacial erratics were carried along and dumped, sometimes hundreds of miles away, in geologically alien terrain. Because glaciers carved depressions in the land and dammed ancient drainages, the present-day landscape boasts an abundance of lakes, ponds, and wetlands.

Plowing areas that are now ocean bottoms, the glaciers left large ridges of unconsolidated gravel, sand, and clay hundreds of feet tall; these form the low hills of Cape Cod, Martha's Vineyard, Nantucket, and Block Island. When they encountered resistant granite ridges, the glaciers climbed over them, often breaking off the southern faces and creating steep ridges like those found in western Rhode Island. The glaciers shaped their own debris into smooth oval hills known as drumlins—which today form many of the islands in Boston Harbor—or carried it in streams beneath the ice, leaving long, sinuous deposits known as eskers. They scoured the soil from the land, left countless rocks behind, and produced the stony terrain that New England farmers have cursed for generations.

The most recent ice sheet melted from the region about 12,000 years ago. Pollen analyses of bog deposits from this time reveal that a northern boreal forest of spruce and arctic birch existed here some 10,000 years ago, about the time the first humans arrived. Many of the area's large animals—mastodons, giant ground sloths, camels, saber-toothed tigers, horses—died out then, perhaps hunted to extinction by Paleo-Indians. If so, these first New Englanders soon developed a lifestyle more in balance with their environment. Recent ecohistorians have documented how Native Americans used and changed the landscape in ways compatible with its resources.

OVERLEAF: *English oaks lift their stately limbs above a luminous swath of Queen Anne's lace. Both of these European immigrants seem perfectly at home at World's End Reservation in Hingham, Massachusetts.*

Southern New England

Although relations between the first European settlers and the indigenous inhabitants were generally peaceful, disease, appropriation of land, and cultural disruption fragmented and decimated the native peoples within decades of the Europeans' arrival. But a number of tribes—the Gay Head and Mashpee Wampanoag in Massachusetts, the Mashantocket in eastern Connecticut, the Narragansett in Rhode Island—managed to maintain their cultural identity and continuity over the centuries. Original Indian names suffuse the map of southern New England, including from Webster, Massachusetts, the longest place name in the country, Lake Chargoggagoggman-chauggagoggchaubunagungamaugg (said to mean, "You fish on your side, I fish on my side, nobody fishes in the middle, no trouble").

The first Europeans settled along the coast and major river valleys during the 1600s. By the early 1700s colonists were pushing into the hills and remote valleys in search of farmland, and by the mid-1800s the original forests of southern New England were virtually gone. As fertile lands opened to the West, much of New England's hard-won farmland was abandoned; after the Civil War only a few areas, such as the Connecticut Valley, continued to support agriculture on a large scale. Pines seeded into the untended fields, and then hardwood sprouts recolonized the pastureland. Today forests cover southern New England to a greater degree than at any time since the arrival of the Pilgrims and their contemporaries.

Biologically speaking, southern New England is a transitional region. Predominating in most of Connecticut and Rhode Island are southern hardwood forests, characterized by oak, hickory, yellow poplar, red maple, black birch, and dogwood. The Berkshires and the top tier of Massachusetts, on the other hand, are home to pure stands of northern hardwoods—beech, sugar maple, white birch, spruce, hemlock, and white pine. The forests of central Massachusetts are a judicious mixture of the two, and on Cape Cod and the islands, pitch-pine and scrub-oak forests are the rule.

Southern New England's glacial history and generous rainfall (about 42 inches annually) are responsible for its abundance of wetland habitats, including maple and cedar swamps, sphagnum and spruce bogs, salt marshes, and vernal pools. Cape Cod also represents an important marine boundary. Because the waters in Cape Cod Bay average some 10 degrees colder than those immediately to the south, northern species (cod, winter flounder, blue mussels) share the waters with more southerly species (blue crabs, striped bass, tuna).

Southern New England has generally temperate (although notoriously changeable) weather, ranging from an average summer temperature in the

70s to about 30 degrees Fahrenheit in winter, depending on location. Because the ocean functions as a massive heat reservoir, temperatures along the coast are relatively stable, warmer in winter and cooler in summer than at inland sites. Extreme winter lows, for example, can range from 10 degrees in coastal areas such as Nantucket to minus 30 degrees in the northern Berkshires. Spring months on the coast are foggy and wetter than they are inland, but fall is generally warmer and more extended. The ocean affects not only coastal weather, but geography as well. Northeast storms and the occasional hurricane batter the coastline, often causing severe property damage. One of the most destructive storms to hit the region was the 1938 hurricane, which killed hundreds of people, destroyed numerous coastal homes and bridges, and toppled vast swaths of forest. In Rhode Island and central Massachusetts today, one can still find groves of fallen trunks pointing northwest like giant compass needles, mute weathervanes of the legendary storm that felled them more than a half century ago.

Even though southern New England has experienced heavy residential and commercial development during the last 50 years, some of the oldest state, local, and private conservation groups in the country have significantly stemmed the loss of natural areas. These include the Massachusetts Audubon Society, the Trustees of Reservations, the Nature Conservancy, and the Connecticut Parks and Forest Association. Several of the country's first state forests were created here from abandoned farmland. Still, the vast majority of southern New England's natural areas are small—thousands of refuges, preserves, and conservation areas often occupying only a few acres. (Middlesex County alone, encompassing the western suburbs of Boston, contains more than 700 municipal conservation areas.) As a result, many sites take some effort to find, but the unexpected solitude and wildness they offer is all the more rewarding.

Southern New England possesses more birders per acre than any other region in the country—and for good reason. Some 400 species of birds can be sighted here, 333 in Rhode Island alone. The most spectacular avian concentrations occur during spring and fall migration periods. Ducks and warblers move through river bottoms and coastal areas in April and May. In late summer tens of thousands of shorebirds and waterfowl stop in coastal refuges like the North Shore's Plum Island and Monomoy Island on the southeastern tip of Cape Cod. In early fall, along ridges in the central and western hills, thousands of hawks and other raptors soar southward on thermal air currents.

Thanks to the reforestation of much of the region in this century and the

growth of wildlife conservation programs, many species—such as bears, bobcats, ospreys, piping plover, and timber rattlesnakes—have been saved from extinction; others—beavers, salmon, wild turkeys, bald eagles—have been successfully reintroduced. Several species have increased or arrived on their own, including white-tailed deer, moose, cardinals, opossums, cormorants, and coyotes.

Despite such advances, on many fronts environmental losses still outweigh gains. Development continues to consume open space and agricultural land and threaten water quality in many areas, particularly along the coast. And although the automobiles of a mobile populace increasingly clog the highways, access to the land is more difficult than in the past. A telling comparison appears in two early auto-tour books, *Massachusetts Beautiful* and *Connecticut Beautiful,* written by Wallace Nutting and published in 1923. Reading them today, one is struck by the casual freedom with which the author pulls off the road to explore a scenic pond, meadow, or beach that catches his eye. Today, unless such an area is clearly designated for public access, the motorist risks a fine or towing. Public access to beaches has become especially restricted in Massachusetts in recent decades. An old colonial law extends private property rights down to the mean low-tide line, and a boundary can extend up to a mile offshore. Thus, although in Connecticut and Rhode Island walkers can legally stroll most beaches below the high-tide line, in Massachusetts many private beaches are off limits to the public.

Some environmental losses seem beyond local or even regional control. During the last few years, for instance, migratory songbird populations have declined. Birds such as wood thrushes, warblers, and towhees seem to have been hit with a double whammy: development and fragmentation of their forest breeding grounds here and deforestation of their wintering grounds in the tropics. The numbers of some native salamander and frog species have also noticeably decreased, probably due to the increasing acidification of the region's ponds and wetlands. Offshore, over the last 30 years, commercial fish stocks of cod, haddock, and yellowtail flounder have been seriously—perhaps irretrievably—depleted by overfishing.

Numerous habitats have been invaded by alien plants and animals, resulting in a decline of native species and of biodiversity. During this cen-

LEFT: *In the fall, marsh samphire, a glasswort, glows like a bed of red coals among the feathery grasses at the Parker River preserve on Plum Island, the northernmost link in a rich chain of migratory bird refuges.*

tury New England has already lost two major trees—the elm and the chestnut—to imported diseases. Today, several more tree species are seriously threatened by invasive alien organisms, most notably the native eastern hemlock by an insect parasite known as the woolly adelgid.

Because human beings have been altering and affecting the environment here for at least 10,000 years, distinguishing the natural from the artificial is often difficult. Such distinctions, however, are probably futile. Humans are now an integral—and inevitable—ingredient of any landscape in southern New England. In the end, we must determine what level of human impact best fosters the long-term survival of the rich diversity of life and habitats that are a particular region's heritage, and then adapt our population, behavior, and use appropriately. Nowhere is this question more pressing than in southern New England.

Today there is still enough natural wealth for all, although most of it is not visible through the windshield. The landscape demands a gentle approach, on foot, and an informed gaze primed to appreciate the small. Raised on photographs of the earth's most spectacular locales, we need to refocus our eyes a bit to see and appreciate the richness of the world close beside us. The rewards are singular and abundant.

As Hudson River naturalist John Burroughs remarked, "In the West one lifts his eyes to grand sizes and vistas; here in the Northeast we look down at our feet to see Nature." The region's most famous naturalist, Henry David Thoreau, chronicled in loving detail the small wonders of his native town, boasting that he had "traveled widely in Concord." The hope and aim of this book are to help you travel more widely and deeply in southern New England.

RIGHT: *Glacial cobblestones and human footprints pattern the dunes at Rhode Island's Block Island National Wildlife Refuge. Fragile but flexible, barrier dunes are natural barricades against the encroaching sea.*

MASSACHUSETTS

PART ONE
MASSACHUSETTS

Massachusetts is better known for its rich cultural and political history than for its natural landscapes. Places such as Bunker Hill, Faneuil Hall, the Old North Church, and Concord's Minute Man Bridge reflect the state's reputation as the birthplace of American liberty. Also the birthplace of America's industrial revolution, Massachusetts is today one of the most densely populated and heavily industrialized states in the nation. Nevertheless, Massachusetts possesses a surprising abundance of natural areas, and its 8,257 square miles contain a greater variety of habitats than any other New England state. Some of the most popular recreational areas in the country—Cape Cod, Nantucket, the Berkshire Hills—are found here, as well as one of the most venerated natural sites in the world: Concord's Walden Pond.

Among northeastern states only Maine has a longer coastline, and Massachusetts's is more varied, encompassing long sandy barrier beaches, island archipelagoes, pitch-pine barrens, sand-plain grasslands, heaths, glacial bluffs, extensive salt marshes, cranberry bogs, cedar swamps, kettle-hole ponds, glacial drumlins, and bold granite headlands. Traveling inland from east to west, visitors encounter rolling farmland and open fields; extensive freshwater marshes and sphagnum bogs; granite gorges and isolated monadnocks; several river valleys, including a portion of the Connecticut, New England's largest; volcanic traprock ridges; old-growth stands; three major forest types; and two mountain ranges, culminating in 3,491-foot Mount Greylock in the northwest corner.

Certain features of the Massachusetts landscape are striking by any standards: the parabolic dunes of the Province Lands on Cape Cod, Martha's Vineyard's colorful Gay Head cliffs, the pearl-like string of the Elizabeth Islands, the autumnal blaze of Nantucket's moors, the great Oxbow of the Connecticut River seen from Mount Holyoke, and the jagged quartz towers of Monument Mountain in the Berkshires. The abundant evidence of past human use in many of the state's dedicated conservation areas often makes them more striking, and some artifacts—lighthouses, cranberry bogs, ancient farmsteads, and white-steepled churches—have been part of the landscape for so long that they seem a natural extension of it.

PRECEDING PAGES: *Native maples, beeches, and birches set the hills of October Mountain State Forest ablaze during the forest's namesake month.*

Interestingly, some of Massachusetts's most valued "natural" landscapes were created by land-use practices that would be frowned upon today. The spectacular dunes of Cape Cod's Province Lands, for example, are the result of overgrazing by cattle in the eighteenth century. The famous moors of Nantucket are likewise the product of the 20,000 sheep that once inhabited that island. The Quabbin Reservoir in central Massachusetts—an artificial body of water on the site of five former towns—is now the largest protected "natural" area in the region and its premier wildlife refuge. In these and many other landscapes across the state, even a limited ability to read the ecological and human history of a place can add a dramatic element to one's appreciation and enjoyment of it.

A variety of Native American tribes of the Algonquian-language group (including the eponymous Massachusetts tribe of the Massachusetts Bay area) inhabited the state for thousands of years before the arrival of the first European settlers in the early seventeenth century. The Puritan leaders of the Massachusetts Bay colony, established in 1630, firmly believed in independent congregational self-rule, a legacy that later translated into a strong political tradition of independent "home rule," or local control, centered on that unique New England institution of participatory democracy, the town meeting.

This tradition of independent local institutions is also evident in the many distinctive home-grown conservation groups that have been instrumental in preserving Massachusetts's natural areas. The Trustees of Reservations, established in 1891 by Charles Eliot of Boston and now the oldest private conservation organization in the country, owns some 12,000 acres of land, much of it former estates of wealthy Boston Brahmins. The Massachusetts Audubon Society, the first such association in America (*not* to be confused with the younger National Audubon Society), owns some 22,000 acres that preserve outstanding examples of the state's landscapes.

Most remarkable, perhaps, are the great number of municipality-owned conservation properties. Statewide nearly 3,000 natural areas totaling more than 86,000 acres are locally owned, the majority in the more densely populated eastern half. Supplemented by conservation restrictions, private land trusts, and state and federal holdings, Massachusetts's natural areas are among the most extensive and varied in the country. Although only a representative selection of so many areas can be included here, brochures, guidebooks, and inventories are available from all the major organizations and most communities. The more obscure areas are well worth seeking out because some of the best are among the least visited.

SOUTHEASTERN MASSACHUSETTS:
THE LEGACY OF THE ICE

The peninsulas, islands, and archipelagoes of southeastern Massachusetts have long been one of America's premier coastal resorts. Each summer millions of space-starved visitors are drawn to long sandy beaches and wind-sculpted dunes, to clear kettle ponds and lush salt marshes, to sheltered harbors, stunted pitch-pine and scrub-oak forests, and wine-colored cranberry bogs. In the mid-nineteenth century Henry David Thoreau wrote that on Cape Cod's outer beaches, "a man may stand and put all America behind him." Although today, on a hot July afternoon, a visitor may feel as if all America is in front of him, solitude and natural beauty still await the traveler here.

Strolling along a sun-drenched strand as a light summer breeze caresses bare limbs, visitors may have difficulty imagining that these soft, gentle lands are the product of violent arctic forces. Yet Cape Cod, Nantucket, Martha's Vineyard, and most of Plymouth County are the handiwork of the Wisconsin Stage Glacier, the last of four massive ice sheets that buried and scraped southern New England's ancient coastal plain for a million and a half years.

Progressing south in three giant lobes, the glacier reached its farthest advance some 25,000 years ago. There it stalled, depositing, in conveyor-belt fashion, millions of tons of glacial till and boulders. Today these terminal moraines form the low hills and ridges of Nantucket and Martha's

LEFT: *Like a meandering tidal creek, a wooden boardwalk at Wellfleet Bay Wildlife Sanctuary winds through a salt marsh to Try Island, home to the northernmost breeding population of diamondback terrapins.*

Vineyard. The ice retreated and a few thousand years later stalled again. The glacier's western arm, the Buzzards Bay lobe, left a spine of rock-strewn hills down the western shore of Cape Cod and the lovely Elizabeth Islands stretching southwest from Woods Hole. The middle or Cape Cod Bay lobe formed the inner shore of Cape Cod Bay and the line of bluffs and ridges ringing it from Plymouth's Manomet Hills to North Truro's High Head. The South Channel lobe, lying east of Cape Cod, produced the "forearm" of the lower Cape from Chatham to Truro.

The landscape of southeastern Massachusetts still displays its glacial legacy. Often stranded far from their place of origin, ice-age boulders called glacial erratics—rocks plucked from mountaintops or plowed up from the ocean floor—dot the terrain, especially along the upper Cape. The region's deep, clear ponds began as giant ice chunks buried in glacial till and debris. Those chunks, melting as the glaciers retreated, left distinctive depressions in the land. Eventually filling with water, the indentations, with no inlet or outlet, became known as kettle-hole ponds.

The rising sea contoured the present shoreline, eroding, smoothing, and elongating the rough edges of the glacial deposits into graceful, often fantastic forms. Facing the open Atlantic and bearing the brunt of the erosion, the eastern shore of the Lower Cape has been sculpted into a superlative 26-mile curve of ocean bluffs known as the Outer Beach of Cape Cod. Material washed from cliffs and coastlines has been reshaped into the numerous barrier beaches and dune systems that fringe southeastern Massachusetts. These beaches, in turn, provide natural barricades that protect the area's extensive salt marshes, which are critical to many species of marine and terrestrial wildlife and one of the most productive ecosystems in the world.

Southeastern Massachusetts is the site of the oldest European settlements in New England. Having touched land at what is now Provincetown in November 1620, the *Mayflower* Pilgrims discovered evidence of even earlier visitors: a skeleton with blond hair in a Wampanoag grave. The Pilgrims eventually settled in Plymouth, but within decades, satellite communities appeared on Cape Cod, where the Europeans found available land, good soil, and abundant salt marshes, which provided natural pastures and sources of hay.

OVERLEAF: *Catching the early morning sun, arching yellow clusters of seaside goldenrod and tall seed heads of American beach grass fringe a barrier beach at Demarest Lloyd State Park on Buzzards Bay.*

ABOVE: *In full plumage, a resplendent tom turkey struts before his less flamboyant harem. Wild turkeys have been successfully reintroduced to much of their former range.*

RIGHT: *Eastern redcedars invade an old pasture at Ellisville State Park. Their berrylike fruit has long been used to flavor gin.*

Thick woodlands once covered all of New England. In this area, from all accounts, large native trees supplied the heavy beams needed for houses and ships. By 1800, however, most of the original forests of southeastern Massachusetts had been cut, loosing the fragile soil, which literally blew away in the constant winds. As early as 1822 a visitor named Timothy Dwight described the hills of outer Cape Cod as "a vast Sahara." The land has taken centuries to recover from this early overcutting, especially on the Cape and Islands, where many areas have been reforested only within the last generation or two.

The itinerary for this chapter begins at Plymouth, proceeds south across the Cape Cod Canal, and turns east along the inner shore of Cape Cod Bay to Orleans. The route then heads north, tracing the "arm" of the Cape up to Provincetown and back to Chatham. Next it travels west along the Cape's southern shore to the canal, continuing to Buzzards Bay, New Bedford, and the Rhode Island line. Separate sections cover the islands of Nantucket and Martha's Vineyard, accessible by ferry from Hyannis or Woods Hole and by air from Hyannis or Boston.

CAPE COD BAY: FROM PLYMOUTH TO ORLEANS

Cape Cod Bay is the most prominent bight in the coastline of Massachusetts. On a clear day, from any coastal promontory—Plymouth's Manomet Hills, Dennis's Scargo Tower, North Truro's High Head—one can discern the entire sickle-shaped shoreline of the Cape Cod peninsula, or to use Thoreau's famous metaphor, "the bare and bended arm of Massachusetts."

Fronting the harbor in Plymouth Center, **Pilgrim Memorial State Park❖** is the smallest property in the Massachusetts park system. It is also the most visited because its nine landscaped acres contain a world-famous boulder. **Plymouth Rock** sits beneath a granite Greek-temple canopy where, according to tradition, the *Mayflower* Pilgrims first set foot ashore in the winter of 1620–21. The rock is also a fine example of a glacial erratic, itself an immigrant that vanished glaciers plucked from mountains to the north and deposited here when the last ice sheet melted.

Just south of Plymouth Center on Route 3A lies **Plymouth Beach❖,** one of a half-dozen prominent barrier beaches along the inner shore of

27

LEFT: *Great blue herons nest in colonies called rookeries. These majestic birds, with their seven-foot wingspans, are North America's largest herons.*

RIGHT: *An old jeep trail winds beside the Great Marshes of Barnstable at Sandy Neck, Cape Cod's largest salt marsh. These wetlands were highly valued as pastureland by early European settlers.*

Cape Cod Bay. Perhaps the most dynamic of all coastal systems, barrier beaches constantly shift in response to wind and wave, in time actually rolling over upon themselves. The process begins when severe storms breach the dune line, allowing tons of sand and fragments of plant material to be carried into the shallow waters or marshes behind the dunes. Eventually the sand finds purchase, the grasses take root, and a new line of rear dunes forms—only to have the cycle begin again.

In summer at Plymouth Beach, raucous clouds of common terns rise from roped-off nesting areas and swift diminutive piping plover scuttle across the foredunes, uttering their flutelike calls to draw intruders away from their perfectly camouflaged eggs nestled in a depression in the sand.

Piping plover are a success story of recent coastal environmental efforts. After World War II, numbers of the soft-gray shorebirds, one of the few such species to nest in Massachusetts, began to decline precipitously as civilization encroached on their nesting habitat. (Because they nest on the bare sand of upper beaches, the small plover are peculiarly vulnerable to development, beach buggies, dogs, and other disturbances.) When the piping plover was declared a federally threatened species in 1985, critical stretches of beach were closed during nesting season, and educational campaigns made the public aware of the bird's plight. The result has been a dramatic increase in the number of nesting birds and fledged chicks over the past decade. In the Cape Cod National Seashore alone, plover nests have increased from only 15 in the late 1980s to more than 100 by the mid-1990s.

From Plymouth, head south on Route 3 to Exit 5. Some three miles west on Long Pond Road is **Myles Standish State Forest❖.** Dotting the forest's gently rolling 15,000 acres are 16 glacial kettle-hole ponds; several contain

LEFT: *In early summer female diamond-back terrapins leave estuaries to lay their eggs in nearby dunes. Sand temperature during incubation may well determine the sex of the hatchlings.*

rare floral species, such as the Plymouth gentian and Maryland meadow beauty, and one of the few known populations of the Plymouth redbelly turtle, another federally endangered reptile. Purchased by the state in 1916 as "wasteland," Myles Standish is now one of only four major pine-barren ecosystems in the country, and a fire-maintained coastal pitch-pine community increasingly rare in the region. The acorn crop from extensive oak woods supports the first successfully reintroduced wild turkeys in eastern Massachusetts.

In South Plymouth, east of Route 3A on Ellisville Road, is **Ellisville State Park❖,** an old coastal farm with bluffs encircling picturesque Ellisville Harbor and its surrounding salt marshes. From the beach impressive views of the Manomet Hills stretch north and south.

Continue south on Route 3, cross the Sagamore Bridge over the Cape Cod Canal (opened in 1914 as the world's longest sea-level canal), and head east on Route 6A. From the canal to Orleans, Route 6A is known as the Old King's Highway; authorized by England's Charles II and laid out in 1660, it winds through Cape Cod's oldest villages, by ancient cemeteries, beside grassy seas of salt marsh, and around small boat harbors.

At the Sandwich-Barnstable line, Sandy Neck Road leads north to **Sandy Neck Reservation❖** on Cape Cod Bay. Seven miles of cobble beaches flank the bay, and a convoluted series of fantastic wind-sculpted dunes stretch the length of the spit. After northeast storms, the beach is an excellent spot to see pelagic birds swept into the bay by winds. The spit encloses the 3,000-acre **Great Marshes,** one of the oldest and largest salt marsh systems in the state, which contains peat deposits up to 60 feet thick.

Salt marshes are the Cape's saltwater prairies, where high tasseled cordgrass borders tidal creeks and ditches, and shorter, finer salt hay tumbles in cowlicks along higher stretches. Besides providing habitat for large numbers of marsh and wading birds, waterfowl, and shorebirds, the marshes at Sandy Neck support one of the northernmost breeding populations of diamondback terrapins, a state-threatened reptile. Once hunted in great num-

RIGHT: *The pale, cryptic coloration of the piping plover is perfect camouflage for this diminutive shorebird, which places its speckled eggs above high water, in simple scrapes in the sand.*

bers for their delicate flavor, these saltwater turtles, whose shells display elaborate namesake patterns, are protected here; each spring they leave telltale claw marks on the dunes where they crawl to lay their rubbery eggs.

During warm weather, the bay side of the beach can be clogged with beach buggies and other ORVs, although stretches are fenced to protect nesting least terns and piping plover. But on the inner side, an old marsh road, off limits to vehicles, winds between the ever-changing Great Marshes and the waters of Barnstable Harbor on one side, and dunes, widely spaced old cottages, and unusual maritime forests on the other. Unlike most other barrier beaches, Sandy Neck has retreated little over the centuries, and mature forests of oak, beech, and hickory grow in hollows between the dunes, sustaining wildflowers such as trillium and columbine, which are more typical of mainland forests.

From Sandy Neck, Route 6A proceeds east through classic Cape Cod villages. In West Brewster, just past the **Cape Cod Museum of Natural History** is the valley of the north-flowing Stony Brook, which connects one of the Cape's best preserved and most varied coastal ecosystems. More than 1,500 acres of ponds, woodlands, freshwater wetlands, salt marshes, marsh islands, and barrier beaches are protected through a cooperative partnership between the town of Brewster and the museum.

Directly behind the museum is the John Wing Trail, which crosses an ancient marsh causeway to **Wing Island❖,** 22 acres surrounded by salt marsh and barrier beach. During the early nineteenth century the island was dotted with saltworks, elaborate wooden structures that extracted salt through solar evaporation. Today this relatively secluded stretch of beach on Cape Cod Bay is home to deer, rabbits, and songbirds, notably the prairie warbler.

Across Route 6A, the museum's **South Trail** meanders through brackish marshes on dikes that once enclosed working cranberry bogs and leads across Stony Brook into a lovely mature beech grove. In spring, the ubiquitous herring and black-backed gulls circle the marshes here, herald-

31

ABOVE: *Found along sandy pond fringes, the lavender Plymouth gentian is globally endangered. Of 61 known sites, 45 are in Massachusetts.*

ing the beginning of the Cape's celebrated annual alewife run.

Foot-long members of the herring family, alewives migrate up coastal creeks and rivers each spring to spawn in freshwater ponds and lakes. The bridge across Stony Brook is a good vantage point, but the spectacle is most dramatic at the **Stony Brook Mill Sites❖** on Stony Brook Road. In late April and early May of a good migration year, the fish ladder here is the scene of concentrated natural energy as thousands upon thousands of fish fight their way through the rushing waters toward the spawning ponds above. It is, in the words of Brewster author John Hay, "a scene to force the heart." Above the herring run a series of ponds border the **Punkhorn Parklands❖,** an 835-acre preserve containing two miles of pond shoreline, extensive pine barrens, old rock quarries, a beech forest, and a rare quaking bog.

At the eastern end of Brewster on Route 6A is **Roland C. Nickerson State Park❖.** Once a private fish and game preserve, its 2,000 acres include a three-quarter-mile beach on Cape Cod Bay, an ornate and eccentric nineteenth-century mansion, a white-cedar swamp, the only extensive

RIGHT: *Hushed aisles of red pine, planted in the 1930s by the Civilian Conservation Corps, stand tall today in Roland C. Nickerson State Park.*
OVERLEAF: *In Wellfleet, comber after comber reshapes the sand and dunes of Newcomb Hollow Beach, part of the Cape Cod National Seashore.*

stands of white pine on the Lower Cape, and some of the finest kettle-hole ponds in the region. Its woodlands are among the few tracts on the Cape not cut during the last century; the tall pine that Thoreau climbed when he became lost on his 1858 trip to the Cape may still be growing here. In winter immature bald eagles frequent the ponds, as do large concentrations of wintering black ducks.

THE OUTER CAPE: CHATHAM TO PROVINCETOWN

Most visitors to the Cape head for the **Cape Cod National Seashore❖.** Established in 1961, the country's second national seashore is the largest and most popular public resort area in southern New England. Its boundaries, stretching 50 miles from Provincetown south to Chatham, encompass some 44,000 acres, of which about 27,000 are federally preserved property. Its constantly shifting beaches and barrier spits, eroding cliffs, moving dunes, and encroaching wetlands make it an exemplar of natural change, a landscape in motion. Although an estimated five million people visit the seashore annually, most congregate on the larger public beaches and ponds, and even in summer a visitor willing to walk a bit can find solitude on the more remote sand spits, dune fields, wooded roads, and ponds. Between Labor Day and Memorial Day the seashore assumes a substantially less human face.

Off Route 6 in Eastham, follow signs on the right to the **Fort Hill Area❖.** The Fort Hill overlook, on the site of one of the last working farms in the area, provides stunning views across wide grassy meadows to Nauset Harbor (visited by Samuel de Champlain in 1606) and Coast Guard Beach beyond. The national seashore staff maintains these open fields, where bluebirds, meadowlarks, indigo buntings, and other birds now rare on the Cape have been spotted. A 1.5-mile trail traverses open meadows, marsh borders, dense redcedar forests, mixed woods, and an extensive red-maple swamp of grotesquely shaped trees, whose brilliant fall colors rival those of the mainland.

A mile farther north on Route 6 is the **Salt Pond Visitor Center❖,** where bike and foot trails (including one marked in braille) lead through oak and pine hills, past **Doane Rock** (the largest known glacial erratic on Cape Cod), to the old Coast Guard Station, with its panoramic view of Nauset Marsh, Coast Guard Beach, and the Atlantic Ocean. In 1926–27 in a now-demolished beach cottage to the south, Henry Beston wrote *The Outermost House,* which has become a classic of twentieth-century nature writ-

ABOVE: *Despite its name, the prairie warbler (left) frequents dry, scrubby areas of the East. A northern parula warbler (right), which nests in Cape Cod's white cedar swamps, perches among shadbush blossoms.*

ing. During the summer piping plover and least terns nest along the beach and on the marsh islands near its southern tip. In winter the large sluglike bodies of harbor seals can be seen draped languorously along the shore.

The hill where the old coast guard station sits is the beginning of the national seashore's most distinctive feature: an uninterrupted 20-mile stretch of imposing glacial cliffs fronting the Atlantic Ocean from Coast Guard Beach north to High Head in North Truro. Known variously as the Great Beach, Cape Cod Beach, the Outer Beach, and the Backside, this undulating glacial scarp, rising to nearly 200 feet, is a layered tapestry of varicolored sand, gravel, iron conglomerate, and clay deposits. More than 3,000 vessels have come to grief on its treacherous offshore bars and shoals. Constantly eroding at an average rate of three feet a year, its slopes and beaches are littered with human and natural debris: cottage and lighthouse foundations; dwarfed trees from the forests at its ridge; ancient shipwrecks imprisoned by and then released from the sand; animal, fish, and bird carcasses; driftwood; and the increasing plastic legacy of modern civilization.

ABOVE: *Along the Cape Cod National Seashore in Eastham, islands in Nauset Marsh form a green archipelago below Fort Hill, named for a fortification built here in 1605 by French explorer Samuel de Champlain.*

Although the actual route is now some 500 feet offshore, this beach was the site of Thoreau's famous 1849 walk, recorded in his classic account *Cape Cod*. Visitors today may also walk the entire length. The ocean beach is accessible at a number of seashore- and town-owned beaches located at "hollows" punctuating the cliffs.

At the traffic lights in South Wellfleet turn right off Route 6 to the **Marconi Site,** the location of Guglielmo Marconi's first two-way transatlantic wireless transmission in 1903. The road to the site traverses the Wellfleet Plains, a barren stretch of the Outer Cape reminiscent of the last century. West of the Marconi Site, a one-mile trail leads to the **Atlantic White Cedar Swamp❖,** the Cape's largest remaining stand of the trees whose rot-resistant wood once provided the ubiquitous weathered cedar shingles on most Cape houses. In summer, from the boardwalk winding through the swamp's dark and hushed aisles, visitors may hear, or even observe, the northern parula warbler, a slate-colored bird with a bright yellow breast that builds its nest from the old-man's beard lichen (*Usnea*) growing on the cedar boughs.

At **High Head** in North Truro, where Route 6 begins a long, steady decline toward Provincetown, the bluffs on the right mark the northern end of the Lower Cape's glacial deposits. North across Pilgrim Lake is the

ABOVE: *Tall, lacy ferns and velvety mosses adorn the hummocks along a trail in South Wellfleet's Atlantic White Cedar Swamp. Once abundant on Cape Cod, many swamps were cleared for cranberry bogs.*

Province Lands, a postglacial formation created over the past 6,000 years. Materials eroded from the glacial cliffs were carried northward by longshore currents and then shaped by wind and wave into a broad 3,000-acre fist of 100-foot dunes, coastal dune ponds, dwarf and buried forests, and wild cranberry bogs. Today such dune inhabitants as Fowler's toads and sand grasshoppers have adapted their coloration to blend into the sands. The best access to the dunes is from the **Province Lands Visitor Center❖** on Race Point Road.

Some nine miles of paved bike trails snake through the dunes, originally forested hills set loose by overgrazing and clear cutting in the 1700s. Stretching east for several miles are a series of parallel dune ridges dotted with 20 or so distinctive and often whimsical dune shacks. Farther east, the winds have shaped the sands into broad U-shaped bowls known as parabolic dunes.

Also on Race Point Road is the **Province Lands Beech Forest❖,**

OVERLEAF: *On Fort Hill in Eastham, feathery grasses, magenta crown vetch, and native Virginia rose help stabilize the dunes. A relic of a long-gone farm, the old stone wall of glacial erratics is a rarity on the Lower Cape.*

LEFT: *During a seasonal migration a hump-back whale breaches in Cape Cod Bay. Each humpback has unique fluke patterns, enabling individuals to be readily identified.*
RIGHT: *Low tide exposes the shallow burrows of fiddler crabs along Wellfleet's Great Island Trail. Male fiddlers have one enlarged claw, which they wave to attract females.*

which juxtaposes two highly unusual habitats. Hidden in a ravine of encroaching dune walls is a mature beech forest, a remnant of the original woodland. On windy days visitors can stand in the shade of this northern hardwood grove and hear grains of sand falling like dry rain through the leaves, gradually burying the forest.

MacMillan Wharf in Provincetown Center is the jumping-off place for viewing some of the largest and most impressive creatures on the planet. Each day from spring through fall, numerous whale-watching boats head toward **Stellwagen Bank National Marine Sanctuary✥.** This large underwater sand and gravel glacial deposit north of Provincetown is a major feeding ground for a number of North Atlantic whales, including 40-foot humpbacks, 70-foot fin whales, and the globally endangered northern right whale, of which fewer than 300 individuals remain in the North Atlantic population. The humpbacks often leap nearly completely out of the water in spectacular breaching displays.

On the return trip south turn west off Route 6 through Wellfleet Center and out Chequesset Neck Road to the parking area at the head of **Great Island Trail.** Stretching along the outer side of Wellfleet Harbor, the trail leads to perhaps the finest example in New England of a tombolo: a seven-mile series of barrier beaches connecting several large glacial islands. On **Great Island** the site of a late-seventeenth-century whalers' tavern reposes among outstanding examples of coastal pine barrens, the stunted trees twisted by wind and salt into fantastic shapes. At the southern tip of the tombolo is **Jeremy Point,** a haul-out site for a sizable herd of wintering harbor seals.

West off Route 6 in South Wellfleet, just before the Eastham line, is the **Wellfleet Bay Wildlife Sanctuary✥,** where 1,000 acres of pine barrens, old fields, salt marshes, brooks, ponds, islands, and heaths create a premier year-round birding spot. **Try Island** was once used to "try out," or render, the oil from stranded whales.

At Orleans, take Route 28 south to Chatham. The road swings close to **Pleasant Bay,** an ancient glacial riverbed. **North Beach,** the eastern border of the bay, is a long barrier spit that encompasses one of the Cape's most volatile barrier systems. In 1987 North Beach underwent a major transformation when a mile-long break formed opposite Chatham center, exposing much of the village shoreline to the eroding forces of the open ocean. A good place to view this dramatic break, and its constantly changing effects, is the overlook on Bridge Street in front of Chatham Light.

South from the overlook, take Morris Island Road across a causeway and follow signs to the **Monomoy National Wildlife Refuge❖.** The section of the refuge at the south end of Morris Island is accessible by foot from the refuge headquarters; the rest, across a narrow channel on North and South Monomoy islands, must be visited via boat. **Monomoy Island Wilderness Area❖** is the only federally designated wilderness area in southern New England. The island has been repeatedly attached to and detached from the mainland, and in 1978 the so-called Storm of the Century cut it in two.

Monomoy is one of the Northeast's premier birding areas. During the summer, large sections of both islands are posted with warnings to protect a sizable common tern colony and other nesting birds (such as oystercatchers, skimmers, willets, and short-eared owls). From mid-July through September, the flats and marshes on the

ABOVE: *With its long yellow legs, bobbing head, flickering tail, and loud, three-note whistle, the greater yellowlegs is easily recognizable on the beach.*

LEFT: *The pinkish blossoms of saltmarsh fleabane, at the northern limit of its range, edge a brackish pond on South Monomoy Island. In the background is Monomoy Light.*

west side of North Monomoy are a major East Coast gathering spot for thousands of migrating shorebirds—including such rarities as golden plover, whimbrels, and Hudsonian godwits.

South Monomoy, the larger of the two, contains a deer herd, dwarf forests, salt ponds, and a series of artificial waterfowl ponds where virtually every species of East Coast duck, goose, and swan may be spotted in early spring and late fall. The refuge is one of the best places to see migrating peregrine falcons in the fall, and in winter substantial seal

ABOVE: *A flock of sanderlings moves as one along the outer beaches of the Atlantic. Cape Cod author Henry Beston described these birds as "fugitive pleides . . . caught with ourselves in the net of life and time."*

herds—including the southernmost breeding colony of gray seals—congregate along the beaches.

The Wellfleet Bay Wildlife Sanctuary and the Cape Cod Museum of Natural History operate day trips to Monomoy, and the museum offers a limited number of overnight trips to the Monomoy Point Lighthouse on South Monomoy. The restored nineteenth-century lighthouse is an excellent observation tower for viewing waterfowl congregating on the ponds and deer bounding over the beach-grass prairies of the dunes—indeed, the entire shining magnificence of this remote corner of Massachusetts.

NANTUCKET SOUND: CHATHAM TO FALMOUTH

Traveling west along Route 28 from Chatham to Falmouth is a somewhat less than natural experience. Among the strips of motels, tourist shops, restaurants, and minimalls, however, occasional scenic oases reveal the geology and natural history of the Cape's outwash plains. In West Harwich the highway crosses the Herring River, a marsh-bordered tidal creek that flows through one of the series of north-south outwash valleys corru-

ABOVE: *A sampler of Cape Cod shorebirds includes (clockwise from top left): a great black-backed gull with a quahog; a feeding American oystercatcher; an elegant snowy egret; and a nesting pair of laughing gulls.*

gating the Cape's southern shore. In spring the river is full of migratory alewives, or herring, weaving their way upstream to spawn in the ponds above. Much of the Herring River watershed is part of the **Harwich Conservation Lands❖.** The river is a favorite canoeing area, and two large brackish reservoirs on Bells Neck Road afford excellent year-round birding for waterfowl and wading birds.

North of Mashpee Center, off the Sandwich-Cotuit road, a wooded half-mile peninsula known as Conaumet Neck juts between two large ponds, Wakeby and Mashpee, the headwaters of the Mashpee River. Formerly the private preserve of Harvard president Lawrence Lowell, the **Lowell Holly Reservation❖** supports a curious mixture of unusual old-growth forest (mature beech, black gum, black birch, and white pine) and introduced species such as balsam fir and hemlock. In spring the woods are ablaze with flowering rhododendron, mountain laurel, rose-bay, and catawba. The reservation is also home to some 300 native and planted holly trees. Two 60-foot knolls offer dramatic views of the ponds and surrounding shores, especially in October when the vistas are

47

ABOVE: *Traditional lines of berry pickers move across a bog in Eastman Johnson's* The Cranberry Harvest, Nantucket Island, *an outdoor genre*

framed by the golden veil of the beeches' changing foliage.

A few miles southwest of the Mashpee rotary on Route 28 is the head-quarters of **Waquoit Bay National Estuarine Research Reserve❖,** 2,250 acres of open water, marshes, islands, barrier beaches, and coastal upland. Botanical studies have located several rare species here, including sand-plain gerardia, a coastal plant species found in only about a dozen loca-tions worldwide. Within the reserve at the southern end of Great Neck Road lies **South Cape Beach State Park❖,** a 500-acre public complex of extensive barrier beaches, salt marshes, and a large salt pond. On the west side of Waquoit Bay, 355-acre **Washburn Island❖** is easily reachable by canoe or small boat and offers a few primitive camping sites.

NANTUCKET

From the air, the offshore islands of Nantucket and Martha's Vineyard re-semble a pair of flip-flopped pork chops lying south of Nantucket Sound.

scene painted in 1880. Cranberry production is still important in Massachusetts, but most bogs are now flooded and harvested mechanically.

Although both islands were created by the farthest advance of the Laurentide glaciation (and thus are called terminal moraines), they are dramatically different in character, topography, vegetation, and fauna.

Nantucket, 18 miles from the mainland, is a low sandy poem of fantastic landforms. Its landscapes are among the most beautiful and fragile on the East Coast, incorporating some of the largest remaining areas of coastal heath and grassland in the country. Settled by Quakers in the mid-1600s, the island soon lost its original forests to timber, and much of its thin soil then blew away. In *Moby Dick* Herman Melville described Nantucket as "a mere hillock and elbow of sand, all beach, without a background." Today, although much of the island is reforested, its flora and fauna maintain a unique character because of the maritime climate, lack of mainland predators, and introduction of exotic species such as the black-tailed jackrabbit, which was originally imported from the West for sportsmen in the late 1800s and reintroduced in the 1930s.

In recent decades Nantucket has experienced heavy development pressure. In response, nearly a third of its 32,000 acres and varied habitats—many home to rare and endangered species—are now protected, the largest portion by the private Nantucket Conservation Foundation. Beyond human pressure, the island is subject to implacable natural forces that give its extraordinary beauty an evanescent quality. Large portions of coastline are lost to erosion (in many places more than 20 feet a year). Peter Dunwiddie, a plant ecologist for Massachusetts Audubon, has predicted that "with global warming and the potential for a future rise in sea level, the entire island is likely to vanish beneath the waves in another few centuries."

One of the first sights to greet island visitors is Coatue, the elegantly scalloped sandy beach that encloses Nantucket Harbor. Coatue is part of the 1,400-acre **Coskata–Coatue, Great Point Wildlife Refuge System❖,** a barrier-beach system shaped like a barbed harpoon. Incorporating more than 18 miles of the loveliest shoreline anywhere, Coskata–Coatue contains large breeding populations of gulls, terns, oystercatchers, and other shorebirds. In early summer its delicate dune ridges explode in a colorful profusion of blossoms, including the easternmost prickly pear population in the United States. During the winter the harbor waters, rich in aquatic life, attract large numbers of winter ducks and other waterfowl. The scrubby woods of Coskata offer cover to Nantucket's large deer herd, said to be descendants of a buck found swimming across Muskeget Channel from Martha's Vineyard Island in 1922 and two does imported from Michigan in 1926 (presumably to give the buck company). One of the state's major tern colonies nests at Great Point near the venerable beacon of Great Point Light.

In the east-central section of the island are more than ten square miles of privately protected natural areas, including the famous rolling heathlands known as Nantucket's "moors." At the heart of the island, the **Middle Moors❖** encompass a vast tract of hills, plains, outwash valleys, and ponds that form Nantucket's largest remaining area of heathlands. In autumn especially, these former sheep pastures glow with a magical intensity, afire with the vibrant reds and golds of blueberry, huckleberry, bearberry, and other heath plants. Originally forested, these heathlands were so thoroughly denuded by sheep herds in the nineteenth century that the native pitch pine had to be reintroduced to the island in the late

---

LEFT: *In the golden light of late afternoon, intriguing patterns appear on the flanks of sand dunes: sinuous wind ripples, small animal tracks, and graceful arcs traced by the tips of beach, or compass, grass.*

1800s. Ironically, natural reforestation now reclaims so much original moorland each year that land managers are conducting controlled burns and considering reintroducing sheep to preserve this "natural" landscape. Southeast of Middle Moors off Milestone Road is **Milestone Bog❖**, a square mile that was the largest natural cranberry bog in the world, until in the 1950s it was subdivided by a system of dikes and ditches to conserve water. Nearly a third of the bog is still under cultivation, and its trails are open to walkers and cyclists.

The largest native coastal grassland on Nantucket is off Madaket Road in the island's southwest corner. On a large peninsula jutting into Hummock Pond, **Ram Pasture❖,** one of several contiguous conservation parcels, encompasses the island's largest outwash plain pond, barrier beaches, extensive tracts of woodland, swamps, moors, and grasslands. Said to be the easternmost natural prairie in the United States, the "pasture"—several hundred acres of coastal grassland at the southern end of the peninsula—is dominated by little bluestem, blueberry, and other native shrubs and grasses. Originally used to separate rams from ewes, the area is a good place to glimpse northern harriers as well as a rare diurnal short-eared owl, a grassland hunter and nester. At Nantucket's far western end, **Eel Point❖** harbors nesting piping plover and abundant shorebirds, including snow buntings, short-eared owls, and Lapland longspurs in winter. A few introduced jack rabbits live in this area.

MARTHA'S VINEYARD

Although born of the same glacier and roughly the same size as Nantucket, Martha's Vineyard resembles the mainland more than its island neighbor. Hilly, rocky, and heavily wooded, the Vineyard seems larger than its 100 square miles, and its varied terrain includes geologic formations and floral communities found nowhere else in the region. Within its diminutive boundaries are impressive barrier beaches, dramatic coastal bluffs, extensive heaths and grasslands, colorful tapestries of Cretaceous clay, a wealth of endangered species, and numerous ponds and streams. Knitting it all together, scenic country roads provide vistas of farms, fields, and ocean at nearly every turn.

One of the best introductions to the island's diversified coastal habitats is provided by **Felix Neck Wildlife Sanctuary❖,** on the road from Vineyard Haven to Edgartown. This 350-acre Massachusetts Audubon property sits on Sengekontacet Pond, one of the island's many enclosed saltwater estuaries. An extensive network of well-marked trails afford excellent access to the rich marshes, open fields, secluded woodland ponds, and Waterfowl Pond, which attracts a year-round pageant of nesting and migratory water birds.

Felix Neck is also the setting for one of the state's most successful species recovery stories. During the 1960s the effects of DDT had reduced the New England osprey population to dangerously low levels. After the ban on such pesticides, the numbers of these large fish-catching hawks began to increase slowly, aided by a breeding protection program and the erection of artificial osprey nesting poles in their former range. From a precarious beginning with two nesting pairs in 1971, Felix Neck pioneered this program; in 1995, 75 osprey pairs were counted. At the sanctuary visitors can watch, at close range, the courting, mating, breeding, and hunting rituals of these dramatically handsome birds.

On the Vineyard's eastern end are two spectacular coastal preserves. From Edgartown, the ferry *On Time* makes a daring 35-second crossing to Chappaquiddick Island. At this island's far end is **Cape Poge Wildlife Refuge✧,** a barrier-beach system boasting more than ten miles of fantastically shaped, delicate sand spits that enclose the vast tidal flats, marshes, glacial knolls, and fertile waters of Cape Poge Bay. Almost any day finds its beaches and waters aswirl in kinetic avian energy: migratory hawks and warblers, hunting harriers and short-eared owls, nesting terns, ospreys, and piping plover. Autumn brings prodigious gatherings of swallows, shorebirds—including Forster's terns, a western prairie species—and wintering sea ducks.

At the end of Wasque Road in Chappaquiddick's southeastern corner is **Wasque Reservation✧.** Its 200 acres contain walking trails that skirt the crest of Wasque Bluffs, a dramatic marine escarpment where ospreys nest in summer. Sweeping vistas of Katama Bay appear across wide expanses of heath and grasslands, where such potentially endangered native wildflowers as the spectacular New England blazing star are protected in a habitat restoration project.

On the main island, off the Edgartown–West Tisbury road is a remote and surpassingly beautiful area, the 633-acre **Long Point Wildlife Refuge✧.** The preserve straddles Long Cove, one of many former saltwater inlets whose entrances are closed by barrier beaches. The isthmus on the refuge's east side is largely heathland; the western isthmus, between Long Cove and Tisbury Great Pond, is a rippling expanse of native grassland surrounded on three sides by water. The bracketing ponds attract year-round populations of ducks, geese, swans, shorebirds, muskrat, and otters. Connecting the two areas is an unbroken mile-long dune ridge. Long Point's heaths and grasslands present a showcase of biodiversity and endangered species, supporting nesting harriers, meadowlarks and ospreys, little red-bellied snakes and rare tiger beetles, as well as a wealth of moths and butterflies.

ABOVE: *An osprey holds a fresh catch in its talons. These raptors build nests on dead trees or nesting poles, and then add material to them each year.*

RIGHT: *In early spring a stand of tupelos leafs out along Brine's Pond on Chappaquiddick Island. On Martha's Vineyard these graceful trees are known as "beetlebungs."*

At the western tip of the island are the 150-foot **Gay Head Clay Cliffs❖,** a National Historic Landmark and the most unusual and visually stunning stretch of marine escarpment in the region. Composed of Cretaceous and Tertiary deposits more than 70 million years old, the varied layers of vividly colored sands and clays contain fossil remains of ancient marine life and horses. Maushop Beach on Maushop Trail Road provides access to the shore, where a one-mile round trip walk winds beneath the psychedelic cliffs, a strange combination of badlands and coastal painted desert. In an amazing tapestry, pinks, mauve, chalk white, grays, greens, solid blacks, deep reds, beiges, and various shades in between rise into miniature sierras, cirques, cracked and fissured cliff faces, spatter-paint murals, and canyon walls.

Return to Vineyard Haven along North Road, which follows one of three narrow parallel glacial valleys. On the left look for the entrance to **Menemsha Hills Reservation❖;** about a mile from the parking area is 308-foot **Prospect Hill.** And from here the vista extends forever: west across Menemsha and Squibnocket ponds to Gay Head, out across Vineyard Sound to Nomans Land Island, and north to Cuttyhunk and the entire sweep of the Elizabeth Islands. Continuing through the rocky wooded headlands, the trail descends to the beach through a steep boulder-strewn ravine. Even in summer this is one of the island's most secluded public beaches, where visitors can rest on huge glacial boulders to watch the terns and local fishing boats ply their respective trades offshore.

In North Tisbury, one mile off Indian Hill Road on Obed Daggett Road—a windy, bumpy dirt track—is **Cedar Tree Neck,** a 216-acre headland stretching into Vineyard Sound. Its extensive trail system leads through dwarfed forests of fantastically twisted oaks to dunes enclosing Cedar Tree Neck Pond and an impressive headland overlook. The heavily cobbled beach is the rocky remnant of the glacial till that here spills out onto the shore like a giant's broken beanbag. In the hills above, **Ames Pond** is a secluded spot where kingfishers and dragonflies dart and turtles laze between sparkling sunlit waters and bordering beech trees.

ABOVE: *A fluffy common tern chick peeks warily from behind its protective parent. Common terns are one of four tern species that nest along the Massachusetts shore.*

LEFT: *At the far western end of Martha's Vineyard, the ancient, fossil-filled ramparts of Gay Head's clay cliffs glow lavender, rust, and gold when lit by the rays of the evening sun.*

BUZZARDS BAY: THE UNDISCOVERED COAST

Between the Cape Cod Canal and the Rhode Island line is a stretch of highly indented and often overlooked coastline. Its many historic boatbuilding, whaling, and industrial towns—such as Mattapoisett, New Bedford, and Fall River—have overshadowed its considerable although sometimes elusive natural attractions. The Dartmouth and Westport shores especially present a bewildering and beautiful labyrinth of protected bays, estuaries, marshes, rivers, islands, and creeks. Many vegetable and dairy farms still flourish here, their long fields of rich reddish-brown earth interrupted by low slabs of gray bedrock that surface through the plowed waves of soil like the backs of whales. In contrast to the geologically young formations of the Cape and Islands, these outcroppings represent some of the oldest exposed rock in southern New England: Precambrian metamorphic schist and granite nearly a billion years old.

Continue west on I-195 to New Bedford, where a ferry and a seaplane service the remote community of **Cuttyhunk Island❖.** Cuttyhunk is the last of the Elizabeth Island archipelago, 16 islands stretching southwest from Woods Hole. Most of Cuttyhunk's western half is undeveloped, and although not formally protected, it is maintained by private owners as a nature sanctuary open to visitors on foot. Numerous barrier beaches and oyster ponds offer fine shorebirding. The high bayberry and witchgrass vegetation provides cover for a large and fairly tame deer population, often encountered at dusk. Bartholomew Gosnold first attempted a European settlement in New England here in 1602, and Shakespeare may have used Goswold's descriptions of the island as a model for Prospero's magic island in *The Tempest.* Certainly the remote and windswept seascape evokes a magical atmosphere unlike any other spot in southern New England.

Back on the mainland, west of New Bedford off Potomska Road in South Dartmouth is the **Lloyd Center for Environmental Studies❖.** On its 55 acres are a variety of characteristic area habitats and wildlife, including a kettle-hole pond with bird blind, former farmland laced with stone walls, lovely small coves with delicate fringe marshes, Osprey Point (named for the fish hawks that frequent the area in summer and fall), the remains of a stone causeway road destroyed in the 1938 hurricane, two of the largest holly trees in Massachusetts, spotted turtles, and spotted salamanders.

From the lookout atop the center's main building, one can see to the west the long brilliant crescent of beach that is part of the natural preserve at **Demarest Lloyd State Park❖,** one of the better-kept coastal secrets in Massachusetts. Its lovely stretches of lengthening barrier spits cradle fringe marshes that are host to numerous cattle egrets and other wading birds.

Continue west on I-195 to Westport and take Exit 10 south on Route 88 to **Horseneck Beach State Reservation❖,** the most extensive state beach on the southern coast of Massachusetts. Once dotted with summer cottages and shacks, its two miles of barrier beach were wiped out by Hurricane Carol in 1954. Today Horseneck is a popular swimming beach in summer and home to flocks of glossy ibis and nesting pairs of the threatened piping plover. At the more secluded eastern end, a causeway provides foot access to **Gooseberry Island,** a former military installation whose blind concrete watchtowers now loom incongruously above hundreds of acres of low dunes, small marshes, and shingle beaches. Watching ibis fly across a summer sunset here confirms a turn-of-the-century promotional brochure that pronounced, "All cheap and childish waste sinks into oblivion before its magnificence."

Right: *Bright yellow seaside goldenrod lines the beaches at Demarest Lloyd State Park near Buzzards Bay. The plant's fleshy leaves and succulent stems help prevent desiccation from the constant salt spray.*

EASTERN MASSACHUSETTS:
URBAN WILDS AND ROCKY SHORES

The area roughly bounded by Interstate 495 is a large and diverse region that includes Greater Boston, the South Shore, and the North Shore. Most of this section of Massachusetts is relatively low (below 200 feet) and heavily influenced by the sea, from its fishing fleets to the massive sea walls that protect coastal property from fierce northeast storms.

The South Shore—the coast from Plymouth to Greater Boston—is a transition zone between the glacial landscape and coastal plain of Cape Cod and the islands and the ancient bedrock of the remaining Massachusetts coast. Although winding tidal rivers, barrier beaches, and salt marshes still characterize much of it, granite outcrops and ledges begin to push up along the coast, some of them providing bases for offshore lighthouses. Taller, straighter oaks and white pines increasingly replace the stunted oaks and pitch pines seen to the south.

The most densely urban area of southern New England, Greater Boston is better known for its rich cultural traditions, historical sites, horrendous traffic jams, and the fickle fortunes of the Boston Red Sox than for its natural attractions. In fact, there are many natural areas dotting the region (Middlesex County alone, in Boston's western suburbs, contains 729 municipal conservation areas), often found on country lanes that wind through surprisingly rural landscapes.

Geologically, the area within Route 128's loop is known as the Boston

---

LEFT: *A rich blue and green tapestry of water and sky, wetland and woodland, the Ipswich River Wildlife Sanctuary includes Bunker Meadows, a freshwater marsh, among its diversified wildlife habitats.*

61

Basin, a distinct formation of low, soft Cretaceous soils surrounded by hills of metamorphic rock that rise 200 to 600 feet above the basin lowland. A dramatic showcase of glacial sculpture, the Boston Basin encompasses New England's greatest concentrations of eskers (long snakelike deposits), drumlins (oval or tear-shaped hills), and other glacial features.

Some of the finest and largest natural areas in Greater Boston are managed by the Metropolitan Parks Commission, conceived in 1892 by Harvard president Charles Eliot to provide parks and recreational facilities for Bostonians—then a revolutionary idea in this country. The great nineteenth-century landscape architect Frederick Law Olmsted designed Boston's "Emerald Necklace" of linked green spaces. Although in many places degraded and overrun, Olmsted's jewel still provides a continuous, if narrow, greenway in Boston's urban heart, as well as access to the much-maligned but surprisingly lovely Charles River.

West and north of Boston, between Route 128 and I-495, lies a region of gently rolling hills, quiet rivers, extensive freshwater marshes, and numerous small lakes. Historically this area supported produce and dairy farms and country retreats for Boston's wealthier families. Since World War II most of the farms have given way to urban sprawl and suburban development, but a significant portion of open land has been preserved.

The North Shore, stretching from Boston to the New Hampshire line, is an area whose forte is variety. Between Lynn and Gloucester, the coastline is indented with small harbors, pocket beaches, and offshore islands. Gloucester and Rockport form Cape Ann, a shield of granite thrusting into the Atlantic. Thoreau, comparing it to Cape Cod's outstretched arm, described Cape Ann as Massachusetts's "other fist, which keeps guard the while upon her breast." Its dramatic and scenic coast looks more like Maine than Massachusetts. By contrast, the region north from Gloucester to Newburyport is rich in marshes, estuaries, dune systems, and barrier beaches—and home to the abundant birdlife associated with such varied environments.

This chapter begins in Duxbury and follows the South Shore north. After exploring some of the major Greater Boston natural areas inside Route 128, it works its way clockwise through the region between Route 128 and I-495, stops at Cape Ann, and concludes on the North Shore.

Overleaf: *The showy flowers and three-lobed leaves of swamp rose mallows line a path at World's End Reservation. Settlers once extracted a sticky white paste from this plant to make marshmallow confections.*

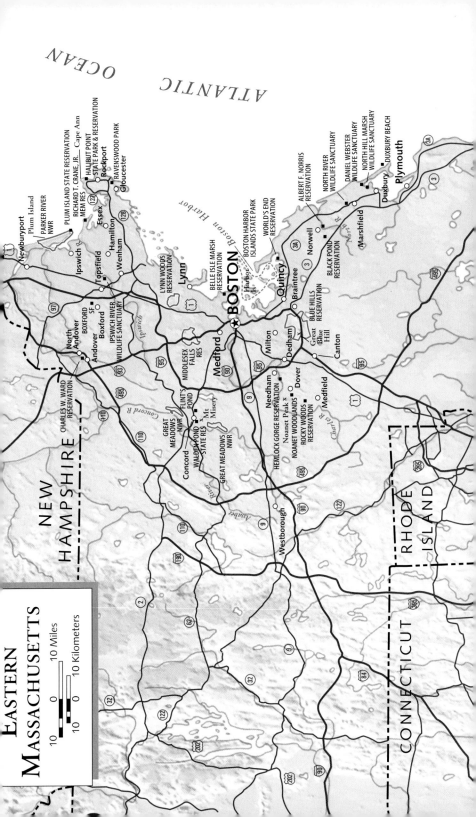

THE SOUTH SHORE: DUXBURY TO HINGHAM

Historic Duxbury on Route 3A boasts an extensive system of preserved open spaces, including more than a thousand contiguous acres in the center of town. The superb white pine and hemlock forests of **North Hill Marsh Wildlife Sanctuary❖** enclose a 90-acre lake rich in nesting and migratory wildfowl. **Duxbury Beach❖,** a fishhook-shaped seven-mile spit, is the largest and least spoiled barrier beach on the South Shore. Its fine gray sands, multicolored stones, and shingles provide habitat for nesting least terns and piping plover.

ABOVE: *In autumn monarchs migrating south frequently stop at New England beaches to feed from plants such as seaside goldenrod.*

RIGHT: *Gravel carriage paths, originally designed for the wealthy elite, now beckon walkers beneath canopies of mixed hardwoods at World's End Reservation.*

Just north in Marshfield, between Green Harbor River and Wharf Creek, is **Daniel Webster Wildlife Sanctuary❖,** named for the famous Massachusetts orator who purchased the property in 1832. Although it is one of the oldest working farms in the country, today the 474-acre property is managed primarily as a wildlife refuge. Its extensive grasslands attract numerous ground-nesting birds and avian predators—including harriers, peregrines, and bald eagles—as well as spectacular congregations of migrating tree swallows and monarch butterflies each fall. Observation blinds at an artificial wetland provide excellent viewing of sandpipers, plover, and herons.

Snaking its way between Marshfield and Norwell is the splendid **North River Watershed❖,** a National Natural Landmark river system that drains 60,000 acres in seven towns. On Route 3, at a dip in the road on the Marshfield-Norwell line, a magnificent vista between two hills appears to the east: The wide, meandering tidal river runs through knobby glacial hills, and pristine salt marshes—their ever-changing displays of color swelling and contracting through the year—sweep to the horizon.

The best way to see the North River is by canoe or kayak, a leisurely paddle along calm, flat water where stunning views appear at every turn. Between 1650 and 1871 dozens of local boatyards produced some one thousand vessels along this stretch. Today, among the rippling marshes

LEFT: *From Blue Hills Reservation, a view of Boston's skyline looms in the distance. The city's venerable PBS station, WGBH, derives its call letters from the transmitter located here on (G)reat (B)lue (H)ill.*
RIGHT: *A medium-sized bird with long wings, the short-eared owl hunts at dawn and dusk, gliding silently over marshes with a low, shifting flight.*

and second-growth woodlands, canoeists may spot occasional shipyard plaques or the rotting remnant of an ancient "corduroy" log road leading down to the river's edge. Noncanoeists can also access the river at more than 50 public sites along its snaky length. Two of the most interesting are the 175-acre **North River Wildlife Sanctuary**❖ off Route 3A in Marshfield and the 117-acre **Albert F. Norris Reservation**❖ off Route 123 in Norwell. In addition to riverside trails, both preserves offer a variety of upland habitat hiking.

Norwell's **Black Pond Reservation**❖, off Mount Blue Street, highlights the sphagnum bog, a wetland uncommon in southern New England. Showcasing a textbook example of pond-bog-swamp succession, a sturdy boardwalk leads to a deep kettle-hole pond edged with a thick floating sphagnum mat. Protected by the Nature Conservancy, this nutrient-poor "quaking bog" supports unusual insectivorous plant species, including pitcher plants and sundews, as well as several orchids. Beyond the bog are bands of white-cedar and then red-maple swamps.

On the water at the end of Martin's Lane in Hingham is **World's End Reservation**❖, a jewel of the Greater Boston landscape. Four superb glacial hills jut into Boston Harbor, providing unparalleled views of the Harbor Islands, the Boston skyline, the encircling arm of Nantasket Beach to the east, and the broad Atlantic beyond. World's End encompasses some of the most perfect examples of tear-shaped glacial drumlins anywhere. The great landscape architect Frederick Law Olmsted designed the grassy knolls, winding carriage roads lined with English oaks, and rocky cliff paths for a private estate that was never built. The result is a grand country park in a magnificent seaside setting.

THE BOSTON BASIN: URBAN WILD LANDS

Anyone taking off from Logan Airport on a clear day cannot fail to notice the impressive array of islands in Boston Harbor. A diverse, unstrung necklace of glacial leavings and bedrock outcrops, some 75 harbor islands range from small bare rocks to forested hills of several hundred acres. Some are deposits of glacial till, the only marine drumlin field in the United States; others are largely slate, the uplifted remains of ancient lake-bed deposits. Many outer islands are solid granite bedrock presided over by lighthouses, including the country's first, Boston Light, built in 1716.

Seven of the islands—Georges, Gallops, Lovell, Peddocks, Bumpkin, Grape, and Little Brewster—constitute the actively managed portion of the **Boston Harbor Islands State Park❖.** A ferry from the city's Long Wharf calls at Georges Island, dominated by a massive Civil War–era fort. From Georges, a free water taxi stops at five other islands. With permits, camping is free on Lovell, Peddocks, Bumpkin, and Grape, where visitors enjoy the remarkable experience of sleeping on a remote ocean island and awaking to the shining skyline of a major city. (Only day use is permitted on Gallops, also accessible by water taxi). On Grape and Bumpkin, both small wooded drumlins, trails wander through miniature forests, along marsh edges, and over rocky outcrops.

Logan International Airport absorbed three Boston Harbor islands. Just north of Logan off Route 145, a small but rich pocket of marsh in East Boston escaped destruction. The only remaining natural salt marsh within the city limits (shared with Winthrop and Revere), **Belle Isle Marsh Reservation❖** was established in 1986 on the former site of the Suffolk Downs Drive-In. Now, amid rusting rail cars, racetracks, and an endless stream of jet traffic, a surprisingly varied congregation of shorebirds, herons, and waterfowl gather. Seasonal visitors include glossy ibis, short-eared owls, and snowy owls—the latter an occasional winter visitor from the Arctic that prefers flat coastal areas (including the airport runways).

Boston's two biggest "urban wild lands," both Metropolitan District Commission properties, sit on opposite ends of the granite hills surrounding the Boston Basin. The larger of the two, **Blue Hills Reservation❖,** spans the towns of Braintree, Milton, Quincy, Randolph, Canton, and Dedham. Forming the southern terminus of Olmsted's "Emerald Necklace" of urban green space, the Blue Hills' ten square miles are the largest public open space in the metropolitan Boston area. Some 150 miles of trails link the reservation's 22 hills, providing abundant opportunities for hiking, solitude, birding, and perhaps even a glimpse of the reservation's endangered timber rattlesnake population. **Great Blue Hill❖,** a 635-foot granite dome, is the highest summit on the eastern coastline south of Maine.

About 11 miles north of downtown Boston is **Middlesex Fells Reserva-**

ABOVE: *Lying just south of busy Route 128, the broad waters of Ponkapoag Pond in the Blue Hills Reservation attract canoers, kayakers, and anglers. Along one edge a boardwalk leads to a quaking bog.*

tion❖, a 2,000-acre park bisected by I-93 that dramatically juxtaposes natural and man-made environments—five reservoirs, a hospital, and a zoo. From the entrance on South Border Road west of I-93, a short trail leads to the summit of Pine Hill, an excellent place to survey the area's geology. Middlesex Fells sits on a dramatic fault line that drops off abruptly to the southwest, providing a splendid vista of the Boston Basin, the surrounding granite rim, and the Blue Hills rising distantly in the south. This is a good place to start a circuit of the reservation's western section across the "fells," or stony hills, that gave the park its name.

East of I-93 is the reservation's **Spot Pond Brook Archaeological District;** a self-guided trail begins at park headquarters on Woodland Road. Now quiet and secluded, this area has historically been the center of intense human activity. Following a meandering stream through oak and hemlock forests, the trail leads past stone-wall pasture boundaries from the 1600s, mill dams and spillways from the 1700s, and the remains of a nineteenth-century rubber-making plant named after its owner, Nathaniel Hayward, who in 1836 discovered the modern process of rubber production with his partner, Charles Goodyear.

71

The 2,200-acre **Lynn Woods Reservation❖,** just east of Route 1 in Lynn, was established in the 1880s as a "healthful resort" for the working population of Lynn and the surrounding industrial towns. One of the first and largest municipal parks in the country, Lynn Woods is three times the size of Manhattan's Central Park. Most of it appears to be a single enormous outcropping of felsite and syenite, rocks so hard and barren that the area was soon designated a "commons" by default. Today its valleys are sprinkled with small swamps and shaded by mature hardwood forests. Sprout birches and maples (multitrunked trees growing from cut stumps), carpets of moss, and tiny fens dot its rocky ridges, or "burnt lands," which offer fine views south to Boston Harbor and north to wooded hills. Dozens of glacial boulders, covered with toadskin lichen and flanked by showy lady's slipper orchids in the spring, balance precariously atop bedrock ledges where glaciers dropped them thousands of years ago.

In the center of Lynn Woods is **Dungeon Rock,** a house-sized granite outcrop with a colorful—and bizarre—pirate legend attached. In 1658, the story goes, pirate Tom Veal was hiding in a cave with stolen treasure when he was entombed by a rockfall. Two hundred years later confirmed spiritualist Hiram Marble was told of the treasure by a fortune-teller and spent the next 12 years digging a 200-foot tunnel in the rock. He never found a single doubloon.

WEST OF BOSTON: NATURE BETWEEN THE INTERSTATES

"The river is my highway, the only wild and unfenced part of the world hereabouts," wrote Henry David Thoreau in his journal. Indeed, Thoreau's world today, the region between Route 128 and I-495, is still filigreed with two major river watersheds: the **Charles River** and the **Assabet-Sudbury-Concord River system.**

The Charles is Boston's river, and like the harbor, it was for years a bad environmental joke. So polluted were its waters from industrial discharge and sewage that it inspired the Shandrells' 1960s rock song "Dirty Water." During the past two decades, however, the water has improved so greatly that now most of it is clean enough for fishing and swimming. Despite its urban associations, the Charles travels through largely natural settings rarely seen by the motorist, and even though it flows over some

---

RIGHT: *Beneath the shade of young hemlocks, Mill Falls, which once provided water power for a long-vanished sawmill, spills over a fieldstone dam at the Broadmoor Wildlife Sanctuary in South Natick.*

LEFT: *With its webbed feet and fishy meal, this young river otter already shows its predilection for aquatic life. Once hunted nearly to extinction, river otters are making a comeback throughout much of their former range.*
RIGHT: *Bold black-and-white coloration warns potential predators not to fool with a striped skunk. Beyond the pungency of its rank defensive spray, this species is also a prime carrier of rabies in the United States.*

20 dams, a canoe is the best way to see its considerable attractions. There are numerous access points, easy portages, and waters quiet and reliable enough to permit attentive nature watching. Many interesting protected areas bordering the river and its watershed are also accessible by foot.

Between Needham and Newton Upper Falls, just inside Route 128 south of Route 9, is **Hemlock Gorge Reservation❖.** Surrounded by urban development, these 23 acres are perhaps the wildest stretch of the Charles. Here the river cuts through a steep rocky gorge where dark stands of hemlock perch on granite outcroppings, as if a small stretch of a wild Maine river had suddenly been spliced into an otherwise tamed and harnessed waterway.

Southwest of Needham in Dover, off Dedham Street, is **Noanet Woodlands❖,** a 695-acre park whose trails follow Noanet Brook, a tributary of the Charles. From 1815 to 1876, this stream powered the Dover Union Iron Company; today, however, the massive stone dam at Noanet Falls, reconstructed in 1954, seems an anomaly in these remote woods. Moderately steep ridges rise from the valley and culminate in 387-foot **Noanet Peak,** where in a remarkable view northeast, the Boston skyline appears to float like the city of Oz on an unbroken sea of green foliage. In fall these ridges create thermal updrafts, attracting numerous migrating hawks.

The **Broodmoor Wildlife Sanctuary❖,** in South Natick and Sherborn, provides 600 acres of pastures, fields, woodlands, ponds, and a lovely stretch of river shoreline where ospreys, wood ducks, and foxes, among other wildlife, can be viewed from hemlock-shaded banks.

Farther south, **Rocky Woods Reservation**❖ off Hartford Road in Medfield is well named because the site encompasses many former rock quarries. The granite ridges of this 488-acre preserve also constitute the divide between the Charles and Neponset River watersheds. Forming a remarkable natural sculpture, a 200-foot-long outcropping called **Whale Rock,** with its broad, smooth striations, rises like a giant cetacean from an ocean of earth and trees.

Nowhere else in southern New England do history, culture, and nature intersect more richly than in the valley of the Concord River and its two major tributaries, the Assabet and the Sudbury. Rising within a mile or two of each other in Westborough, the Assabet and Sudbury rivers diverge and then come together again in Concord Center to form the Concord River, which then flows north to its confluence with the Merrimack at Lowell. Like the Charles to the south, these waterways are winding, slow-moving, and heavily vegetated. (The Sudbury is so unaggressive that during spring floods the runoff from its larger brother, the Assabet, actually causes it to flow backward.) Six millennia ago Native Americans dubbed the Concord Musketaquid, meaning grassy banks, and these "great meadows," arable after spring floods receded, attracted farmers early on to the valley.

Slicing through deep pieces of time and history, these rivers today meander north through well-to-do Boston suburbs. They flow by historic houses and farms; beneath mill sites, dams, graceful nineteenth-century arches, and Concord's Old North Bridge; under railroad bridges and modern highways; beside abandoned factories and a modern missile plant;

and finally through the intricate canal system in Lowell, America's first industrial mill town.

Among the wealth of natural areas in this region, the jewel is the **Great Meadows National Wildlife Refuge❖.** Only 20 minutes west of Boston, it is one of the country's great migratory bird sanctuaries. Established in 1944, its 3,400 acres of river, bays, marshes, and upland incorporate 12 miles in two distinct sections of the Sudbury and Concord rivers. In spring and particularly fall, the refuge is a stopover for thousands of Canada geese, wood ducks, green-winged teal, black ducks, mallard, blue-winged teal, gadwalls, wigeon, ring-necked ducks, and a host of less numerous waterfowl and wading birds, many of which nest along its banks during the summer. Year-round the refuge attracts some 220 species of birds, 25 species of freshwater fish, snapping turtles, water snakes, at least 4 species of salamanders, 7 species of bats, flying squirrels and jumping mice, river otters, white-tailed deer, and even an occasional bobcat.

Like the Charles, this riverine refuge is best seen by canoe. (There is a canoe rental place in Concord and numerous pedestrian access points along the rivers' paths.) In the Sudbury Unit, at refuge headquarters at the end of Weir Hill–Sudbury Road, a mile-long trail winds by a red maple swamp and a waterfowl pond, along marshes and riverbank, through some impressive pine woods, and by a kettle-hole pond to the top of **Weir Hill,** a 12,000-year-old drumlin. Its 200-foot summit provides a fine view. The Concord Unit, at the end of Monson Road off Route 62 in Concord, encompasses the **Concord Impoundments,** two large marsh-bordered pools surrounded and split by earthen dikes that separate them from the Concord River. The pools are off limits to boats, but the dikes, bordered by natural blinds of high cattails and an observation tower, provide visitors with excellent birding vantage points, especially during fall and spring migration.

Two miles south of the Concord dike pools, off Route 126, is **Walden**

Pond State Reservation❖, encompassing arguably the most famous pond in the world. The site of Henry David Thoreau's classic account of his life in the woods includes a reconstruction of his small cabin. Although altered by a state swimming beach and other public facilities, the deep, clear pond is still an exceptionally lovely place to visit; white pine woods surround it, and **Emerson's Cliff,** steep rocky outcrops broken off by glaciers, and the **Andromeda Ponds** (actually a series of shrub swamps) are nearby.

East of Walden Pond is the town of Lincoln, which more than any other Boston suburb has managed to preserve a large portion of its rural character and natural resources. Some 80 parcels incorporating more than 2,000 acres of farm fields, wetlands, woods, riverfront, ponds, and hills are owned by the town and the Lincoln Land Conservation Trust. **Flint's Pond❖,** a beautiful 156-acre reservoir surrounded by walking trails, was Thoreau's first choice for his stay in the woods (allegedly the owner refused permission). A somewhat misnamed preserve, **Mount Misery❖** includes a canoe landing on the Sudbury River and an extensive network of trails that wind along the natural and man-made dams of Beaver Dam Brook and through noble oak, beech, and pine woods to the gentle summit of 360-foot Mount Misery, which offers a fine view of Fairhaven Bay, one of Thoreau's favorite haunts.

North of Boston: The "Green Region"

North of Route 128 and east of I-93, the inland towns of Andover, North Andover, Boxford, Topsfield, Hamilton, and Wenham contain a wealth of large state forests and intriguing private preserves. Many sites now occupy former estates and farms of old North Shore families or turn-of-the-century entrepreneurs, and larger tracts of land are often still privately owned. The result is a splendidly "green region" between the loop highways of Route 128 and I-495, a rural mosaic of forested hills, winding rivers, lakes, dairy farms, orchards, and horse farms.

Off Prospect Street in Andover and North Andover, the **Charles W. Ward Reservation❖** provides a fine introduction to a classic northern spruce–tamarack quaking bog. Full of sundews and other carnivorous plants, the refuge is distinguished by tall, dark spires of black spruce and larch, or tamarack, a deciduous conifer with needles that turn a brilliant honey-gold in autumn. Around the bog stretches a square mile of woodland paths and lovely hillside orchards and pastures. From the summit of Holt Hill, the highest in Essex County, an ocean of trees, unbroken except for a few water towers and church steeples, sweeps toward a diminutive outline of the Boston skyline some 20 miles south.

Boxford State Forest❖, off Middleton Road in Boxford, contains one of the region's most biologically interesting areas: the 355-acre **John C. Phillips Wildlife Sanctuary,** which sustains an unusual diversity of bird and plant life. Its calcium-rich epidote gneiss bedrock gives the swamps and woodlands an unusually sweet soil that supports abundant fern species and spleenworts, as well as sweet pepperbush, buttonbush, basswood, sugar maples, and six species of birches. More species of birds breed here than in comparable surrounding areas, including such uncommon nesters as goshawks, red-shouldered hawks, broad-winged hawks, barred owls, Louisiana waterthrushes, and the spectacular red-crested pileated woodpecker, the largest woodpecker in North America.

A major ecosystem in this region, the Ipswich River flows 35 miles, most of which is navigable by canoe. In the town of Topsfield, off Route 97 on Perkins Row, lies the wholly magnificent **Ipswich River Wildlife Sanctuary❖,** the largest of the Massachusetts Audubon preserves. Within its 2,800 acres of meadows, swamps, ponds, islands, and eskers, some

RIGHT: *After beavers caused the flooding of this trail at Audubon's Ipswich River Wildlife Sanctuary, purple loosestrife, a nonnative invasive plant, quickly moved in to colonize the moist edges of the path.*

eight miles of river wind through dramatically contrasting habitats. On the west is a prime example of a river floodplain forest swamp—populated primarily by silver maple—unusual because most of the area's forested floodplains were drained for farmland or developed. The trees' tall arching branches and huge upended stumps are home to a cornucopia of nesting woodland birds: veeries, wood thrushes, orioles, yellowthroats, yellow warblers, swamp sparrows, black-throated green warblers, blackpolls, kingbirds, great crested flycatchers, and spectacularly colorful wood ducks. Canoeists with sanctuary permits may camp on **Perkins Island,** a parklike 50-acre isle of white pines.

In the eastern half of the sanctuary, the Ipswich River crosses into an area of open swamp and wet meadows, revealing a world of wide swinging energy, of water, sky, grass, light, and space. As the enclosed forest falls away and sunlight floods the river, wide vistas of glacial hills and islands emerge. The surrounding marshes teem with their own distinctive avian fauna: red-winged blackbirds, marsh wrens, snowy and great egrets, goldeneyes, red-tailed hawks, and soaring peregrine falcons.

CAPE ANN AND THE NORTH SHORE

The granite headlands and rocky offshore islands of Cape Ann offer some of the most dramatic seascapes on the Massachusetts coast. **Halibut Point State Park❖** and **Halibut Point Reservation❖,** at the north tip of Rockport, are contiguous preserves whose 66 acres are the quintessence of Cape Ann—50-foot slabs of granite bedrock sloping steeply down into the sea. At the edge of these massive ledges grow delicate trout lilies and violets, just a few feet from tidal pools crawling with hermit crabs, periwinkles, and starfish. Impressive anytime, Halibut Point is best seen after a northeaster, when crashing waves create a symphony of sight and sound. Winter months bring parti-colored harlequin ducks, which hang about on the offshore rocks.

Back along Route 127 in the historic and colorful fishing community of Gloucester lie the 500 beautifully landscaped acres of **Ravenswood Park❖.** Carefully designed and maintained carriage roads and trails wander among tall groves of hemlock and white pine, through patches of pink lady's slippers and the diminutive pink and white blossoms of trail-

---

LEFT: *Augmenting the North Shore's scenic and rocky coastline at Halibut Point State Park is an enormous jumble of granite debris, tailings from Babson's Quarry, a major nineteenth-century industrial site.*

ABOVE: *Elaborate courting rituals and fish exchanges precede the actual moment of copulation for a pair of least terns. This smallest of tern species winters in Brazil and Venezuela.*

RIGHT: *Early morning light casts boardwalk shadows over Hellcat Swamp on Plum Island. Here "sunken forests" between the dunes provide cover for the island's populous deer herd.*

ing arbutus, over ledges strewn with delicately balanced glacial boulders, and down into **Magnolia Swamp,** an extensive wetland that shelters the northernmost stand of sweet bay magnolia in New England (in Massachusetts it is listed by the state as endangered).

North of Cape Ann the rocky coastline gives way to a softer, labyrinthine landscape of brilliant white barrier beaches, sweeping dunes, extensive salt marshes, and an unparalleled example of nineteenth-century opulence. One of the largest of the Trustees of Reservations properties, the combined **Richard T. Crane, Jr., Memorial Reservation❖** and **Cornelius and Miné S. Crane Wildlife Refuge❖** in Ipswich and Essex covers more than 2,000 acres and includes one of the most popular beaches on the North Shore. Each summer, just south of the beach parking area, the air fills with the scissoring flight and calls of a major least tern colony, while tiny nesting piping plover run about on little mechanical feet. Beach access through the fragile dunes is strictly controlled. Wide parklike stands of pitch pine, a series of maple swamps, and wild cranberry bogs line the hollows behind the dunes. A stand of river birch, a tree of coastal plains and rivers with diamond-shaped leaves and heavily peeling bark, is a disjunctive population—the nearest similar coastal stand grows on Long Island, 150 miles south. Intervening populations were probably swallowed up by rising sea levels when the last glaciers melted, stranding this northern island population.

Brooding above the refuge's parking lot at the northern end of Castle Neck are the heavily wooded slopes of **Castle Hill,** which is surmounted by the 59-room baroque mansion known as Great House. Behind the mansion, the **Grand Allée,** a wide lawn bordered by classical statuary, rolls down between spruce and maple plantations and back up to the summit of **Steep Hill,** where it carries the eye over the steep bluffs and across the sparkling waters of the Castle Neck River, north to the sand spits, dunes, and marshes of Plum Island.

North of Crane's Beach is the 4,662-acre **Parker River National Wildlife Refuge❖,** the northernmost significant barrier-beach system on the East Coast and a major coastal migratory bird refuge. Here a bowl of gentle glacial hills and steepled New England villages enclose long white beaches, forested and moving dunes, and vistas of bogs, swamps, marshes, and estuaries.

Unlike Cape Cod's remote Monomoy Island refuge, Parker River is readily accessible both to pedestrians and vehicles. A paved access road runs the length of **Plum Island,** a seven-mile barrier beach composed of several low glacial drumlins connected by dunes, maritime forests, and

---

OVERLEAF: *American beach grass holds down fragile dune lines at Crane's Beach. New plants form from underground runners, creating a gridlike system of roots that can reach eight feet deep in the sand.*

LEFT: *A Canada goose (top) performs low-impact aerobics, stretching its wing. A dabbling duck that feeds on aquatic plants, this male American wigeon (bottom) sports breeding plumage: a white crown and iridescent green band.*

RIGHT: *This bucolic scene at the Parker River National Wildlife Refuge looks much as it has for centuries. Surrounding fields are now maintained for waterfowl, which graze on the gleanings.*

swamps. In summer Plum Island's beaches overflow with swimmers and sunbathers, who share the sand with nesting terns and piping plover. The refuge's natural spectacles, however, reach their height in the spring and fall, when thousands of Canada and snow geese, American black ducks, green- and blue-winged teal, northern shovelers, gadwalls, wigeon, old-squaws and mergansers, harriers and falcons, sandpipers, plover, swallows, and dozens of other species of migratory birds move through the coastal refuge.

One of the best spots to experience the refuge's varied habitats is **Hellcat Swamp,** where an impressive network of well-maintained trails and boardwalks lead the visitor through shrub swamps of alder, birch, and winterberry to an observation blind beside a freshwater marsh. The marsh edges are strewn with cut poplar-tree stumps, the work of beavers that were introduced to the area about 15 years ago. Today the beavers make their home in the refuge's freshwater pools.

At the southern tip of the barrier beach, **Sandy Point State Reservation❖,** a Massachusetts Wildlands Site, contains **Bar Head,** a 50-foot glacial drumlin, as well as the **Emerson Rocks,** an extensive natural stone field formed from the sea-sifted remains of former drumlins. The rocks lie on an expansive, gently sloping beach glistening with mica and garnet flakes and dotted with sand dollars—the round shells of a spiny echinoderm related to sea urchins. In fall, purple sandpipers and other shorebirds pick among the stones and tidal pools for periwinkles, worms, mussels, and other food.

CENTRAL MASSACHUSETTS:
THE PLATEAU AND THE CONNECTICUT RIVER VALLEY

L ying between the Boston Basin and the Connecticut River valley, Massachusetts's Central Plateau is part of the erosion surface region, the worn-down roots of ancient mountain ranges that once towered 20,000 feet or more. Over hundreds of millions of years, erosion has reduced the mountains to a fairly uniform plateau—averaging about 1,000 feet in height—with moderate hills and valleys carved by glaciers and postglacial rivers. Considered a geologic extension of New Hampshire's White Mountains, the Central Plateau contains remnants of ancient granite peaks, most notably Mounts Wachusett and Watatic. The region's major "natural" feature is the Quabbin Reservoir, 40,000 acres set aside in 1937 to augment the water supply for the Greater Boston area. It subsequently became what writer Tom Conuel calls "the accidental wilderness"—and one of the great wildlife preserves in southern New England.

Until fairly recently the Central Plateau was the small-farm heartland of the state. Post–World War II development has enveloped much of the former farmland, and second-growth white-pine forests have claimed other abandoned tracts. The region's transitional forests include some pure southern hardwood (oak-hickory-white pine) forests in the south and east and northern hardwood (maple-birch-beech) stands in the north. Since the old shade elms succumbed to Dutch elm disease, the largest trees are now

LEFT: *The forested islands and peninsulas of the vast Quabbin Reservoir rise above a colorful autumnal sea of birches, maples, and white pines in this sweeping view looking north from the Quabbin Tower.*

sugar maples, whose stately silhouettes border the country roads, their rough, gnarled majesty flanked by the parallel shoulders of old stone walls. The Connecticut River, New England's largest, winds south 68 miles through scenic countryside dotted with outstanding examples of traprock geology, river geography, floodplain ecology, and even dinosaur fossils. In northern Massachusetts the Connecticut is a fairly straight, fast-flowing river coursing through a narrow valley and floodplain. Below Greenfield, however, the valley broadens and the river slows as it reaches the ancient sedimentary bed of glacial Lake Hitchcock. By Northampton, where the valley spreads 15 to 20 miles wide, the river meanders slowly across its ancient floodplain, creating oxbows and sloughs as it runs through some of southern New England's most fertile farmland, its soil replenished each spring by snowmelt and runoff flooding.

Several traprock ridges, the remains of 300-million-year-old lava flows, have been preserved in the Connecticut's valley, affording the visitor excellent opportunities to explore these interesting geologic formations and providing fine views of the river and surrounding landscape.

This itinerary traces a counterclockwise circuit, beginning just outside Route 495, heading west across the northern tier of central Massachusetts, down the Connecticut Valley to Northampton, then east to the Quabbin Reservoir, the Quaboag River valley, and finally southeast to the Blackstone River valley.

The Central Plateau

At the end of Still River Depot Road off Route 110 in Harvard is an area that presents a strange conjunction of the man-made and the natural. **Oxbow National Wildlife Refuge❖,** bordering the eastern banks of the Nashua River, is a 711-acre preserve of marsh, woodland, swamp, and oxbows. One of the state's less-frequented birding spots, it attracts numerous breeding and migratory land birds and waterfowl, including the uncommon worm-eating and hybrid "Brewster's" warblers (a cross between golden-winged and blue-winged warblers), in the spring, as well as rich populations of dragonflies and butterflies. The refuge was once an artillery range for the now deactivated Fort Devens Military Reservation, and the U.S. Fish and Wildlife handbook still cautions visitors, "Do not touch unusual metallic objects."

From Route 110 take Route 62 west to the lovely hilltop town of Princeton. One mile down Goodnow Road is the **Wachusett Meadow Wildlife Sanctuary❖,** an old farm preserve of more than 1,000 acres of

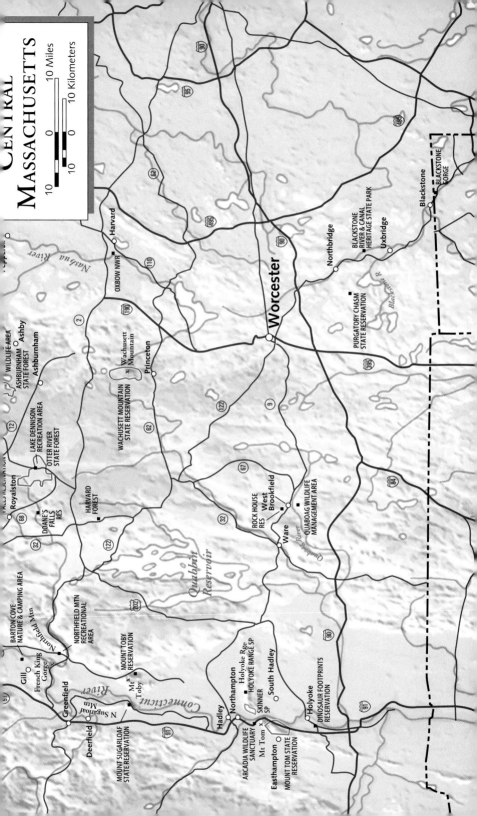

10 Miles

10 Kilometers

0

0

10

10

Blackstone Gorge

Blackstone

BLACKSTONE GORGE

Uxbridge

BLACKSTONE RIVER & CANAL HERITAGE STATE PARK

Northbridge

PURGATORY CHASM STATE RESERVATION

Nashua River

Harvard

OXBOW NWR

Worcester

Ashby

WILDLIFE AREA

ASHBURNHAM STATE FOREST

Ashburnham

Princeton

Wachusett Mountain

WACHUSETT MTN STATE RESERVATION

Blackstone R

LAKE DENNISON RECREATION AREA

OTTER RIVER STATE FOREST

Royalston

HARVARD FOREST

DOANE'S FALLS RES

ROCK HOUSE RES

West Brookfield

QUABOAG WILDLIFE MANAGEMENT AREA

Ware

Quaboag River

BARTON COVE NATURE & CAMPING AREA

Northfield Mtn

NORTHFIELD MTN RECREATIONAL AREA

MOUNT TOBY RESERVATION

Mt Toby

Quabbin Reservoir

Gill

French King Gorge

Greenfield

N Sugarloaf Mtn

Connecticut River

Deerfield

MOUNT SUGARLOAF STATE RESERVATION

Hadley

Northampton

Holyoke Rge

HOLYOKE RANGE SP

SKINNER SP

South Hadley

Holyoke

DINOSAUR FOOTPRINTS RESERVATION

ARCADIA WILDLIFE SANCTUARY

Mt Tom

Easthampton

MOUNT TOM STATE RESERVATION

LEFT: *With its tall nodding red flowers, the carnivorous pitcher plant is unmistakable in sphagnum bogs. The large, hollow, pitcher-shaped leaves are lined with down-curved hairs and partially filled with a sticky liquid in which curious insects are trapped and digested.*

woodlands, orchards, hay fields, pastures, stone walls, and an eighteenth-century farmhouse and barn. In summer Wachusett Meadow exudes a lush abundance. Bobolinks, tree swallows, and barn swallows flit about the hay fields, which are not mowed until after the nesting bobolinks' broods have fledged.

Above the farmhouse a trail leads through a large field of golden-topped hay to the **Crocker Maple,** whose 15-foot circumference makes the 250-year-old tree one of the largest maples in the country. Left for shade when the fields were cleared in 1786, its enormous bulk—its crown rotted off and its massive horizontal limbs supported by cables like some sylvan marionette—has weathered the blows of the ages, reminding us that trees, unlike people, show all their wounds.

Three miles north of Princeton Center on Mountain Road is the entrance to **Wachusett Mountain State Reservation❖.** A monadnock, or isolated mountain that has escaped erosion, Wachusett at 2,006 feet is the highest point in southern New England east of the Connecticut River and the southernmost peak of New Hampshire's White Mountain range. (From the top, New Hampshire's Mount Monadnock—which gave its name to such peaks—is visible to the northwest.) Composed primarily of granite, Wachusett's resistant core was once a part of a towering massif. Of special note on its higher elevations are stands of northern spruce–hemlock forests quite rare in eastern Massachusetts, and at its northern

RIGHT: As if flying into a red sun, a male tiger swallowtail (top) is attracted to a scarlet flower to feed. A black swallowtail (bottom) clings to a withered milkweed stalk. Darker female forms of both species mimic the distasteful pipevine butterfly, dissuading potential predators.

edge a grove of old-growth northern red oak protected under the Massachusetts Wildlands Project.

Each September Wachusett hosts one of New England's great natural spectacles when it becomes the premier hawk-watching spot in eastern Massachusetts. As early fall sunlight heats the granite ledges, warm air currents called thermals rise into the cool air. Migrating hawks ride the thermals south along the ridges, often arriving in impressive concentrations called kettles. During peak migration days, usually just after a cold front arrives, up to 10,000 hawks, ospreys, falcons, and eagles may swoop and soar over Wachusett on a single day. Most of these birds are broad-winged hawks, medium-sized buteos with broad banded tails and white underwings bordered in black. They seem to materialize out of thin air by the hundreds, rising in corkscrew gyres high over the summit, then gliding gracefully southward on their wide wings to the next thermal. Even the presence of hundreds of birders and a forest of radio antennae cannot diminish the splendor of this annual natural event.

THE NORTHERN TIER: MOUNT WATATIC TO THE CONNECTICUT RIVER

The border towns of north-central Massachusetts, from Pepperell to Royalston, boast some of the state's most attractive and least-visited villages and natural areas. Rich concentrations of glacial lakes surround Ashburnham and nearby towns. Large state forests—such as **Lake Dennison Recre-**

LEFT: *Usually seen soaring effortlessly overhead in wide spirals, the common red-tailed hawk is known by its sharp, descending "kee-arr" call.* **RIGHT:** *In fall, a vivid red maple presides over the broad, grassy entrance to the Jug End Trail at the Northfield Mountain recreational area.*

ation Area✧ and **Otter River State Forest**✧ both near Winchendon—offer extensive camping, hiking, fishing, boating, and swimming opportunities. Here also the true northern hardwood forests begin, providing spectacular fall displays of maple, beech, birch, and other trees.

Ten miles north of Wachusett, near the towns of Ashby and Ashburnham, lies eastern Massachusetts's other monadnock, Mount Watatic. Less well known and a bit lower than Wachusett Mountain, Watatic's slopes of northern hardwoods straddle **Ashburnham State Forest**✧ and **Watatic Mountain Wildlife Sanctuary**✧. The 1,832-foot summit, privately owned but open to the public, affords another good vantage point for watching migrating hawks wheel and soar in September and October. From Watatic's bald peak, a mix of granite outcrops and quartz-shot schist, magnificent vistas sweep in every direction. The rolling hills extend south, broken by the sole promontory of Wachusett. To the northwest, New Hampshire's Mount Monadnock stands in solitary splendor; to the east-southeast, the distant skyline of Boston and the blue waters of Boston Harbor materialize. And as far as the eye can see to the north-northeast, a series of genuine mountain ranges—Barret Mountain, the Pack Monadnocks, Crotched Mountain, the Uncanoonucs—culminate 100 miles away in the White Mountains' Presidential Range.

Farther west, the town of Royalston on the New Hampshire border boasts two impressive and contrasting waterfalls. Off Falls Road north of Route 68, **Royalston Falls Reservation**✧ is the more remote. Many consider Royalston the region's loveliest waterfall: The 70-foot cataract plummets into a granite gorge bordered with dark, towering hemlocks; in summer, lush ferns and the songs of Swainson's thrushes abound. Although best seen in early spring during snowmelt, the falls offer solitude almost all year, shared only with a beaver or two swimming at the base of the falls.

Doane's Falls Reservation❖, south of Royalston Center at the intersection of Doane's Hill Road and the Athol-Royalston road, includes an impressive series of cascades. Here Lawrence Brook emerges beneath an arched stone bridge and in five separate falls drops 200 feet through northern hardwoods and hemlocks to the valley of the Tully River. Such power was not lost on the early colonists, and the gorge is littered with impressive stone foundations and millstones of historic mills set below rock ledges so steep that one wonders how the mills were ever built.

Continue on the Athol-Royalston Road to Route 32 and head south. One mile past the Petersham town line look for the entrance to the **Harvard Forest❖** on the left. Donated by James L. Brooks to the Harvard University Forestry School in 1907, the forest is a unique outdoor laboratory for those seriously interested in the dynamics of forest processes. Its 2,000 acres encompass textbook tracts of second-growth forests, hurricane blowdowns, natural hardwood succession, and planted pine plantations. Some of the pines, their trunks bent but not broken by the devastating 1938 hurricane, grow in tilted and recurved patterns, like sinuous stands of seaweed. Return north on Route 32 to Route 2 and follow it west beside the scenic Millers River.

Less than a mile before reaching the Connecticut River, take Route 63 two miles north to the entrance of the **Northfield Mountain Recreation and Environmental Center❖,** a 2,000-acre "preserve" owned by Northeast Utilities. An environmentalist's conundrum, the mountain has been gouged out to create an enormous artificial reservoir that supplies supplementary hydroelectric power for coal, oil, and nuclear power plants. Transformers and high tension wires pattern the landscape, and turbines pumping water from the Connecticut River to the reservoir sometimes trap young salmon smolts introduced in a federal salmon restoration program. However, the utility is making efforts to improve the smolts' downstream passage.

Despite transformers and turbines, however, Northfield Mountain is a well-planned and excellently maintained recreational area with outstanding natural environments and a fine system of marked trails. The grassy hills near the visitor center, for instance, are actually fossilized sand dunes from Lake Hitchcock, an enormous glacial lake that once flooded much of the upper Connecticut Valley.

Northfield's **Rose Ledges Trail** leads to 80-foot-high gneiss outcrops. Like schist, gneiss is a metamorphic rock, but coarser, exhibiting thicker and more prominent layering that resembles the wet, swollen leaves of a giant book. Named perhaps for the reddish foliose lichen covering their faces, the ledges provide dramatic views of the upper Connecticut Valley and delight local rock climbers. The pink and white blossoms of trailing arbutus, or mayflower—Massachusetts's state flower—delicately scent the air in April and May, and in June the hills erupt with pink nosegays of mountain laurel.

THE CONNECTICUT RIVER VALLEY

On a strikingly graceful 750-foot steelwork span 140 feet above the water, Route 2 crosses the Connecticut River at **French King Gorge❖.** Steep-sided and constricted, this granite gorge encloses the wildest and most scenic stretch of the river in the state. On the north side of the bridge, hemlock and paper birch grow along rock ledges that step down and into the river's currents. The view to the south is sometimes marred by the black waters of the merging Millers River, which spreads dark tendrils of paper-plant pollution into the green Connecticut.

Generally, the Connecticut River winds through Massachusetts in less dramatic, less hurried settings such as the **Barton Cove Nature and Camping Area❖,** a few miles below the gorge on Route 2 in Gill. Owned by Northeast Utilities, Barton Cove sits on a wide embayment where the Connecticut jogs sharply west around Turners Falls. From a miniature inlet reminiscent of the Maine coast, steep sandstone ridges covered with hemlocks rise sheer above a narrow fjordlike body of water. When a pair of bald eagles built their large stick nest here, Barton's Cove became the most accessible place in the state to view the breeding behavior of these majestic birds. Canoe rentals are available for exploring the cove and French King Gorge above.

A few miles south, three prominent peaks flank the Connecticut River: Mount Toby to the east near Sunderland, and North and South Sugarloaf mountains to the west near Deerfield. These peaks are the northernmost of a long series within the Connecticut River valley. Unlike most of the others, however, they are not basalt traprock ridges but remnants of a peculiarly resistant layer of pudding stone and sandstone known as the Mount Toby conglomerate, deposited by streams eroding the faulted Connecticut Valley lowland 200 million years ago. Cranberry Pond, on the left at the entrance to **Mount Toby Reservation❖,** rests on the valley's ancient fault line. At 1,269 feet, **Mount Toby** is one of the highest peaks in the Connecticut Valley, and its exposed ledges, especially near the summit, are an impressive sight. Equally formidable is its botanical variety, among the most diverse in the state. Known as a paradise for fern lovers, the reservation contains 42 of the region's 45 indigenous fern species.

Across the Connecticut in Deerfield is **Mount Sugarloaf State Reservation❖.** Although North Sugarloaf is higher, 652-foot South Sugarloaf provides a superb view of the Connecticut Valley (or Pioneer Valley, as the Massachusetts portion is known) extending southward, its agricultural fields and bucolic towns flanking the broad, winding river. Earlier in this century the valley was dominated by tobacco farms, their distinctive shade netting stretched over the plants and rows of long wooden drying sheds. Today the remaining sheds stand weathered and abandoned in fields that grow corn, potatoes, and Chinese vegetables.

Straddling the Connecticut River to the south are the humped massifs of the Holyoke Range and Mount Tom, two of the most dramatic geologic formations in Massachusetts. The northernmost extensions of the Metacomet Ridge, these two traprock formations stand at right angles like great, galloping forms of shaggy behemoths frozen in their migration down the valley. Encompassing **Skinner State Park❖** and **Holyoke Range State Park❖** in Hadley and South Hadley, the nine-mile Holyoke Range is a prime and unusual example of a basalt traprock ridge. Whereas other Connecticut Valley traprock ridges run north-south, nearly the entire Holyoke Range was twisted into an odd east-west orientation some 200 million years ago.

A portion of the Metacomet-Monadnock Trail traverses the ridge, and strung along its center section is a series of peaks called the Seven Sisters. Appearing much higher than its 942-foot summit, **Mount Holyoke,** the westernmost, provides one of the best overlooks in the valley, its panoramic views stretching from New Hampshire to Connecticut on clear days. Because of its dramatic rise and east-west orientation, the range offers a vivid contrast of forest types. Dominating the warmer southern slopes is a typical oak-hickory southern hardwood forest, and the cooler, moister northern slopes support a northern hardwood-hemlock-white pine community unusual in the valley. The long snaking ridge also creates thermals, or uplifts of warmer air, that attract numerous kettles of migrating hawks in the spring and fall. In September, up to 10,000 broad-winged hawks have been recorded here. The Holyoke Range, especially Mount Tom, supports populations of state-endangered timber rattlesnakes and copperheads.

RIGHT: *The fertile floodplain of the broad Connecticut River attracted the first European settlers to the state's interior in the late 1600s.*

OVERLEAF: *Thomas Cole painted* **View from Mount Holyoke, Northampton, Massachusetts, after a Thunderstorm (The Oxbow)** *in 1836.*

Above: *Resilient and highly adaptive to coexistence with humans, the Eastern coyote has reappeared throughout New England. Unlike wolves, coyotes hold their bushy, black-tipped tails down when running.*

Looking west from Mount Holyoke's summit reveals a scene familiar to students of American landscape painting: **Oxbow Lake,** the subject of a famous 1836 painting by Hudson River School painter Thomas Cole. Then a circular bend in the Connecticut River, Oxbow Lake was cut off when the river took a newer, straighter course during an 1841 flood and has been further bisected by the construction of Route 5 and I-91.

Much of the Oxbow today is included in **Massachusetts Audubon at Arcadia❖,** across the river from Mount Holyoke on Fort Hill Road in East-hampton. This 550-acre sanctuary shelters a wealth of lowland habitats, in-cluding old fields and orchards, rare examples of undisturbed river-plain forest and swamps, duck ponds, and lush groves of ostrich, cinnamon, and royal ferns along the riverbank. The old field off Horseshoe Trail attracts numerous species of sulphur, swallowtail, and skipper butterflies in sum-mer. An observation tower overlooking Arcadia Marsh is an excellent place to view the sanctuary's abundant water life, including muskrat, kingfishers, nesting wood ducks, Canada geese, and green and great blue herons.

Return to Route 5 and follow it south about three miles to **Mount Tom Reservation❖** on the right. Another basalt traprock ridge and the taller western twin of Mount Holyoke, Mount Tom affords even more breathtaking views. The dramatic basalt cliffs on the western slopes—hard, columnar, crystalline—seem to possess a frozen energy, a thrust and upward yearning that bespeaks their volcanic origins. The exposed tops of the polygonal basalt columns are frequently crisscrossed with networks of glacial scratches. Although highly resistant to weathering, these angular cliffs are not resistant to gravity-induced rock falls, and their bases are lined with skirts of talus—basalt fragments that clink like a xylophone junkyard underfoot.

Along the ridge trail, which rises southward toward the 1,202-foot summit of Mount Tom along increasingly open and more dramatic exposed basalt ridges, hikers often encounter resident ravens, larger, wilder relatives of common crows. Their spectacular courtship antics in early summer include bouts of upside-down flying. Unfortunately, the peak of Mount Tom is not included within the reservation, so visitors emerge from relatively unspoiled forest and cliffs into an incongruous phalanx of beacons and radio towers, fenced transmitter stations, and a colorful jungle of graffiti on the exposed basalt just below.

In the shadow of Mount Tom, just a few feet from the roar of traffic on Route 5, is **Dinosaur Footprints Reservation❖.** (Take Route 5 south from the Mount Tom entrance into Holyoke and look for a small unmarked parking area on the east side of the highway, just above the river.) Dinosaur tracks abound in the sandstones and shales of the Connecticut Valley, where saurians roamed the tropical swamps of the Triassic period 200 million years ago. When their fossil footprints were first discovered here in the early nineteenth century, the existence of dinosaurs was unknown. An early investigator, Professor Edward Hitchcock of Amherst College, called them "stony bird feet," speculating that they were made by giant antediluvian ravens that never got onto Noah's ark. (Given the current theory that dinosaurs are the direct ancestors of birds, perhaps he was not far off.) Although only eight acres, this reservation provides a rare opportunity to see footprints of large carnivorous dinosaurs in New England. Follow a graveled path down the embankment to the shale outcrops. Here, between a railroad bed below and the highway above, are several dozen well-preserved prints up to two feet in length of 200-million-year-old three-toed saurians.

LEFT: *Mute testimony to the "lost" villages that disappeared when Quabbin was flooded in the 1930s, bricks and debris are still visible in the clear waters.*

RIGHT: *Where cardinal flowers bloom, hummingbirds are likely to be nearby, pollinating the red tubular blossoms with their long, thin beaks.*

THE QUABBIN RESERVOIR AND SOUTH-CENTRAL MASSACHUSETTS

From Holyoke, take Route 202 east to Route 9, then continue east to the park entrance at the south end of the **Quabbin Reservoir❖.** A major feature on the southern New England landscape, Quabbin is the largest body of open water and one of the largest public open spaces in the region. Designed to provide a municipal water supply for metropolitan Boston in the 1930s, the Quabbin was formed by flooding the Swift River valley, wiping four townships—Enfield, Dana, Prescott, and Greenwich—from the Massachusetts map, along with their attendant villages, roads, and cemeteries. Reminders of the once-thriving communities are everywhere: Old roads disappear into the water; the remains of town centers evoke vanished ghosts of buildings and commerce; "ghost" ponds and lakes are still marked on the official reservoir map, connected beneath Quabbin's overarching waters.

As an unintended byproduct of its creation, Quabbin is the largest and one of the most important wildlife refuges in the state, an "accidental wilderness." Its 39 square miles of surface water and 56,000 acres of surrounding watershed are home to deer, otters, fishers, mink, bobcat, turkeys, pileated woodpeckers, beavers, coyotes, and even mountain lions. Bald eagles, however, are probably Quabbin's most remarkable success story. Scientists speculate that southern New England's bald eagle population began to decline during the 1800s, when dams and industrial development disturbed and polluted the birds' traditional nesting and feeding areas. Even so, there are very few authenticated sightings of these impressive birds in nineteenth-century Massachusetts. During the 1960s bald eagles were virtually extirpated in New England by the deleterious effects of DDT and other pesticides on egg development. Since harmful pesticides have been banned, a sizable wintering population has gradually formed around Quabbin. In 1982 biologists began importing eagle young to be raised artificially

105

ABOVE: *Bordered by a stately red maple, Quabbin Reservoir epitomizes the paradox of southern New England's natural areas: The "natural" aspect of their wild landscapes is often the work of human engineering.*

and released at Quabbin, in hopes that they would return as adults to nest. In 1988 the first nesting pairs of bald eagles in Massachusetts in more than 80 years successfully fledged chicks. By 1993 nine nesting pairs of these magnificent birds were returning to Quabbin each summer.

Breeding birds are quiet and secretive, and the best time to see these majestic eagles is during the winter, especially from the **Enfield Lookout** or the **Quabbin Hill Lookout Tower** at the reservoir's south end. With its arms stretching northward out of sight, its long pine-crested peninsulas, its archipelago of dozens of islands, and its surrounding bowl of low, wooded hills, Quabbin might well be one of the larger lakes in northern Maine. From the main visitor center one can make a complete clockwise motor loop of the reservoir on Routes 9 west, 202 north, 122 east, and 32A and 32 south, and hikers will find trails at many gates.

Continue east on Route 9 into West Brookfield and the **Rock House Reservation❖,** where large glacial erratics surround **Rock House,** a massive granitic augen gneiss outcrop (*augen,* German for "eye," refers to the large crystals of feldspar embedded in the rock) whose overhanging rock ledge and southeast exposure made it a favored winter camp for prehistoric Native Americans. Its diverse habitats, including an artificial pond, attract a wide variety of wildlife, including great blue herons, deer, coyotes, and wild turkeys.

Two miles east of Rock House, where Routes 67 and 9 join, the Quaboag River Watershed provides canoeists with an unspoiled and accessi-

106

ABOVE: *Hank's Picnic Place, with its spreading maple trees, is a popular gathering spot at Quabbin. The nearby hardwood forests are now home to a growing population of fishers, a type of arboreal weasel.*

ble stretch of flat water. Typical of the quiet, marsh-bordered rivers of south-central Massachusetts, the Quaboag allows paddlers to concentrate on the abundant bird and animal life along its winding course, including such specialties as breeding American bitterns. Unless flushed, these secretive medium-sized herons are hard to spot among their favored cattail reeds, where their brown streaked plumage and habit of freezing with neck and bill extended upward provide almost perfect camouflage.

Muskrat, yellow warblers, painted turtles, and the occasional beaver frequent the river, also known for its populations of pike, bass, catfish, and panfish. In midsummer the ubiquitous foliage of the beautiful but invasive purple loosestrife brings a blaze of color to the marshes. Several bridges give visitors without a canoe a chance to admire the river's beauty and wildlife. Most of the gentle hills south of the river are protected in the 1,100-acre **Quaboag Wildlife Management Area❖,** which includes several hiking trails off Long Hill Road.

South of Worcester, a portion of western Rhode Island's extensive granite bedrock shield pushes into Massachusetts. A dramatic portion of this bedrock is exposed at **Purgatory Chasm State Reservation❖,** in Sutton State Forest west of Route 146. Although the chasm—a 60-foot-wide geologic fault eroded out of the granite bedrock—extends less than an eighth of a mile, within that space the devastation of the ages might well have occurred. Over time, huge slabs of rock have sheared off the

107

70-foot walls, forming a chaotic jumble of boulders at the bottom and treacherous footing for visitors. (The chasm trail is closed in the winter months.) Towering hemlocks, their roots grappling the rock ledges, soar a hundred feet out of the canyon, like dark spirits ascending to heaven. Water remains frozen in this natural refrigerator late into the spring—when little rills and seeps collect at the outlet—then issues forth in a clear stream that swerves softly down through the forest beyond, sweetness and clarity flowing from rocky chaos and dark earth.

Just east of Sutton, Route 122 follows the course of the Blackstone River, once one of the wildest—and most powerful—rivers in southern New England. From its headwaters in Worcester to its mouth at Narragansett Bay, the Blackstone drops 438 feet in 46 miles, more than the Colorado River falls in a similar stretch through the Grand Canyon. Situated in one of the country's first industrial valleys and called "the hardest-working river in America," the waterway in this century has been characterized by industrial pollution and decay. Recent federal legislation, however, established the **Blackstone River Valley National Heritage Corridor❖;** under its provisions, Massachusetts and Rhode Island are creating a greenway along the river, preserving its historic legacy and restoring many of its natural assets. The **Blackstone River and Canal Heritage State Park❖** already encompasses nearly a thousand acres on the Uxbridge-Northbridge line. Here visitors can explore an eighteenth-century barge landing, canoe the river or portions of the 1828 Blackstone Canal, follow the barge towpath, or observe upland and wetland wildlife in the 900-acre **Rice City Pond Natural Area,** which supports abundant waterfowl, especially wood ducks and teal.

On the Massachusetts–Rhode Island border, between the towns of Blackstone and North Smithfield, is **Blackstone Gorge State Park❖,** a dramatic stretch of free-flowing river. Access and a small parking area are at the end of County Road off Route 122 (Main Street) in Blackstone. Here the river narrows and plunges through rugged hundred-foot granite walls lined with dark hemlocks. During high water in spring, this unexpectedly wild quarter-mile stretch of the Blackstone reminds viewers of the unfettered power that fed the first great industrial valley in North America.

Left: *With the banning of such pesticides as DDT, the bald eagle is thriving and has returned to nest near the Quabbin Reservoir again.*
Overleaf: *Natural and artificial blend seamlessly at Rock House Reservation. The huge boulders were left by glaciers; the pond is man-made.*

WESTERN MASSACHUSETTS:
THE BERKSHIRE HILLS AND MARBLE VALLEYS

The Berkshire Hills have a distinct identity defined more by culture and tradition than by strict political or geographic boundaries. Lying primarily in Berkshire County, but also in western portions of Franklin, Hampshire, and Hampden counties, the Berkshires are unquestionably the most rugged area in southern New England. They contain the region's highest peaks, including the tallest, Mount Greylock; the largest tracts of state forest in Massachusetts, comprising some recently identified stands of old-growth timber; some of the most unusual botanical communities in New England; all of the Massachusetts portion of the Appalachian Trail; the lion's share of the state's waterfalls and white-water rivers; and its largest populations of beavers, bobcats, wild turkeys, porcupines, and black bears, as well as a large number of fishers, weasel relatives once hunted for their fur.

Having weathered the ages gives the Berkshires a force and presence greater than their modest elevations. Averaging slightly more than 2,000 feet, these ridges have undeniable muscle and character, the result of millions of years of erosion that has reduced the original elevated peaks to their hard, resistant gneiss and schist cores. In contrast, the softer, more easily eroded rocks in the Hoosic and Housatonic river valleys to the west include large deposits of marble, a metamorphic form of limestone, that was deposited eons ago when the area was part of an inland sea. Because of their composition, they are frequently called Massachusetts's Marble Valleys.

LEFT: *In the central Berkshires, a stand of paper, or white, birches flourishes amid a lush understory of ferns. The distinctive peeling bark of this native tree was used to cover the lightweight canoes of Native Americans.*

113

Both the valleys and the mountain ranges were once part of the Berkshire erosion surface, an uplifted shield that represents the ancient roots of the original Appalachian range. The Berkshires are composed of such irreducible bedrock that postglacial rivers were unable to breach the north-south ranges, which for more than a century after European arrival in New England remained an obstacle to westward expansion from the Connecticut Valley. This geologic barrier also created anomalies such as the Hoosic, the only significant river in southern New England to flow northwest. Thus the Hoosic and the Housatonic (which, more conventionally, flows south) drain the area in opposite directions.

On the westernmost border of Berkshire County loom the eastern flanks of New York's Taconic Range: higher, younger, angular, and dramatic. Geologists now believe that the rocks of the Taconics originated east of what are now the Berkshires and through some massive ancient lateral displacement of bedrock called thrust-faulting were flipped over them to the west, so that the younger metamorphic shales and slates now rest atop older deposits.

Because of its rugged terrain and generally poor soils, this region was less suited to farming than other portions of the state, and during the eighteenth and nineteenth centuries much of the forest was logged off. Since then second-growth forest has re-covered the hillsides, and today the region seems heavily wooded, even in river valleys. Populated predominantly by northern hardwoods and some boreal spruce-fir stands in the northwest corner, the Berkshires have the look and feel of northern New England—as well as its brilliant fall colors.

This exploration of western Massachusetts follows Route 2 west up the Deerfield River valley to the summit of the Hoosac Range at Mount Greylock and then swings south along the Housatonic River, with a loop east into the Berkshire plateau. The itinerary then heads south again into the southern Berkshires, ending at the Connecticut border.

THE MOHAWK TRAIL:
THE DEERFIELD RIVER VALLEY AND THE HOOSAC RANGE

The hill town of Shelburne on the Deerfield River was incorporated in 1768. Only 30 miles west in the Hoosic Valley lies Williamstown, site of

---

OVERLEAF: *The Berkshires have long attracted artists and writers. Monument Mountain, rendered here by Asher Durand (1796–1886), is where Nathaniel Hawthorne and Herman Melville first met, in 1850.*

Williams College, settled in 1753. Yet not until 1914 did a highway—present-day Route 2, which follows the Mohawk Trail, a route used by the Mohawk in the French and Indian War—connect the two towns and the distinct regions they represent.

Affording spectacular vistas and a good view of this ancient travel corridor, **High Ledges Wildlife Sanctuary❖** is off Route 2 in Shelburne, on the upper slopes of 1,600-foot Massaemett Mountain. Sheer rock outcrops—which attract the ravens often seen here—offer dramatic scenes of the Deerfield River as it winds westward into the Berkshires and of Mount Greylock, some 25 miles to the west. An extensive trail system through steep northern hardwood and hemlock forests provides challenging wilderness hiking. The sanctuary's vertical diversity of habitat enables its 400 acres to support some 500 plant species, including an abundance of pink, yellow, and even rare white lady's slippers in June.

South of Shelburne Center, off Bardwell's Ferry Road in Conway, is **South River State Forest❖,** a deceptively wild area encompassing a 300-foot gorge heavily forested with hemlocks and hardwoods. A series of 128 wooden steps leads down to one of the state's most impressive waterfalls: an 80-foot-high cataract of Niagaralike symmetry that roars through a primeval-looking gorge. A closer look, however, reveals that the falls are actually an abandoned dam—built in 1910 to provide power for the Conway Electric Street Railway. Behind the dam the reservoir has silted in over the years, creating a marsh full of peepers, turtles, redwings, coots, wood ducks, and herons. Near the steps back up to the road is one of the largest black oaks in Massachusetts, measuring more than five feet in diameter at breast height.

Return to Route 2 and head west to the village of Shelburne Falls, site of the **Salmon Falls Glacial Potholes❖.** Although the falls have been converted into a rather unattractive power dam, below them sprawl acres of beautifully sculpted blue granite ledges striated with ribbonlike intrusions of orange and white quartz. Carved by glaciers millennia ago, these ledges are pockmarked with smooth circular holes hollowed out by the whirlpool action of glacial grindstones, many of which remain in the holes. Among the more than 50 glacial potholes here is the world's largest, 39 feet in diameter.

West on Route 2, the hills become steeper and the Deerfield River more

---

Rɪɢʜᴛ: *Dwarfed by the steep, forested slopes of the Hoosac Range, two energetic kayakers on the wild upper reaches of the Deerfield River enjoy one of the best white-water stretches in Massachusetts.*

rapid. At the town line of Charlemont and Savoy visitors enter Berkshire County—and the heart of the Hoosac Range. The Cold River branches from the Deerfield, and the highway follows it for several miles through **Mohawk Trail State Forest❖,** a wild river corridor featuring some of the most rugged scenery in Massachusetts. Impressive most times of the year, the Cold River is especially dramatic in winter, when it is often choked with jumbled slabs of ice. Inaccessible slopes rising more than 500 feet from the south banks of the river probably preserved the **Cold River Old Growth Forest❖,** one of the largest stands of old-growth hemlock, yellow birch, and sugar maple in the state, now designated a Massachusetts Wildlands Site. A portion of this forest is visible from Black Brook Road, just off Route 2. In the town of Florida, the **Reed Brook Preserve❖** protects what the Nature Conservancy calls "one of the most unusual bedrock geologic features in Massachusetts": a 400-foot outcrop of orange-gray serpentine, a rock that is a portion of the earth's deep mantle. The rock's heavy metal content produces a harsh soil that only a few plants, such as the maidenhair spleenwort, can adapt to. A marvelous view of the upper Deerfield River can be had from the summit. Near Florida, farther west on Route 2, rises the Whitcomb Summit—at 2,240 feet the highest point on the Mohawk Trail—where breathtaking views stretch north across the upper Deerfield Valley and into the Green Mountains of southern Vermont.

THE NORTHERN BERKSHIRES

From the western summit of the Hoosac Range, Route 2 begins a steep seven-mile descent—including the notorious Hairpin Turn—into the industrial city of North Adams. Just before entering the city proper, turn north on Route 8 and follow signs for **Natural Bridge State Park❖,** which contains the only water-carved natural marble bridge in North America. Formed from limestone laid down nearly half a billion years ago, the marble chasm is a chiaroscuro of black and white rock reminiscent of the smooth, wind-sculpted canyons of the Southwest. This miniature gorge, carved by the waters of melting glaciers thousands of years ago, is home to Hudson Brook, which spills over a dam onto gleaming marble ledges, then switchbacks down the 60-foot chasm, creating a symphony of sound and mesmerizing plays of light. The walls of the ravine sustain such un-

---

LEFT: *In a moist hemlock ravine, Reed Brook cascades over moss-covered rocks. An old wagon road beside the stream climbs to a rare and ancient outcrop of magnesium that originated deep in the earth's crust.*

ABOVE: *A high meadow in the Green River Valley provides stunning views of the wooded western flanks of the Mount Greylock State Reservation, considered the crown jewel of the Massachusetts park system.*

usual plants as maidenhair spleenwort, bulbet fern, and dwarf horsetail. The "bridge" itself, some 30 feet long, is nearly obscured by a complex web of walkways and fencing.

Crouched between the Hoosic and Green River valleys is **Mount Greylock,** at 3,491 feet the highest point in southern New England and the lion of Massachusetts mountains. (Herman Melville, who lived in nearby Pittsfield, dedicated his novel *Pierre* to Greylock, calling it "His Majestic Eminence.") Surrounding the mountain is 11,000-acre **Mount Greylock State Reservation❖,** the flagship of the state's forest and parks system, which concentrates in one area many superb natural attractions, including five major peaks and a long stretch of the Appalachian Trail.

The Greylock massif is actually an outlying spur of New York's Taconic Range, separated when erosion wore down the softer schists and marbles between them and formed the present Green River valley. The rocky summits of Greylock's north-south ridges, composed of hard, quartzite-laden metamorphic schists, provide spectacular hundred-mile views in all directions. In winter these heights are frequently rimmed in silver hoarfrost, per-

122

haps resembling locks of hair and suggesting the name "grey lock." The peak also has its own weather, nearly always windy and frequently swathed in thick clouds when the lower slopes remain clear. Several prominent manifestations of man's presence at the summit include the still-operating Bascom Lodge, a stone edifice that the Civilian Conservation Corps built in the 1930s from Mount Greylock schist and spruce.

In its great diversity of habitats, Greylock supports 46 species of rare, threatened, or endangered Massachusetts plants and animals, as well as a forest community unique in southern New England. Stunted balsam fir, red spruce, yellow and white birch, and northern mountain ash inhabit a true boreal forest flourishing here at the southern limit of its range. In May and June a rich variety of wildflowers brighten Greylock's slopes: lovely yellow trout lilies and pink-veined spring beauties, small yellow lilylike blossoms of clintonia, Canadian and smooth yellow violets, wild ginger, jack-in-the pulpits with their green or purplish-brown hooded floral leaves, and red and painted trilliums (the former possessing a flower that looks and smells like carrion to attract pollinating carrion flies). Also common is hobblebush, whose tips bend over and root in the ground and are thus likely to trip, or "hobble," a horse.

June and early July bring nesting birds, including the blackpoll warbler—a handsome black-capped bird that nests in the mountain's boreal forest and nowhere else in the state—and four species of nesting thrushes. Among the frequently seen larger avian species are wild turkeys, pileated woodpeckers, ruffed grouse, and barred owls. White-tailed deer and porcupines abound, as do snowshoe hares, whose fur turns white in winter. In addition, black bears, coyotes, and fishers are making a comeback, and Greylock is one of the best places in the state to glimpse the elusive bobcat. The reddish-gray streaked or spotted form of this nocturnal predator is most often seen in the glare of car headlights.

Of Greylock's more than 40 miles of maintained trails, a few are especially interesting. At the end of Sperry Campground Road, **Stony Ledge Trail,** a favorite congregating point for Greylock's increasing population of ravens, offers a magnificent view of the **Hopper.** A National Natural Landmark, the Hopper (its converging slopes reminded early farmers of a grain hopper) is a massive cirque, or circular valley, carved by mile-high glaciers. Its steep slopes support nearly 2,000 acres of old-growth hardwoods and conifers. On Greylock's northern face, west of Mount Williams, **Money Brook Trail** leads from the Appalachian Trail to **Money Brook Falls,** a tall, narrow cascade named for a gang of local

ABOVE: *Mount Greylock's rich vertical zonation attracts diverse species. The indigo bunting (left) frequents its lower woodland clearings. The evening grosbeak (right) inhabits the summit's colder boreal forests.*

counterfeiters who hid their equipment here during the depression. The trail passes a stand of old-growth red spruce known as **Tall Spruces,** which in June is suffused with the delicate scent of mountain azalea.

South of Mount Greylock and east of Dalton Center on Route 9, follow Waconah Falls Road to **Waconah Falls State Park✤,** where water from the Windsor Reservoir less than a half mile upstream makes the falls impressive in all seasons. Hemlocks and yellow birches form a perfect amphitheater for the cascade, which plunges through several gateways of talc schist—a stratified greenish-gray rock—into a deep pool below. At the top of the falls are the remains of a mine shaft where talc was processed in the last century. Encircling the pool is a jumble of large erratics, including one five-foot boulder of nearly pure quartzite.

THE BERKSHIRE PLATEAU

The route now follows a wide loop east into the hill towns of the Berkshire plateau. Some 40 miles long and 20 miles wide, the plateau lies east of the Housatonic River valley and south of the Hoosac Range; although nearly 2,000 feet high, it looks like a gently rolling wooded plain because the underlying bedrock has worn down fairly evenly. Despite its flat appearance, the plateau is divided by deep northwest-southeast valleys carved by the three branches of the Westfield River. Often a thousand feet below the surrounding ridges, these river valleys have isolated many towns, which are connected to adjacent communities only by steep mountain roads.

From Waconah Falls, return to Route 9 and drive east into the township of Windsor, often called the icebox of the Berkshires because it con-

---

RIGHT: *Distinguished by its white blazes, the 2,000-mile Appalachian Trail crosses many of the highest peaks from Maine to Georgia. This section in Massachusetts leads to the 3,491-foot summit of Mount Greylock.*

124

LEFT: In early autumn, the Westfield River surges between the sheer gray granite walls of Chesterfield Gorge, a dramatic product of ancient ice sheets as well as more recent river erosion.

RIGHT: Although it weighed less than a pound at birth, this cub may grow to 600 pounds. Good climbers, black bears often use rough-barked "bear trees" such as this oak to sharpen their teeth and claws and to rub off any loose fur.

tains some of the region's coldest habitats. One mile east of the junction of Routes 9 and 8A is the entrance to **Notchview Reservation❖.** The largest of the Trustees of Reservations' properties, Notchview's 3,000 acres include 2,297-foot **Judge's Hill,** northern hardwood and boreal conifer forests, and habitat for bears, turkeys, and porcupines. Near the summit of Judge's Hill, a small meadow provides a fine vista of the notch carved by the Westfield River as it courses through the Cummington hills, an impressive prospect that gave the property its name. From a visitors' lodge, 25 miles of cross-country ski trails, offering fine hiking and exceptional opportunities for winter exploration, wind through broad fields, dark hemlock ravines, and bright open woodlands; across frozen brooks; and among spruce plantations whose symmetrical radiating aisles resemble expressionist sets for a Grimm fairy tale.

Return on Route 9 to Windsor Center and take Route 8A north for three-quarters of a mile to the **Eugene D. Moran Wildlife Management Area❖,** which straddles the highway. The refuge's 1,147 acres—a mixture of pastures, hay fields, marshes, heath, mixed hardwood forest, and pockets of boreal conifer forest—is a mecca for birders, particularly in winter. Cold-weather months regularly attract such northern and boreal species as evening and pine grosbeaks, white-winged and red crossbills, and the rare boreal chickadee, a denizen of northern coniferous forests that sports a brownish-gray cap and a more nasal call than Massachusetts's state bird, the common black-capped chickadee. In residence year-round are wild turkeys, ruffed grouse, snowshoe hares, porcupines, beavers, and mink.

In the northwest corner of Windsor is 2,000-acre **Windsor State**

127

ABOVE: *The hooded merganser is an uncommon but striking duck that nests in the Berkshires. Here a male displays its dramatic breeding crest in a painting by American artist Louis Agassiz Fuertes (1874–1927).*

Forest❖, whose highlight is **Windsor Jambs,** off Schoolhouse Road. A natural icebox, Windsor Jambs is a hemlock-spruce gorge that can remain 20 degrees cooler than the surrounding land, often holding ice and snow well into May. The sides of the gorge, sheer 70- to 80-foot walls of gray schist and quartzite, gradually narrow into the "jambs," a steplike canyon only 25 feet wide, where the waters of Windsor Jambs Brook are squeezed into a tumbling, reverberating torrent, especially during the meltwater months of late spring. An intricate mosaic of hemlock roots, rocks, thick mosses, and ferns patterns the cliff walls.

A different kind of ravine is the centerpiece of **Chesterfield Gorge Reservation❖,** on River Road south of Route 143 in the town of Chesterfield. Here the East Branch of the Westfield River flows through glacier-carved walls crowned with hemlocks. The riverbed retains artistic examples of the glacier's handiwork: Long granite ridges undulating through the gorge create a frozen sculpture of an Ice Age river, its smooth contours occasionally pocked with ancient potholes. On the east side, a large tightly fitted stone wall is all that remains of a 1739 bridge, once part of the original Boston-Albany Post Road. Southwest of Chesterfield, in the town of Middlefield, the Middle Branch of the Westfield River has cut a route a thousand feet below the surrounding plateau of hills. Overlooking the river on Clark Wright Road, one of the most remote Trustees of Reservations

128

properties, **Glendale Falls Reservation✤,** offers solitude as well as scenic beauty. A tapestry of braided cascades unrolls over giant natural stone steps, here flowing over wide ledges, there squeezed between deep rock crevices. From the head of the falls, the river gorge and unbroken stretches of forest beyond seem as close to an untouched wilderness as a traveler is likely to find in Massachusetts. A little exploration, however, reveals that "wilderness" is often simply an illusion created by the recuperative powers of nature. Just to the left of the falls stands the substantial stone foundation of an eighteenth-century sawmill, its diversion ditch still intact.

The Central Berkshires

Pittsfield, the county seat and largest city in the Berkshires, is rimmed with lakes formed by damming natural basins carved by glaciers. These large bodies of water—Pontoosuc, Onota, and Richmond—are splendid places to observe migratory waterfowl in spring and especially fall. From late October to freeze-up, numerous loons, grebes, teal, wigeon, canvasbacks, scaup, scoters, old-squaws, ruddy ducks, and other migrants ply their waters. At **Onota Lake✤,** northwest of the city, a short causeway (Dan Casey Memorial Drive) provides an excellent vantage point to observe Onota's sizable population of wood ducks. Each year these vividly colored birds build nests in tree cavities in the wooded marshy areas north of the causeway. From emerald head and crest to speckled maroon breast feathers and teal-blue wing scapulae—all dramatically outlined in white—male wood ducks sport a jeweled array of iridescent breeding colors unsurpassed among waterfowl.

Just southeast of downtown Pittsfield off Holmes Road is **Canoe Meadows Wildlife Sanctuary✤,** a fine urban-area preserve whose 298 pastoral acres of broad rolling fields are pungent with the smell of new-cut hay in summer and bubbling with the songs of bobolinks. Sacred Way Trail runs beside the Housatonic River, at this point a sluggish stream, through an open meadow rife with milkweed, phlox, and honeysuckle, whose lavender and white blossoms attract numerous butterfly species. Farther along, hikers may spot a small oxbow swamp, painted turtles basking in the sun, impressively large maples and birches, and a beaver dam. Another trail leads past West Pond, where great blue herons stalk fish and amphibians,

---

Overleaf: *Bleached tree skeletons stand watch in a bog near Halfway Pond in October Mountain State Forest. Beavers create such ponds to protect their lodges and provide ready access to surrounding trees.*

129

Left: *A denizen of wet heaths and bogs, the rhodora bears magenta flowers before its leaves unfurl.* Right: **Clearing for agricultural fields once nearly eliminated the white-tailed deer, which is now the Northeast's most common game animal.**

to **Wolf Pine,** an imposing hulk of a white pine. (The spreading branches of a "wolf tree" typically hog, or "wolf," the sunlight from neighboring trees.)

Appropriately enough, one of the most rewarding canoe trips in the Housatonic River Valley begins at Canoe Meadows, where it abuts the Housatonic River Wildlife Management Area. From this point a six-mile canoe trip on a flatwater stretch of the river leads through marshes, farmland, riverine forest, backwaters, and oxbows south to Woods Pond in **October Mountain State Forest❖.** Birdlife is abundant year-round, but the area's specialty is its marsh nesters: American bitterns, Virginia rails, and sora rails. Unfortunately, PCB contamination has made the river's fish dangerous to consume.

Continue south on Holmes Road and take Route 7/20 south toward Lenox; turn right on West Dugway Road and follow signs to **Pleasant Valley Wildlife Sanctuary❖.** Generally considered the source of most of the present generation of beavers in Massachusetts, the 1,500-acre refuge includes portions of **Lenox Mountain,** which, like Greylock, is an outlying ridge of the Taconic Range. Along Yokun Brook are several active beaver ponds, including **Pike's Pond,** site of the first reintroduced beaver colony in Massachusetts in 1932 and still one of the most reliable spots in the state to view the continent's largest rodent. Once hunted to extirpation for their fur, beavers often annoy landowners because they fell young trees and flood lowlands with their dams. Some of the prime land first farmed by European settlers in this region, however, was the silted-in sites of former beaver ponds, which provided flat, fertile, and stoneless loam.

Pleasant Valley also encompasses the nation's first dedicated salamander sanctuary, established to protect these amphibians whose breeding success is thought to have been damaged by the acidification of the region's lakes

and ponds, or possibly by ozone depletion. On warm, rainy nights in late spring, legions of spotted, four-toed, and Jefferson's salamanders can be seen scurrying across the roads and wet fields of the sanctuary.

THE SOUTHERN BERKSHIRES

Just over the Lee line on Route 20 is a small graveled parking area for the Appalachian Trail and the start of a 1.6-mile hike south to **Upper Goose Pond❖.** The trek begins on a footbridge over the Massachusetts Turnpike. Then a short, steep trail heads up and over a 300-foot ridge to the pond's pristine northern shore. Less than a mile from one of the busiest highways in New England, hikers find a remarkably undisturbed shore lined with hemlocks, beeches, yellow birches, sugar maples, and white pines. Of interest here is the unusual Goose Pond bladderwort, which grows in abundance with other aquatic plants at the eastern end of the pond and in summer carpets portions of Upper Goose with its diminutive yellow blossoms. This carnivorous plant captures tiny aquatic crustaceans called water fleas (genus *Daphnia*) through the sucking action of small underwater bladders.

Returning west on Route 20, take Route 102 west in Lee, immediately turning left onto Tyringham Road. A lovely pastoral combe full of working farms and horse pastures, the Tyringham valley is a "hot spot" among local birders because it contains woods and open fields. Its outstanding natural attraction, however, is **Tyringham Cobble❖,** a 400-foot rounded hill that dominates the valley. (The entrance and parking area are .3 miles south of Tyringham Center on Jerusalem Road.) Sometimes called an upside-down hill, Tyringham Cobble was formed when a section of the adjoining Back-bone Mountain broke off and flipped over, leaving older strata of gneiss atop the younger layers.

A two-mile loop trail leads through hillside pastures full of bobolinks (the only eastern bird that is white on top and black below) and grazing cows and up onto the rocky cobble, where hilltop ledges covered with stunted yew provide a fine view of the idyllic valley. The cobble's north-ern slopes are covered with hemlocks and an eastern hop hornbeam, or ironwood, normally a small understory tree with smooth, muscular limbs. This impressive specimen has a trunk some 16 inches in diameter and a grotesque skeletal appearance, its twisted arms reaching tortuously up through the dark hemlocks toward the light. Carpeting the ground are lush swaths of maidenhair and Christmas fern (its smooth-edged leaflets are shaped like miniature Christmas stockings).

Route 102 goes west into Stockbridge, a town made famous by the paintings of longtime resident Norman Rockwell. Within walking distance of the bustling town center lies one of the wildest settings in the Berkshires: **Ice Glen❖.** (At the end of Park Street, just south of town off Route 7, cross a footbridge over the Housatonic and follow the trail as it bears right into the glen.) A dark, rugged granite-gneiss cleft in the earth, Ice Glen was formed by a fracture in the earth's crust and widened by glaciers. An over-whelmingly primeval aura still clings to this wet, shaded ravine. Although the legend that ice remains here throughout the summer is inaccurate, frozen remnants often last well into May and even June. The glen's north-south orientation admits little sunlight, and even that is blocked by the tow-ering trunks of hemlocks and white pines, three to four feet in diameter. Although only about a hundred yards long, the trail through the glen pre-sents a challenge, even when not icy. It winds between sheer 80-foot rock walls, across footbridges, and over mammoth boulders and massive fallen trunks. Ice Glen's druidic atmosphere was not lost on the villagers, who in years past staged a torch-lit Halloween trek through its dark passage.

Route 7 leads south from Stockbridge into Monument Valley, bounded by

RIGHT: *On the dry, wintry summit of Monument Mountain, pitch pines thrive; below Monument Valley stretches north toward Mount Greylock.*

OVERLEAF: *Monument Mountain's crooked peak rises above the cattails and lush waterlilies at Fountain Pond in Great Barrington State Park.*

Beartown State Forest contains an abundance of diversified wetlands, such as this phragmites reed bog (right). Many of the forest's ponds and marshes were created by its beavers (above).

the massive bulge of Beartown Mountain on the east and by the unmistakable silhouette of Monument Mountain on the west. **Monument Mountain** is a magnificent geologic oddity: an isolated formation set between the Taconic Range and the Berkshire plateau that resembles no other peak in the region. Looming over the landscape, its white and pink ridges and crags suggest origins very different from those of the smooth forest-draped slopes of the Berkshires. Its quartzite and marble rocks were formed deep in the earth from sedimentary sandstone and limestone, then thrust upward along a fault. Because quartzite is one of the hardest rocks in the Berkshires, the mountain's rough outlines have resisted even the sculpting forces of the glaciers.

From the base of **Monument Mountain Reservation**❖ (about three miles south of Stockbridge on Route 7), trails climb to the top of **Squaw Peak** (1,642 feet). Crowned with a stunted forest of pitch pines, the summit provides stunning views, spanning the Housatonic River valley from Connecticut's Litchfield Hills in the south to Greylock in the north. Sheer cliffs and dramatic rock pillars drop off to the east.

According to Massachusetts Audubon master naturalist Tom Tyning, Monument Mountain provides the finest spring hawk-watching in the

138

Berkshires. Winter wrens, with their high bubbling trills, are also a spring specialty. Peregrine falcons are often spotted in migration, and ravens have now returned to the mountain to nest. The recent report of a timber rattlesnake is the northernmost sighting of this species in the Berkshires.

Across the valley to the east are the rolling hills of **Beartown State Forest❖** (the main entrance is on Blue Hill Road in Monterey). Because Beartown's nearly 11,000 acres contain only 12 campsites, solitude is a primary attraction. Turkeys, grouse, deer, beavers, and muskrat abound, and there is a good chance of sighting the elusive bobcat and the forest's namesake, the black bear. Swamps, beaver ponds, and bogs border the forest's roads. Near the entrance, **Benedict Pond** is a fine place to observe little brown bats chasing mosquitoes and other insects at dawn and dusk during the summer. A portion of the Appalachian Trail winds around the pond's southern end and up the southern slopes of Mount Wilcox to the **Ledges,** rocky outcrops that provide an excellent view of the valleys and Mount Everett to the south.

West of Great Barrington, just past the historic village of South Egremont, take Route 41 south and then immediately turn right on Mount

Washington Road. (The pond on the right is the only nesting site of the common moorhen in the Berkshires.) About three miles up the road on the left is exquisite **Guilder Pond,** the second-highest natural body of water in the state. Steep hemlock groves, massive schist ledges, and beaver lodges border the water, along with a wreath of mountain laurel that bursts into explosive bloom in mid-June. Late spring visitors may also spot a wild turkey hen waddling along the shore, her brood of eight to ten large fluffy chicks tumbling along behind.

About three miles farther, south of the village of Mount Washington, is the entrance to **Mount Everett State Reservation❖.** From here a three-mile drive (or walk, depending on the state of the gravel road) leads to 2,608-foot **Mount Everett,** the highest peak in the southern Berkshires. Just below the summit, a stone shelter offers protection from nearly constant wind as well as a spectacular panorama up the Housatonic River valley to the saddleback form of Mount Greylock 40 miles north. The Taconics and the Berkshires roll across the landscape like some giant land-storm of hills, and along their slopes and crests clouds and frequent summer thunderstorms create dazzling light shows. The summit of Mount Everett affords a virtually unobstructed 360-degree view and some of the best fall hawk-watching in the state. To the south, Mount Frissell straddles the Massachusetts-Connecticut border; just beyond it is Bear Mountain, Connecticut's highest peak, and the Litchfield Hills.

Sage's Ravine❖, an unusual east-west cleft in the hills and one of the loveliest and least-visited natural areas in the region, lies three miles to the south and 2,000 feet down. A strenuous hike covers the ten miles to Sage's Ravine via the Appalachian Trail, which crosses Mount Everett here. To reach it by car, follow the Appalachian Trail via access points off Route 41. The Racebrook Falls Trail in Massachusetts and the Under Mountain Trail in Connecticut both have parking lots.

Sage's Ravine Brook, the descendant of the glacial floodwaters that carved this steep valley, is a wild mountain stream that drops some 400 feet in a mile. Above a moist forest floor lush with ferns, the woods are remarkably open and parklike, and the brook twists and tumbles over moss-covered rocks in a series of seemingly landscaped cascades and clear pools. Above the myriad voices of the brook listen for the ringing song of the

---

RIGHT: *Spring and autumn find Bash Bish Falls near Mount Washington at full volume. Afternoon hours bring fascinating plays of light and sound as the sun declines westward and slants through the gorge.*

Louisiana waterthrush: high, slurred notes followed by a descending jumble. Actually a large warbler, the bird has thrushlike markings—olive-brown back, streaked breast—and is an uncommon nester in Massachusetts.

After returning to Mount Washington village center, take Falls Road west to **Bash Bish Falls State Park❖.** The park is within Mount Washington State Forest, which abuts Taconic State Park in New York; together they form the largest preserved natural area in the Taconic Range. From the upper parking lot, perhaps the pinnacle of all views in the Berkshires stretches into the distance. To the west, the steep slopes of Bash Bish Mountain on the left and Cedar Mountain on the right frame a 900-foot-deep gorge. Bash Bish Brook, the convergence of a dozen streams draining the town of Mount Washington, weaves downward through the dark foliage like a silver thread. Farther west, beyond this gigantic cleft in the Taconic Range, extends the broad plain of the Hudson River valley and the humped purple ridges of the Catskill Mountains. Devotees of this su-

LEFT: *The moist climate and environmental diversity of the Berkshire Hills create a multi-season cornucopia of wildflowers at Bartholomew's Cobble. Clockwise from top left: spring beauty, an early blossom of the moist woods; fire pink, with sticky hairs to trap insects; the exquisite white-fringed orchis, found in wet meadows and bogs; painted trillium, reflecting its name in trios of petals, sepals, and leaves; round-lobed hepatica, an early spring flower of dry, rocky woods; and the golden-flowered trout lily, named for its brownish, mottled leaves.*

RIGHT: *Thick stands of ferns, such as these on Mount Everett, indicate alkaline soils. Owing to their extensive limestone deposits, the southern Berkshires possess some of the richest fern habitat in the country.*

perb panorama often throng the parking lot at sunset.

Deservedly famous as the most photogenic waterfall in southern New England, **Bash Bish Falls** plummets 200 feet, splitting around a large outcrop of granite and plunging in two cascades into a deep emerald pool, part of a natural rock amphitheater. The left cataract is more powerful, spouting and bubbling in gushing fountains; the right is more delicate, sending lacy veils of water over moss-covered rocks and creating a symphonic complexity of volume, speed, and texture. Bash Bish's many ledges and shady ravines also provide habitat for unusual species, including timber rattlesnakes and worm-eating warblers, usually found much farther south.

From Bash Bish Falls, go back to Great Barrington and take Route 7 south into Sheffield, which shelters more state-endangered plant species than any other town in Massachusetts. Of the unusual limestone outcrops that foster such diversity, the most accessible is **Bartholomew's Cobble❖,** a National Natural Landmark world-famous for its outstanding floral community. Two mounds, or cobbles, composed of the same erosion-resistant quartzite and marble as Monument Mountain, create a varied alkaline and acid habitat for some 700 species of plants. An amazing 53 species of ferns, some growing nowhere else, form reputedly the greatest natural fern collection in the country.

Visitors needn't be polypodiophiles to appreciate Bartholomew's Cobble, however. Bordering two miles of the Housatonic's River's winding banks, the idyllic reservation embraces a wide range of habitats: floodplain, riverine forest, ancient oxbows, old pastures, climax forest, and rock ledges. This diversity produces "edge habitats," which are particularly attractive to birds. As riverine forest changes to sunny open fields, listen for the notes of wood-nesting redstarts and thrushes and the bright, bubbling songs of bobolinks and meadowlarks. Watch for the darting iridescent shapes of tree swallows and bank swallows (the latter nest in cavities excavated in mud banks along the river); for flocks of migrating Canada geese, mergansers, and wood ducks; and for the soaring forms of red-tailed and broad-winged hawks. Turkey vultures roost along the riverbanks, and there have been recent sightings of a black vulture, a rare visitor to the Berkshires that appears to be spreading its range northward.

Unlike many other sites in the Berkshires, Bartholomew's Cobble is not visually dramatic. Its richness is best appreciated over time, in the grand sweep of flowers, ferns, trees, and wildlife in the four seasons. Through the year its ledges and fields present an ever-changing parade of more than 500 different wildflower blossoms. In early spring the Ledges Trail displays the snowy white flowers of bloodroot, the yellow trumpets of trout lilies, the three-sepaled flags of red trilliums, and the miniature white pantaloons of Dutchman's-breeches. During the summer, the ledges sport bluebells and the pink blossoms of four-leaved milkweed; moist lowlands gush showy three-foot-high spires of great blue lobelia while pastures and fields blaze with such naturalized "aliens" as oxeye daisies, black-eyed Susans, devil's paintbrush, cinquefoils, and butter-and-eggs. Late summer through early November brings 16 species of goldenrod and the vivid purple and gold flowers of New England aster, and after the leaves have fallen, the curling yellow blossoms of witch hazel add a splash of color to the graying woods.

RIGHT: *Corbins Neck at Bartholomew's Cobble in Sheffield borders the meandering Housatonic River. Here the floodplain supports unusual southern tree species, such as the yellow poplar and giant cottonwoods.*

CONNECTICUT

PART TWO

C O N N E C T I C U T

Quietly conscious of and conscientious about its natural and human history, Connecticut, the Nutmeg State, has generally eschewed Massachusetts's dramatic history of fiery preachers, Revolutionary War battles, and abolitionist fervor, garnering itself the nickname State of Steady Habits. Its landscape too, containing 5,009 square miles, presents a relatively settled and quiet look. Few places in Connecticut can be termed rugged.

Connecticut's shoreline, fronting Long Island Sound, is a largely sheltered coast, encompassing numerous salt marshes, pocket beaches, offshore islands, and quiet coves. The state is divided into two large areas of low metamorphic and granite hills—the Eastern and Western Highlands—which flank the broad Central Valley, once the bed of glacial Lake Hitchcock. Sediments from this ancient lake bottom created the fertile soils that made the Central Valley the richest agricultural area in New England. In its northern reaches, the broad Connecticut River meanders sedately through the valley, bordered by productive farmland and old canal routes; some 40 miles above its mouth, however, the river unexpectedly leaves its cozy valley bed, cutting its way through forested hills of metamorphic rock and winding past enchanting old river towns to Long Island Sound. Navigable from its mouth to the state capital at Hartford, the Connecticut River has always been the state's most important waterway, and in places river ferries operating for centuries still carry travelers across its wide waters.

Dividing the Central Valley is the Metacomet Ridge, probably the most distinctive feature of the Connecticut landscape: a nearly continuous line of volcanic ridges called traprock that rise a thousand feet or more above the valley. Because of its geological and historical significance, the Metacomet Ridge also divides the two Connecticut chapters in this book.

Connecticut's ready access from the coast and more moderate climate attracted settlers considerably earlier than its neighbors to the north. European colonists moved first up the river valleys and then into the hills,

---

PRECEDING PAGES: *On a foggy morning, spiderwebs glisten at Selden Creek, a secluded inlet of quiet beauty along the Connecticut River.*

particularly in the western sections of the state. As in many other New England locales, most of the native forests were cut for timber or cleared for farmland during the eighteenth and nineteenth centuries. After the Civil War, when the population moved into burgeoning mill towns along the region's fast-flowing rivers, many farms were abandoned. Some of the state forests, in fact, were created when Connecticut acquired these forsaken properties for nonpayment of taxes during the Great Depression. Today, second-growth woodlands—predominantly a southern hardwood community of oak, hickory, yellow poplar, dogwood, black birch, and red maple—flourish in the region.

Individual trees seem especially dear to Connecticut residents. Indeed, a cherished historical legend relates that in 1686, when the English government tried to revoke the colony's original charter, Hartford patriots hid the document in a hollow oak tree that became known as the Charter Oak. The tree later acquired an almost religious significance: Scions of the great oak were carefully propagated, and their genealogies recorded as meticulously as those of the first families. Hartford resident Mark Twain once commented that he had seen enough venerated objects supposedly made from the original Charter Oak "to build a plank road from Hartford to Salt Lake City." In any case, Connecticut has always valued its "specimen trees," and several natural areas were specifically established to recognize and preserve the state's record holders.

Nature in Connecticut tends to be a local, often humanly influenced presence. The state's natural areas form a complex patchwork quilt of state, federal, local, and privately held properties. Offering more than 40 sites for the visitor, the Nature Conservancy has been particularly active in Connecticut, as have private municipal land trusts. No one publication describes them all, and only a selection are included here, but local inquiries are usually rewarded with some unusual and sparsely visited sites.

Perhaps Connecticut's most distinctive conservation organization is the venerable Connecticut Forest and Park Association, which maintains headquarters in Middletown. Formed in 1929, the association manages more than 500 miles of trails—the famous Blue-Blazed Hiking Trail System, one of the most extensive private networks in the nation. Running primarily across private land whose owners allow public access, the trails follow ridges, watercourses, valleys, and pond shores. They connect many of the larger public natural areas, enabling the adventurous walker to travel most of the state on public-access trails.

WESTERN CONNECTICUT:
THE METACOMET RIDGE AND WESTERN HIGHLANDS

Western Connecticut encompasses four distinct geographic regions: the northwest highlands; the southwest hills; the western coastal slope, from Greenwich to New Haven; and the western half of the Central Valley. The most rugged and scenic part of Connecticut, the northwest highlands boast impressive waterfalls, sizable wild turkey flocks, and the only true northern hardwood forests in the state. The area's Litchfield Hills are a southern extension of the Berkshire Range, and a small section of New York's Taconic Mountains penetrates the far northwestern corner, culminating at 2,380-foot Mount Frissell, the highest spot in Connecticut. (Nearby Bear Mountain, at 2,316 feet, is the tallest summit lying wholly within the state.)

Also in this northwestern region, western Connecticut's major river, the Housatonic, enters from Massachusetts. In places the Housatonic ambles through fertile farmlands; in other spots it slashes through steep hillsides, producing white-water runs in spring freshets. Limestone deposits underlying the area, which give it the name Marble Valley (marble is a metamorphic form of limestone), support several large calcareous, or alkaline, wetlands where a number of rare and endangered plants flourish. East of the Housatonic along the Shepaug River lie some of the most scenic and least visited natural areas in the state.

Settled early in the 1600s, the coastline from Greenwich to New Haven is today the state's most heavily populated and industrialized shore area

LEFT: *The Housatonic is a placid, meandering river through most of western Connecticut. As it nears the Saint Johns Ledges in Kent, it begins to cut a steep, narrow gorge through the ancient Housatonic highlands.*

151

and the site of most of the major seaports. Composed of metamorphic and granite bedrock outcrops overlain with glacial till, this strip, with a few notable exceptions, is the least "natural" stretch of shore in southern New England. Still, a few coastal preserves provide fine shorebirding opportunities, and just a few miles inland some of Connecticut's oldest preserves offer an unexpectedly rugged and rich respite from urban sprawl.

East of New Haven and sweeping north into Massachusetts is the Metacomet Ridge, a nearly unbroken line of exposed traprock that divides the state's Central Valley in two. Originally called Connecticut's Great Wall, the ridge, rising in places to more than a thousand feet, posed an effective barrier to trade and cultural exchange between Hartford and New Haven in colonial days. Today I-91 and other highways, their roadbeds lined with crushed basalt mined from traprock quarries, connect the state's two largest metropolitan areas.

These traprock ridges are actually the exposed edges of lava flows that spilled over the sedimentary floor of the valley during the Triassic and Jurassic periods. The Metacomet, named for a Wampanoag sachem (leader) who conducted King Philip's War in 1675–76, can best be seen from Route 10, which parallels the ridge on its western side. Here the uptilted rust-colored basalt cliffs and talus slopes rise precipitously above the western Central Valley, forming dramatic backdrops to scenic towns such as Farmington and Simsbury and providing some of the best fall viewing of hawk migrations in the state. At Tariffville, near the Massachusetts border, the Farmington River slices through the ridge in jagged Tariffville Gorge.

On the western edge of the Central Valley are several isolated traprock ridges called intrusive outcrops. These formations, including New Haven's Sleeping Giant and the Barndoor Hills near Tariffville, were created when magma flows punched vertically through the surface of the ancient sandstone layers that once filled the valley. As the sandstone eroded, these structures, darker and knobbier than the ridges to the east, were left exposed.

From the Massachusetts line, this chapter follows the Housatonic River valley south, loops east to sites on the Shepaug River, and then heads southwest to the shore. From Greenwich, the route traces the coast east to New Haven and then travels north up the western side of the Central Valley, concluding at sites along the Farmington River.

CONNECTICUT'S "ICEBOX" AND THE NORTHWEST HILLS

Norfolk township sits among hard hills of gray and white banded metamorphic rock shot through with intrusions of white quartz. Although not

ABOVE: *A delight to the eye but a bane to environmentalists, purple loosestrife, shown here blooming along the misty Housatonic River south of Kent, is an aggressive alien that crowds out native plants.*

the highest region in the state, Norfolk is called the icebox of Connecticut for its unusually cold environment and supports one of the state's few extensive areas of northern hardwood–hemlock. Its dense conifers and shaded stream banks are home to rare nesting northern bird species, including grosbeaks, pine siskins, and northern waterthrushes. Straddling the Massachusetts-Connecticut line off Route 272 near Norfolk, **Campbell Falls State Park❖** features an impressive 50-foot cascade. (The falls are actually in Massachusetts, but the best access is from Connecticut.) A trail winds a third of a mile through a northern hardwood forest—hemlock, white pine, beech, sugar maple, mountain maple, black birch, and a noticeable absence of oaks—descending into a rocky gorge. Here the falls plunge in a braided cascade into a dark pool and are transformed in winter into fantastic ice sculptures.

West of Canaan Center on Route 44, turn south on Route 126 and follow it 1.5 miles to the intersection of Sand Road and the railroad tracks at the Hollenbeck River. Despite appearances, **Robbins Swamp Wildlife Management Area❖** is Connecticut's largest natural inland wetland, a 1,500-acre diverse calcareous, or lime-rich, wetland partially owned by the state and the Nature Conservancy. A walk north alongside the still-used tracks when the trees are bare affords a fine view of limestone outcroppings that support both commercial limestone plants along Sand Road on

ABOVE: *Breaking gently around one of the many green wooded islands that dot its course, the Housatonic flows softly over the wide, easily eroded limestone that forms the bedrock of the northern Marble Valley.*

the bluffs to the west and such rare botanical plants as bur oak and northern white cedar in the swamp to the east.

Follow Route 44 west to Salisbury and take Route 41 north for 3.2 miles to a parking area on the left. Here the **Under Mountain Feeder Trail** begins a 6-mile loop to the top of 2,316-foot **Bear Mountain❖,** Connecticut's highest summit, part of the small section of the Taconic Range that brushes the corner the state. This challenging trail, worth the climb simply for the view, is bordered by the giant hulks of a once-mighty chestnut forest. In the fall, the summit affords great hawk-watching.

Continuing south to Lakeville and Sharon, Route 41 traverses some of the most picturesque farm and horse country in western Connecticut. In Sharon head east on Route 4 for two miles to the entrance of the **Sharon Audubon Center❖.** One of the National Audubon Society's education centers, this 700-acre preserve features two large ponds, maple swamps, open meadows, and upland forest. In the fall, Bog Meadow Pond attracts huge flocks of migrating Canada geese, and Ford Pond provides nesting sites for colorful wood ducks and hooded mergansers each summer. Both ponds support active beaver populations, which fell trees to build their dams and lodges along the shore. An unusual example of wildlife improving on human endeavors is sometimes apparent at the western end

155

Above: *A sea of dark late-autumn foliage washes over the overlapping ranges of Connecticut's rolling Litchfield Hills, seen here from Mohawk*

of Ford Pond, where these resourceful animals occasionally raise a concrete dam to higher levels.

Continue east on Route 4 to its intersection with Route 7 at the southern end of **Housatonic Meadows State Park❖.** Here, after its wide, meandering course through the northern Marble Valley, the Housatonic River has cut a moderately steep gorge through the schists and granite of the Housatonic highlands. Hardly a wild river on its 132-mile passage through Connecticut, the Housatonic is a fairly fast-flowing stream along this stretch, which is a favorite of canoeists and trout-fishing enthusiasts. Although numerous dams and hydroelectric facilities cause water levels to fluctuate and portions have been contaminated by PCBs (polychlorinated biphenyls) and other industrial waste, the park encompasses one of the Housatonic's cleaner and more scenic portions. On the west side of Route 7 just below the park campground is the trailhead for the 2.5-mile **Pine Knob Loop,** which provides a fine view of the river gorge and the towered crest of Mohawk Mountain to the east.

156

Mountain. Once several miles high, these hills are the remnants of mountains formed eons ago by the collision of continental plates.

Remaining on Route 4, continue east into Cornwall through classic New England landscapes of rolling hills, fertile valleys, and church-spired villages. In Cornwall Center turn right on Pine Street and left on Valley Road, then bear left on Essex Road and look for a small parking area on the left. Connecticut's famed **Cathedral Pines❖,** a 42-acre Nature Conservancy preserve, once boasted the most extensive stand of old-growth white pine and eastern hemlock in New England. A devastating 1989 tornado destroyed much of the grove—including the largest white pine in the state—and subsequent coring showed many of the downed giants to be more than 300 years old. Enough of the stand survives to create beneath its dense shade and massive columns an atmosphere of hushed mystery found in few other places in the region.

Some three miles east of Cornwall on Route 4 lies the entrance to **Mohawk Mountain State Park and State Forest❖.** A park road winds through its 3,600 acres to the summit, where a splendid panorama—from Massachusetts's Mount Everett to the traprock ridges of the Central Valley—

157

is being slowly obscured by a regenerating oak forest. Mohawk Mountain's claim to botanical fame, however, is an unusual two-acre **Black Spruce Bog.** Perched at an elevation of 1,500 feet, this type of wetland, although common in northern New England, is rarely found in Connecticut. A foot trail wanders through thick stands of mountain laurel decked out with white and pink blossoms early each June, as well as through stands of dark hemlock whose twisted roots grasp the rocky ground. A sturdy boardwalk crosses the bog, where a floating mat of soft sphagnum moss covers the wetland. Here typical bog plants such as sheep laurel and leatherleaf grow in the dense shade of black spruces, tall, thin conifers rising 30 feet or more.

ABOVE: *Not normally a tree climber, this chipmunk has scampered out on a cherry limb for a look-see. In winter chipmunks hibernate only lightly.*

RIGHT: *A serpentine tangle of tree roots and sphagnum moss carpets the floor of Black Spruce Bog. Early settlers brewed tea from spruce needles to treat cases of scurvy.*

To the southeast, about two miles west of Litchfield on Route 202, **White Memorial Foundation❖,** a privately owned 4,000-acre preserve, offers extensive woodland walking trails, river and lake canoeing, and a notable natural-history museum and library. Its outstanding natural feature is **Catlin Woods,** a 30-acre grove of 200-year-old hemlocks and white pines. After the destruction of much of Cornwall's Cathedral Pines in 1989, Catlin Woods became the largest old-growth stand in Connecticut. In its eastern section, hemlocks three to four feet in diameter are common. The small mounds and depressions that mark the forest floor—called pillow and cradle topography—are very rare in southern New England; they result from the decayed stumps of an even more ancient forest, providing compelling evidence that this land has never been plowed.

Proceed west to Route 7 and the Housatonic River, via Routes 202, 341, and 45 north. Having cut its way through the Housatonic highlands, the river now flows through a wide stretch dotted with small villages, farms, and pastures. Here, the soft limestone of the river's bedrock has eroded to

LEFT: *Although it's not the most voluminous cascade in the state, Kent Falls, with its multifarious schist and marble terraces, is certainly one of the most aesthetically pleasing.*

RIGHT: *In the wooded western highlands, pink and white native mountain laurel, Connecticut's state flower, reach their glorious peak each June.*

produce several notable waterfalls. One of the most popular and accessible plunges through **Kent Falls State Park❖,** just south on Route 7. Most impressive during spring runoff, the falls plummet 70 feet over a series of marble and schist terraces.

Along the slopes of the Housatonic highlands on the river's western side, sheer rock faces called the **Saint Johns Ledges** emerge from the vegetation. Rising nearly 500 feet above the river, these imposing formations are some of the oldest exposed rocks in Connecticut, pre-Cambrian granitic gneiss more than half a billion years old. For a closer look, cross the Housatonic on Route 341 at the village of Kent and immediately turn right on Skiff Mountain Road. After about a mile, bear left onto River Road, which runs beside the river for 1.7 miles to a parking area and marked trailhead.

Especially in spring, some of the best birding in the state is found on this stretch of the now-placid Housatonic. Migrating ducks rest and feed along the river, hawks ride the crests above it, and several species of nesting warblers—including redstarts and worm-eating, golden-winged, and black-throated blue warblers—arrive. The autumn foliage here is spectacular. This portion along the Housatonic River is included in the National Park Service's **Appalachian Trail Corridor❖** although unfortunately, as in several other areas of the Housatonic, PCBs have contaminated the fish.

One of the most scenic sections of the 2,000-mile Appalachian Trail, the hike to the ledges is short but strenuous. After passing through a mixed

---

OVERLEAF: *Above rows of historic marble gravestones, the half-billion-year-old rock of the Saint Johns Ledges near Kent raise a silent hosanna to the dawn and to the glory that is Connecticut in the fall.*

hardwood forest, the trail reaches the base of the ledges: sheer 80-foot cliffs and house-sized cantilevered rocks of gray-green gneiss that lean against the side of the mountain like expressionist sculptures of stone skyscrapers. The ledges were formed when ancient sandstone was heated, pressed, and recrystallized into gneiss, then upended by mountain-building processes 400 million years ago. Even with the aid of stone staircases cut into the rock faces, negotiating these ledges is difficult climbing. At the top, hikers are rewarded with marvelous views of the river valley, the glacial terraces on the facing hills, and the Litchfield Hills rising to the east. The large V-shaped forms soaring above the valley in summer are turkey vultures, which lay their eggs on the bare rocks of the ledges.

Just a few miles south of Kent on Route 7, **Bull's Bridge Recreation Area,** owned by Connecticut Light and Power, provides a fascinating juxtaposition of ancient natural and contemporary technological landscapes. Under one of Connecticut's most picturesque covered bridges, the Housatonic—depending on the needs of the hydroelectric plant—either flows gently over ancient rock cascades or gushes in an enormous flume from a diversion dam above the river. During the latter periods, the original riverbed above the bridge is exposed, offering intriguing glimpses of natural potholes that small whirling stones have ground into its marble ledges.

Paralleling the course of the Housatonic some ten miles east, the Shepaug River winds south through the Litchfield Hills. In the township of Washington, the river makes a dramatic oxbow turn, forming the setting for **Steep Rock Reservation** (the entrance is on River Road, off Route 47 in Washington Depot). Rewarding visitors with unexpected solitude and rugged beauty, the reservation encompasses more than 1,500 acres in two separate sections along the Shepaug—**Hidden Valley** to the north and **Steep Rock** to the south. In these areas the Shepaug, one of Connecticut's most unspoiled rivers, twists and turns with what one nineteenth-century traveler called "a luxurious indefiniteness." During spring runoff, the river, whose Indian name means "rocky waters," offers challenging kayaking and canoeing; at other times, it runs glassy smooth between aisles of old-growth hemlock and pines. In the Steep Rock portion, one of the largest protected stretches of free-flowing river in the state, the Shepaug has sliced a deep, narrow valley between high slopes known as the Hartland formation, uplifted bedrock of extremely hard quartz mica schist. Joints and folded patterns in the rock forced the river into a sharp S-curve, creating a magnificent gorge. From the summit of **Steep Rock Cliff,** 400 feet above the river to the south across the gorge is the

Clamshell, a 200-foot hill that bears an uncanny resemblance to a giant bivalve, even down to a hinge-shaped outcrop at the rear. A few miles to the south, off Route 67 west of Roxbury, **Mine Hill Preserve** rises steeply above the Shepaug's western bank. For a decade after the Civil War, this area flourished, supporting a siderite mine (an uncommon iron ore) and a granite quarry. The roasting ovens and blast furnace are well preserved and imposing representatives of the era's grand industrial architecture. Nature, however, always reclaims human enterprise for its own purposes. Wrens and kinglets now flit among the chimney stacks, and grated-off ventilation shafts of long-abandoned mines are home to substantial populations of wintering bats, including the eastern pipistrelle, little and big brown bats, and Keen's bats.

THE SOUTHWEST HILLS

Numerous small rivers flowing south into Long Island Sound drain the hilly region southwest of the lower Housatonic. The Saugatuck River valley, for instance, contains a rich patchwork of public, private, and corporate natural areas linked by an extensive network of paths known as the **Saugatuck Valley Trails.** At the **Saugatuck Falls Natural Area,** north off Route 53 in Redding, a half-mile trail to the falls meanders along the river through towering stands of white pine and an open meadow studded with cedars and white with pear blossoms in the spring, beside a red-maple swamp floodplain, and into a gorge where the path becomes a mosaic of rock and root in a dense, cathedral-like stand of hemlocks. During the spring freshets, Saugatuck Falls is a spreading cascade rushing over schist and granite outcrops. Its upper reaches feature curious "pancake stacks" of granite slabs and the remains of an old mill.

South of the falls Route 53 hugs the west side of the **Saugatuck Reservoir❖.** More reminiscent of a lake in northern Maine than an artificial reservoir, this long, beautiful body of water is studded with small rocky islands and bordered by tall stands of hemlocks, white pines, and mixed hardwoods, along with small swamps and granite outcrops. Several parking turnouts intersect a 5.5-mile trail that snakes along the western shore; a side trail leads to the **Great Ledge,** a massive 200-foot vertical cliff that offers a spectacular view of the water.

A few miles southwest in Weston (via Route 53 and Godfrey and Pent roads) lies the 1,720-acre **Devil's Den Preserve❖,** the largest natural area in southwestern Connecticut. Throughout the preserve large, smooth granite ridges, their shapes planed by eons of erosion, wind north-south

like giant fossil snakes. Their broken-off southern edges trace the southward path of glaciers that plucked the lower ends from the ridges. Mature oaks and shagbark hickories, interspersed with the straight, dark trunks of large black birches, give the woods an open parklike feel.

In late May, dense stands of swamp azalea, bursting with pinkish-white trumpet-shaped blossoms, crowd the low spots. In June, gnarled forests of mountain laurel dressed in clusters of pink and white adorn most of the rocky upland and ridges, and purple and white violets dot the rocky brooks. Devil's Den is one of the best places in the state to see the Louisiana waterthrush, a large, uncommon warbler with streaked breast and bubblegum-pink legs that feeds along streams, bobbing its tail constantly. Some 150 species of birds, including pileated woodpeckers and wood ducks, have been recorded in the preserve. Foxes can be glimpsed there as well.

ABOVE: *This Blackburnian warbler wears its brilliant breeding plumage—an orange throat and head stripes; it is at the southern end of its East Coast breeding range in Connecticut.*

LEFT: *The arching branches of hemlock, maple, and yellow birch form a luminescent tunnel above a leaf-strewn trail at the Mine Hill Preserve in Roxbury, now sylvan but once a thriving center of industrial smelting.*

On the east side of the preserve, Godfrey Brook cascades softly into **Godfrey Pond,** an exquisite tear-shaped pond created during the American Revolution to power a sawmill. Just west of the pond, along Laurel Trail, are relics of the charcoal industry that flourished here in the late 1800s, as well as some unusually high stone walls in areas once used as sheep pens.

In the southwestern "tab" of Connecticut that borders the New York metropolitan area, two National Audubon Society properties provide natural oases in an otherwise suburbanized corner of the state. At the intersection of John Street and Riversville Road, the **Audubon Center in Greenwich**✣ shelters an unmanaged oak and beech forest in its northern half. Strewn with standing and fallen hulks of dead trees up to three feet in diameter, the woods exude a wildness that belies their populous surroundings, reminding visitors of the central role that sylvan corpses play in a natural forest.

167

ABOVE: *Except when denning their pups, red foxes curl up to sleep outside, even in the coldest weather. Their underground tunnels, usually dug in well-drained, south-facing slopes, can be up to 75 feet long.*

RIGHT: *A new blanket of snow softens the rugged outlines of Devil's Den Preserve in Weston. In spring the park's network of streams is bordered by carpets of dark blue bird's-foot violets.*

Just to the south off North Porchuck Road lies the **Audubon Fairchild Garden✣,** a 127-acre wildflower preserve established in 1895. Its wide variety of habitats—including woodland, stream bottom, open fields, and wet meadows—make the Fairchild Garden a favorite birding spot where up to 70 species may appear on a single early-spring day. Of a more southern composition than most other inland sites in the state, the forest here is dominated by tulip trees, which commonly grow more than 100 feet high and 2 feet in girth.

Sprawling along the Meadow Trail are extensive drifts of marsh marigolds, with their large butter-colored flowers, and mayapples, whose fragrant, waxy white blossoms mature into yellowish edible "apples." In a particularly striking formation on Wilderness Road, a sizable granite boulder has split, revealing a geodelike deposit of brilliant white quartz. From this cleft grows a large white oak whose bark has exfoliated over the rock

168

surface, creating a four-foot-wide cowl that covers the top of the boulder.

At the property's northern end a large granite ledge covered with moss dominates a landscaped garden, where wooden bridges and stone steps cross small ponds edged with wild irises and skunk cabbage. Here visitors can rest in the shade of a small wooden pagoda beside the pond or climb to the open stone structure of Cliff House—and give thanks for the foresight of Benjamin T. Fairchild, who established this garden a century ago as "a refuge for all the native plants of Connecticut."

OASES ON THE MAN-MADE COAST: GREENWICH TO NEW HAVEN

Natural areas along this stretch of coastline are few and far between. One of the more picturesque is **Greenwich Point Park,** owned by the town of Greenwich and open year-round only to residents and their guests. In

169

midwinter it can be a magical place. Located on Shore Road in Old Greenwich, Greenwich Point is a barrier spit, a 1.5-mile hook of sand and glacial boulders completely surrounded by water. Its shoreline encompasses an interesting variety of beach types—from fine-grained sand to pebble and cobblestone—and its low dunes and wind-sculpted woods wrap around two small ponds and the remains of an old estate. Dunlins and sanderlings often feed along the tidal wrack, and small rafts of winter sea ducks bob offshore. On a calm winter's day, the solitude of the beach and the play of subdued light off the flat waters of Long Island Sound seem far removed from the towers of Manhattan just 20 miles south.

Off Norwalk Harbor a few miles up the coast lies a broken necklace of glacial leavings known collectively as the **Norwalk Islands❖.** Some 100 acres on Chimon and Sheffield are part of the **Stewart B. McKinney National Wildlife Refuge❖.** Of particular interest to birders, Cockenoe Island each summer shelters one of the largest nesting colonies of wading birds in the Northeast, including snowy egrets, glossy ibis, and other species. Access is restricted during the nesting season, but all-day private boat tours for viewing the birds are available from Norwalk.

Probably the best place along this

LEFT: *An early morning tableau captures familiar elements of the Connecticut landscape: a white-tailed deer, Queen Anne's lace and blue bachelor's buttons, and the shimmering web of an orb weaver spider.*

171

stretch to observe nesting shorebirds and waterfowl is **Milford Point❖**, part of the combined **Smith-Hubbell Wildlife Sanctuary** and the **Charles E. Wheeler Wildlife Refuge** in Milford. Milford Point sits at the mouth of the silt-laden Housatonic River, whose clay deposits have created the state's largest expanse of salt marshes behind a curved mile-long sand spit. After crossing the Smith-Hubbell sanctuary the road to Smith's Point ends at the beach, where the dunes mount a spectacular display of white beach-plum blossoms each May. Although private homes line the sand, state law allows visitors to walk below the high-tide line. In spring or late summer, this beach is an excellent place to observe migratory shorebirds, especially at low tide, when its fine sand, cobblestones, and offshore gravel bars attract a wide variety of species, including plover and sandpipers.

Although the state wildlife refuge property at the western end of the point is closed to foot traffic during the breeding season to protect nesting least terns and plover, a platform at the entrance allows visitors to observe the contrasting courting and breeding rituals of these birds. The least terns, small dynamos with forked tails, black caps, and yellow bills, soar overhead with high-pitched *kips* and dive offshore for sand eels; the shy piping plover, light-beige shorebirds with short bills and a remarkable ability to blend into

Left: *The snowy egret's bright yellow feet distinguish it from other white herons. This species has recently extended its breeding range north, from Long Island to Maine.*

Right: *Found all over the world, the glossy ibis was worshiped in ancient Egypt. Its long down-curved bill and burnished purplish-brown plumage are unmistakable.*

their beach surroundings, trot along the sand like pale feathered ghosts. Snowy egrets, black ducks, and other waterfowl feed in the extensive marsh islands to the north.

From Milford Point, the Wilbur Cross Parkway (Route 15) leads northeast. Just outside New Haven the highway passes through a tunnel; the terrain above is the ancient lava flow of **West Rock,** an extrusive traprock ridge that forms **West Rock Ridge State Park❖.** To explore a more dramatic example of an intrusive traprock formation, take Exit 61 and continue north on Route 10 to **Sleeping Giant State Park❖.** A 700-foot-high dome of knobs, jagged cliffs, and talus slopes, the Sleeping Giant was formed when molten magma intruded itself into cracks and spaces in the sandstone bedrock of the Central Valley. Unlike the long, straight cliffs of surface traprock in the Metacomet Ridge, the intrusive traprock at Sleeping Giant is more irregular, formed by magma that never reached the surface. In southern New England only Monument Mountain in the Berkshires displays more dramatic formations.

The rock is named for its resemblance to a huge supine figure, whose features are easily discernible from the campus of Quinnipiac College, just across from the park entrance. The most rugged is the Giant's Chin, composed of sheer, jagged basalt cliffs topped with scrub oak and cedar. In late spring, one of the best times to visit Sleeping Giant, the chin's sharp stubble is softened by the sweet calls of prairie, yellow, black-and-white, and other migrating warblers. Climbing to the Giant's Chest, the Tower Trail passes through abundant dogwood blooms in May and mountain

Overleaf: *The dramatic, east-facing basalt columns in West Rock Ridge State Park are part of a ancient lava formation that runs beneath New Haven. This traprock ridge emerges east of the city as East Rock.*

173

ABOVE: *The soaring red cliffs of West Rock brood over Connecticut's fertile Central Valley in this detail from an 1849 painting by noted Hudson River School artist Frederic Edwin Church, a native of Hartford.*

laurel in June. American copperhead snakes also emerge in spring to sun on the rock ledges.

At the lumpy gray summit, a large stone tower affords a 360-degree view: The ridges of the Hanging Hills lie to the north, the expansive wetlands of Quinnipiac River State Park to the east, and to the south, the low morainal hills of Long Island's north shore materialize across Long Island Sound on a clear day. Elbow Trail on the west side of the park skirts an immense abandoned traprock quarry once mined for roadbeds. Its artificially exposed rusted rock slopes and soaring columns form one of the largest basalt outcrops on public land in the state.

Sixteen miles east of New Haven off Route 1 in Guilford lies a large, unusual preserve on a rocky stretch of the Connecticut coast. With dense forests, huge fractured outcrops of granite, swamps, and streams spread over 1,000 acres, **Westwoods**❖ boasts some 40 miles of marked but rugged hiking trails that clamber over 100-foot rock ridges separated by deep ravines. Large glacial boulders sit balanced atop these ridges or lie piled on one another, giving the place the massive, titanic playfulness of a giant's playground. Its many interesting features include a rock tunnel, rock carvings, Fallen Cliff (a house-sized fragment), and Rock Canopy, a large curved granite overhang, or hanging wall, formed when compressional stresses in the underlying bedrock caused a reverse fault, or a slipping of one section of the fault up over the other.

The steep ridges are covered with mountain laurel, which opens its showy blossoms in early June. Cool ravines harbor unusual pockets of northern hardwood forest—birch, beech, and sugar maple—more characteristic of New Hampshire than Connecticut. The Green Trail provides a glimpse of the **Great Hemlock,** a two-century-old tree 12 feet in circumference that is one of the largest specimens in the state. Unfortunately, hemlocks here have fallen victim to the woolly adelgid, and dead trees sport giant shelf bracken a foot or more across. At the southern end of the preserve is **Lost Lake,** a large brackish pond cut off from Long Island Sound by Amtrak's railroad bed. Where a stream enters at the northern end of the pond, ospreys, ducks, and large flocks of snowy and great egrets often feed and preen.

THE METACOMET RIDGE

Just above Guilford on Route 77 is the southern terminus of the Metacomet Ridge, the nearly continuous wall of ancient lava deposits that divide the region's Central Valley as far north as the Holyoke Range in Massachusetts. Above North Guilford the highway enters a notch—once a portion of the ancient geologic fault that formed the Central Valley—as steep hills rise on either side. Long, narrow Quonnipaug Lake to the right was created when the eastern end of the valley was offset nearly 10,000 feet along this fault over millions of years. Here, with only the width of the highway between them, lie vastly different rock formations: to the west the sharp, rust-colored talus fragments of lava traprock, formed some 200 million years ago, and to the east layers of coarse dark-gray schist twice that age.

A half mile north of the lake on the left is a parking area for **Bluff Head❖,** the sheared-off northern end of Totoket Mountain, a traprock ridge. Two trails—one gradual, one steep—climb to the 500-foot summit, which provides a fine panorama across the fault to the eastern highlands plateau, as well as a dramatic lesson in the power of erosion. Hundreds of millions of years ago the plateau's now-level ridges rose nearly two miles high. Because the harder basalt of Bluff Head's traprock resisted erosion more effectively than the softer schist of the highlands, today

177

Bluff Head is actually taller than the older hills. To the north, lovely heart-shaped Myer Huber Pond also lies on the fault line.

From Bluff Head, Route 77 continues north through pastoral farm country little changed in 200 years. In Middlefield, off Route 157, is **Wadsworth Falls State Park❖,** site of a majestic cascade. At the western end of the park on Cherry Hill Road is a small parking area. Here, on the backside of the Metacomet Ridge, the Coginchaug River flows over a resistant basalt

shelf, creating a 20-foot-high horseshoe-shaped basin, a miniature Niagara. Starting at the main gate, various trails wander beside the Coginchaug, up onto a traprock ridge, and through a light and lacy hemlock forest. The Main Trail leads to the **Giant Laurel,** a single shrub 15 to 18 feet high and 40 feet wide, whose enormous squiggles of twisted branches explode in a jungle of pink blossoms each June.

A few miles west of the falls, just east of the Wilbur Cross Parkway in Meriden, lies **Mount Higby❖,** a classic traprock ridge of sheer columnar reddish-brown cliffs, which are skirted with talus rubble at the base. The Nature Conservancy's trail (beginning on Preston Avenue near the police academy) traverses lowland woods and pasture, then angles steeply up Preston Notch through talus slopes and tall stands of hemlock. The

ABOVE: *The northern copperhead, one of New England's two poisonous snakes (the other is the timber rattlesnake), is most commonly seen on the rocky basalt outcrops of Connecticut's Metacomet Ridge.*

RIGHT: *In late winter, tenacious clusters of white oak leaves and still-green rhododendron bushes cling to lichen-covered granite ledges at the Westwoods preserve.*

steplike formations of the basalt ledges reflect the origin of the name *traprock:* the Swedish word *trappa* means "step."

As the path climbs to the dry ridges of the summit, some 500 feet above the valley, a typical traprock succession occurs. Moist forests of hemlock and mixed hardwoods give way to old-field redcedars, stunted chestnut oaks and shagbark hickories, and grassy clearings. These ridge-top forests offer refuge to wildlife, including the once-common box turtle,

ABOVE: *The five-petaled lavender wild geranium is a common spring understory wildflower found throughout the woods of Connecticut.*

RIGHT: *The tumult of Wadsworth Falls sweeps fountains of spray downstream, moistening hemlocks perched on the surrounding ledges.*

increasingly endangered in New England due to destruction of its woodland habitat. Higby also boasts an unusual floral community, where northern (such as bearberry) and southern (such as yellow corydalis) plants reach their respective limits.

From Higby's summit, the skyline of New Haven and the dome of Sleeping Giant rise to the southwest; the protruding ridges of the Hanging Hills and the western highlands sweep westward. To the north I-91 cuts through the Metacomet Ridge toward Hartford; Lamentation Mountain holds a fistful of tall antennae, and a large traprock quarry scars one of the hillsides. This is typical Central Valley landscape: islands of natural preserves surrounded by a sea of urban development, highways, and industry.

180

The Hanging Hills, the highest and one of the most dramatic stretches of the Metacomet Ridge, rise a few miles west of Mount Higby in the town of Berlin. Also called the Lion's Paw, the four short parallel ridges—separated by deep notches (actually geologic faults subsequently carved by glaciers)—are now part of **East Peak/West Peak** and town-owned **Hubbard Park❖**. From Main Street, the park road leads through a gate (closed at 5:00 P.M.), under I-691, and beside Merimere Reservoir, whose wooded islets give it the look of a lake in Maine on a misty morning. The road ascends to **Castle Craig**, a stone tower atop the ridge open from April to October. On clear days vistas stretch as far north as Mount Tom and the Holyoke Range in Massachusetts. The prospect can be equally impressive in fog: Like islands in a dream of wilderness, the crags seem craggier, and the sound of traffic below could be the primal moiling of the earth's engines that raised this hardened lava eons ago.

A 1.6-mile section of the Metacomet Trail that leads from Castle Craig to West Peak traverses a steep ravine, a wild draw full of broken basalt boulders and stands of mountain maple and American yew, a bush-sized evergreen at the southern edge of its range here. On the summit of West Peak, at 1,024 feet the highest point on the Metacomet Ridge, rock faces provide some excellent examples of the polygonal shapes of the basalt columns, separated by raised beads of igneous "mortar" cementing them together.

Take I-691 west and then head north on Route 10, which parallels the western cliffs of the Metacomet Ridge and provides fine views of its longest continuous sections. At Farmington the highway enters the Farmington River valley, a fertile agricultural region dotted with picturesque New England villages such as Farmington, Simsbury, and Avon. Thousands of years ago the Farmington River, which rises near the Massachusetts border, flowed south for its entire length, emptying directly into Long Island Sound. During the last glaciation, some 10,000 years ago, the retreating ice sheet left a dam of glacial till south of Farmington. Today the river does an abrupt turnabout at this point, flowing north again in a lazy meandering course to the Tariffville Gorge, where it heads rapidly southeast for its confluence with the Connecticut River.

At the junction of Routes 10 and 185 south of Simsbury, in Weatogue, go east on 185 across the Farmington River; immediately turn right onto Nod Road and park beside the bridge. From this point the 1,000-foot vertical basalt columns of **Talcott Mountain State Park❖** stretch south. Only ten miles from downtown Hartford, this park encompasses, with Penwood State Park to the north, the longest protected section of the Metacomet Ridge in the state. At sunset the rust-colored columns glow with an intensity that suggests ancient Egyptian temples.

Just across Route 185 in a three-acre town-owned park is the **Gifford Pinchot Sycamore❖,** the largest tree in Connecticut. Named for the first head of the U.S. Forest Service, this magnificent tree, with a circumference of nearly 26 feet, covers more than a third of an acre and overhangs the highway like some great speckled sculpture of the mythic serpents that slayed Laocoön.

Continue east on Route 185 to the entrance to **Talcott Mountain.** From the parking area two trails, one steep, one more gradual, climb two miles up the ridge. (Note the pencil-sized holes in the basalt where gas bubbles formed in the cooling lava.) On the easier Tower Trail a massive overhang of columnar basalt looms over the path like a stone tree. At the top, open ridges provide splendid views of the Metacomet Ridge and also a vivid overview of land use in this part of Connecticut, from the fertile Farmington Valley to the rugged western highlands, once intensively farmed and now largely reforested. An even more expansive view awaits atop the 165-foot Bavarian-style **Heublein Tower,** built as part of a private home in 1914 and now open to the public. On clear fall days, migrating broad-winged hawks, peregrines, and other raptors soar on the thermals above the long ridge.

Return to Route 10 and follow the meandering Farmington River north. Turn east on Route 315 to Tariffville, where the river does another abrupt about-face and dramatically cuts its way southeast through the **Tariffville Gorge.** Here the Farmington's character quickly changes from a meandering watercourse to a fast-flowing white-water river slashing through three different layers of basalt. Ledges of dark basalt protrude from hemlock-studded cliffs, and jagged fallen chunks jut from the water like half-sunken wrecks. A steep trail leads to an overlook of the entire gorge.

A few miles to the northwest two prominent ridges—twin 600-foot basalt knobs formed when hot lava intruded into surrounding sandstone—rise on either side of a large U-shaped gap. Called the **Barndoor Hills** because they reminded early settlers of wide-open barn doors, these mounds guard the edge of the Central Valley like entrance doors to the western highlands. The Barndoor Hills straddle the border of the **McClean Game Refuge❖,** a sprawling privately endowed tract of wild land. (The main entrance is on Route 10/202, one mile south of its intersection with Route 20 in Granby.) Containing some of the most diverse terrain in the state, the refuge is home to interesting geologic formations and biological communities. On the west side glacial eskers and sand-plain deposits support an unusual pitch-pine community and such nesting bird rarities as the pine warbler. Although the western Barndoor Hill lies on private land, a trail to the summit of the eastern one provides a fine vista of the small valley between them, cut by a long-vanished stream.

In the western sections of the refuge, visitors pass from the pastoral landscape of the Central Valley—punctuated with traprock ridges—into a wilder, more rugged terrain of ancient schists and gneiss. Oaks, hickories, pitch pines, and cedars of the drier and sandier habitats alternate with stands of sugar maples, black birches, hemlocks, and white pines on the cooler, moister slopes of the highlands, which also attract such northern birds as goshawks and evening grosbeaks.

CHAPTER SIX

EASTERN CONNECTICUT:
THE RIVER, EASTERN SHORE, AND HIGHLANDS

From the Massachusetts border to the town of Rocky Hill, the Connecticut River meanders slowly through the state's broad Central Valley. In this most fertile region of New England, deep alluvial soils and the annual flooding of the Connecticut have nourished intensive farming for some 300 years. (During the last century the long slatted barns and white-netted fields particular to the prized tobacco crop dotted the terrain.) Today, even though development has claimed much former farmland, agriculture is still an important element of this landscape.

The valley's rich soil is formed primarily from the sedimentary rock commonly known as brownstone, a malleable sandstone appearing on historic building facades from New York to San Francisco. Two hundred million years ago this area was a low tropical swamp flanked by towering Andes-sized peaks, the majestic forerunners of today's Litchfield Hills and eastern uplands. Because dinosaurs large and small once roamed these bogs, leaving footprints in the sedimentary brownstone, the region now boasts the most impressive display of saurian fossil prints in New England.

Just below Rocky Hill, site of the glacial dam that created ancient Lake Hitchcock, the Connecticut River makes an abrupt shift to the east through an ancient channel in the bedrock of the Bolton Range and then bounds through the eastern coastal slope to discharge into Long Island Sound at Old

---

LEFT: *From the ramparts of Gillette Castle State Park, autumn hills ablaze with sugar maples and oaks overlook the Connecticut River's Hadlyme ferry, which recalls daily travel in an earlier, slower era.*

Saybrook. As a result, the last 40 miles of the river's narrow course through wooded hills present a much wilder aspect than the hundred miles above it.

The Nature Conservancy, which designated this stretch of the lower Connecticut one of the Western Hemisphere's 40 "Last Great Places," has organized a Tidelands of the Connecticut River Program to preserve its entire ecological system. And more recently, the area was dubbed a Wetlands of International Importance—one of only 13 in the United States—by the Ramsar Convention, a multinational treaty recognizing the importance of wetlands. The state and other private organizations have established a number of scenic parks and preserves along the river here, including an unusual camping opportunity at Selden Neck State Park. Although Route 9, a four-lane highway, parallels the river on the western side, most of the natural areas are on the east, and only one bridge crosses the Connecticut between Middletown and Old Saybrook. Traveling the smaller roads on the eastern side is a delight, however, because they pass through some of the most attractive small towns and rural countryside in the state.

Connecticut's eastern shoreline—barrier beaches and small marshes nestled amid stretches of rocky shore—is generally less developed, better preserved, and more scenic than its western counterpart. Travelers can follow Interstate 95 east, dipping down to shore sites, or take the slower, more picturesque coastal route, which weaves back and forth across Amtrak's New York–Boston line.

New London, at the mouth of the Thames (rhymes with "names") River, is a typical Northeast seaport, an industrial harbor, and the site of a large naval shipyard. It is also home to the Connecticut College Arboretum, one of the country's outstanding botanical research facilities and an unexpected bit of wilderness in an urban setting. Farther up the Thames is the heart of Connecticut's eastern uplands, an area of schist and granite formed on the erosion surface of ancient mountain roots. Today this terrain of low, smoothly sculpted hills and ridges of nearly uniform height slopes gradually from 1,000 to 500 feet from north to south. The Mohegan Range, which crosses the Thames between New London and Norwich, is the only east-west range in southern New England.

Although it contains more unspoiled stretches of woodland, farmland, and river valleys than any other region in Connecticut, the heavily forest-

---

OVERLEAF: *In Hampton, small glacial boulders lie strewn at the dark feet of black oak trunks near a quiet pond in Hurd State Park, one of a half dozen state and private preserves along the lower Connecticut River.*

ed northeast quadrant, fittingly nicknamed the Quiet Corner, is often overlooked by travelers. Of particular interest are the two main rivers, the Shetucket and the Quinebaug, which drain the area from north to south, converging at Norwich to form the Thames. Residents hope to create a National Heritage Corridor to preserve this historic Quinebaug-Shetucket watershed. Fall colors in eastern Connecticut rival those of Vermont and New Hampshire, but this undiscovered area attracts only a fraction of the leaf peepers who annually trek north.

This journey begins at Enfield, near the Massachusetts border, follows the Connecticut River south (circumventing the Hartford area) to its mouth at Old Lyme, and then heads east along the shore to Stonington, at the Rhode Island border. From there the route proceeds up the Thames and Quinebaug Rivers into the eastern uplands and terminates in the northeast corner of the state.

Down the Connecticut: Enfield to Old Lyme

Each spring New England's largest run of shad struggles up the two-mile **Enfield Rapids,** located south of the bridge where Route 190 crosses the Connecticut, the longest stretch of white water on the lower Connecticut and also a site of historical importance. One of the earliest (1829) and best preserved New England canals and its towpath (now a paved bike and walking trail) run along the river's western shore. The 4.5-mile stretch of canal called **Windsor Locks❖** is accessible at its northern end from Canal Road in Suffield. From April to mid-November the canal and towpath are open to the public, affording fine views of both the rapids and King Island to the east, and the still waters of the canal and venerable farmland to the west. The canal banks stage one of the best wildflower displays in the region, making this heavily altered stretch of the river, as one writer put it, a natural "oasis in an urban desert." During the winter the towpath is closed to protect wintering bald eagles, which fish the river and can be observed from the bridge north of Enfield Dam.

Just west of I-91, on the banks of the Farmington River in Windsor, is **Northwest Park❖,** a 473-acre town-owned nature preserve. Earlier in this century, shade-grown tobacco, a fine-textured leaf used for cigar wrappers, was the dominant agricultural crop of the Central Valley. Today only a few tobacco farms remain, but their rich history is preserved and interpreted at the park's **Luddy/Taylor Connecticut Valley Tobacco Museum** and archive building.

Most of the park, however, is devoted to nature trails that explore the Rainbow Reservoir section of the Farmington River. One, a braille trail, circles a large sphagnum bog overflowing with wild grapes, blackberries, and blueberries. Another, a riverside path, visits a sizable hemlock grove, an open marsh frequented by wood ducks and herons, a wetland forest with solid stands of black birch, and a series of mown and unmown fields. Such a variety of edge habitats makes Northwest Park one of the state's best year-round birding spots. A particularly rewarding time to visit is an autumn day, when the fields shimmer with a tobaccolike haze and the giant sugar maples radiate a soft blaze of glory.

Below Hartford, the Connecticut River slowly snakes its way down to Rocky Hill, where an ancient dam created Lake Hitchcock, a glacial impoundment that once filled the Connecticut Valley as far north as the Vermont border. Just east of I-91 (Exit 23) off West Street, **Dinosaur State Park❖** contains the most extensive exhibit of *in situ* fossil dinosaur tracks in North America. Accidentally discovered in 1966 during excavation for a state building, some 500 of more than 2,000 known tracks are housed beneath a large geodesic dome. Set in a broad shield of slanting sandstone, most of the three-toed examples are 10 to 16 inches long and probably belonged to a 20-foot kangaroolike dinosaur known as *Eubrontes,* which inhabited the swamps and shallow lakes of central Connecticut 185 million years ago. Some of the tracks, casts of the entire foot called negative fossils, are so meticulously preserved that individual scales are visible.

Outside, visitors can make their own casts of real dinosaur tracks and hike along a nature trail through a large red maple–white cedar swamp. On a hot, humid summer day, it is easy to imagine that the trees are ancient ginkgoes, cycads, and pines; that the butterflies are primitive two-foot-long dragonflies; and that the dark surface of the water is about to be broken by the ridged snout of some antediluvian crocodile.

After crossing the river—either on the tiny Glastonbury ferry (in continuous operation since 1655) at Rocky Hill or on the Route 66 bridge at Middletown—head for **Hurd State Park❖,** off Route 151 in East Hampton. Occupying the Connecticut River's floodplain and the steep hills that rise to the east behind it, the park's rocky 200-foot bluffs provide a splendid view of the "wild" lower Connecticut as it flows between hills of unbroken forest. **Split Rock Trail**—named for a massive 30-foot-deep granite outcrop cleft by a 2-foot gash—also offers an excellent prospect of the river. Few other places in the state are more gently exhilarating to the spirit than this summit on a clear autumn morning, when a cloud river of fog blankets the

LEFT: *A true native American, the raccoon derives its name from the Algonquian word* aroughconne, *which means "he that scratches with his hands."*

RIGHT: *Chapman Falls tumbles over rocky terraces at Devil's Hopyard State Park—an intriguing name whose origin is lost in the mists of time.*

water, morning light touches the treetops on the far shore, and chestnut oak acorns are scattered underfoot like brown marbles.

Visiting **Chapman Pond❖**, a 700-acre preserve managed jointly by the Nature Conservancy and the East Haddam Land Trust, requires a canoe or small boat. (Canoes can be rented from Down River Canoes, across the swing bridge on Route 154 in Haddam.) There is a state-owned boat launch a mile north of the swing bridge on Route 149.

Going downstream, stay close to the shore and keep the two small offshore islands, Rich and Lord, on the right. The first entrance to the pond is at the southern end of Rich Island. Because of its singular setting, Chapman's Pond is an important refuge for many forms of wildlife. Although located in the tidal portion of the river, the pond is constantly freshened by numerous feeder streams. This popular fishing spot is home to some 25 year-round species, an alewife run, and overwintering fish from the lower river, which conserve energy in its calm waters. Permanent residents include mute swans, river otters, mink, and muskrat, and the secluded location also attracts numerous migratory waterfowl, especially black ducks, scaup, mergansers, mallard, and teal. During the colder months bald eagles winter here, and the pond is closed to visitors. A riverine forest of red and silver maple, cottonwood, and ash lies between the river and pond, and a diverse botanical wetland community includes two rare plants: tidewater arrowhead (*Saggitaria montevidensis*) and Torrey's bulrush (*Scirpus torreyi*).

From East Haddam, head east on Route 82, then take Route 434 (Mount Parnassus Road) east toward Millington. Here in the heart of the eastern uplands, gentle ridges rise and fall through a countryside of well-kept fields, stone walls, and old homesteads. Just past Millington Center, the highway bends sharply to the south and shortly enters **Devil's Hopyard State Park❖.** This large park boasts some of the most rugged scenery in eastern Connecticut: sheer rocky bluffs, large concave rock "cradles,"

solid stands of giant hemlocks and yellow birches, as well as flocks of native wild turkeys and one of the state's few nesting sites for the diminutive Acadian flycatcher. Its most outstanding feature, however, is 60-foot **Chapman Falls,** a rocky cascade that bounds over steps of Scotland schist down to an area of small potholes. Beside the falls are signs of present natural activity (a beaver dam impounding a large marshy area above) and past human endeavors (a flume and circular stone walls that were part of a grist- and sawmill complex in the last century). Below the falls a path follows the scenic Eight Mile River, which is lined with mountain laurel and mica-rich stones that lie broken and glinting in the sun.

Continue south on Route 434 through the park, then west on Routes 82 and 148 to **Gillette Castle State Park❖,** just above the Hadlyme ferry landing. Visitors must apply at the castle, an eccentric 24-room stone mansion built by actor William Gillette during World War I, to obtain overnight camping permits for **Selden Neck State Park❖,** located on Selden Island a mile below the launch at the ferry landing.

Once connected to the mainland by a neck of land, Selden Island, Connecticut's largest, was separated by a great flood in the mid-1800s and today is accessible only by canoe. The state maintains primitive camp sites along Selden Creek on the island's back side. Providing one of the most scenic paddles in southern New England, the river flows beneath 60- to 80-

193

LEFT: *The pink and white showy lady's slipper is the tallest of more than 70 native orchid species growing in New England.* RIGHT: *Accessible only by boat, Selden Neck State Park offers canoers an increasingly rare opportunity for secluded river camping.*

foot granite palisades that line the eastern mainland shore. In early fall wild rice (actually a grass) matures in the bordering wetland, and visitors can shake the seed heads into their canoe as Native Americans have done for centuries.

A massive outcrop of 350-million-year-old (possibly even older) granitic gneiss, the island presents a colorful array of rocks, which were quarried during the late 1800s to pave the streets of major eastern cities. White-tailed deer swim across the creek to the island, and in summer ospreys soar by on crooked wings, snatching prey from the water's surface with their sharp talons. In the fall the park is an excellent spot to watch the wintering population of bald eagles.

Take the Hadlyme ferry across the Connecticut and head south on Route 9 to Exit 2 in Old Saybrook. Off Route 154 on Watrous Point Road, **Turtle Creek Preserve❖**, a small but exquisite sanctuary, straddles the towns of Old Saybrook and Essex. On a series of glacial terraces thick stands of mountain laurel and crowds of pink lady's slippers thrive only a few miles from the coast. The western bluffs offer a good view of South Cove, a favorite stopover for migratory waterfowl, and the lighthouse, docks, church spires, and old houses of Essex, a historic shipbuilding town.

About ten miles west of Old Saybrook off I-95 at Exit 62, **Hammonasset Natural Area** at the eastern end of **Hammonasset Beach State Park❖** includes a series of marsh islands, wooded in sassafras and hickory, that serve as a "bird trap" for migrating warblers and other species in spring and fall. Observation platforms allow viewing of ospreys, egrets, and great blue herons.

ABOVE: *The tricolored heron, shown here in breeding plumage, is one of several heron species that have recently extended their coastal range north into Connecticut.*

RIGHT: *A rich variety of wetlands and the thick vegetation covering its glacial deposits make the coastal Hammonasset Natural Area one of the best birding spots in the state.*

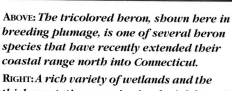

THE EASTERN COAST:
OLD LYME TO STONINGTON

East of Old Saybrook, to the south of the I-95 bridge across the Connecticut River, is one of the most unexpected sights in the Northeast: the unspoiled mouth of a major river. Although navigable to Hartford, the Connecticut never developed a large seaport because of its constantly shifting bars and channels. As a result, the terminus of New England's largest river, discharging more water than the Hudson at New York City, offers an extraordinary and unexpected opportunity for solitude and coastal beauty.

Access to the area is at **Griswold Point** and **Great Island Marsh Preserve❖.** From Old Lyme, take Route 156 south for two miles to Long Island Sound. Canoeists can put in at the state landing on Smith Neck Road; from Labor Day to Memorial Day, motorists may park at the town-owned White Sands Beach and walk west to the preserve. Extending be-

hind Griswold Point, a mile-long barrier spit built on a core of glacial till, are marshes and canoeable channels. Nesting ospreys, piping plover, and a growing least tern colony reside here in summer, and grebes, scoters, and loons paddle about offshore in winter. A curiously etiolated spit, the beach, paved with characteristic round black cobbles, is barely 100 feet wide in places. Constantly lengthening, shortening, and changing position, Griswold Point is among a very few coastal areas still purely and dynamically shaped by natural processes. The western end of the point presents a splendid panorama: Long Island's Orient Point to the south, the village of Old Saybrook to the west, pristine marshes full of egrets and osprey nests to the north, and bucolic farmland dotted with white-clapboard houses to the east.

A very different coastal environment awaits visitors some five miles east at **Rocky Neck State Park✥,** off Route 156 in East Lyme, where a coastal salt pond and marsh lie between two huge granite fingers of land, Rocky and Giant's necks. The wetlands were created when a barrier beach formed across the mouth of Bride's Brook about a century ago, probably accelerated by the construction of the railroad line that runs along the park's southern boundary. From May through September blue crabs may be caught in this tidal creek. This delectable crustacean—whose Latin name, *Callinectes sapidus,* means "beautiful swimmer"—has flattened, paddle-shaped hind legs and a spiked fusiform body that allow it to move rapidly in almost any direction. Although most common in the Delaware Bay region, the crabs spawn in shallow estuaries as far north as Cape Cod.

To reach the half-mile-long crescent barrier beach, walk through the tunnel beneath the railroad bed. To the west, the sculpted granite slabs of Rocky Neck slope steeply down into a small cove at the outlet of Four Mile River. Above the cove, nature trails run along Rocky Neck Ridge through hardwood forests filled with mountain laurel, passing such quaintly named features as Anthony's Nose Lookout.

Old seafaring towns at the mouth of the Thames River, New London and Groton are today home to the Coast Guard Academy, a Navy submarine base, and the **Connecticut College Arboretum❖,** a 425-acre botanical preserve adjoining the main campus. The formal plantings and managed areas showcase some 300 species of woody trees and shrubs native to the southern New England area. The **Bolleswood Natural Area,** on the west side of the campus, features a rocky ravine full of mature hemlocks and contorted giant rhododendrons. Clothed in bright green moss, granite ridges 30 feet high border a rushing stream whose polyphony soon drowns out the roar of nearby I-95. At Bolleswood's southern end is a sizable sphagnum-heath bog, unusual in Connecticut, whose central floating mat of moss supports such rare insectivorous plants as sundews and pitcher plants. East of the campus, the **Mamacoke Natural Area** occupies a high wooded island—its granite outcrops jutting from the west bank of the Thames—connected to the mainland by foot trails through a tidal marsh.

Bluff Point State Park❖ in Groton, perhaps the best-kept secret on Connecticut's coast, is not even shown on some state maps. To reach it, take Route 117 south from I-95, then Route 1 west for a third of a mile. Just past the Groton town hall, turn left onto Depot Street and follow it under a railroad bridge to the Bluff Point picnic ground and parking area. This 800-acre forested neck of schist and gneiss bedrock—the largest wild coastline remaining in the state—affords views of some of Connecticut's most substantial winter waterfowl concentrations, including hundreds of brant, smaller relatives of Canada geese, and rafts of scaup that may number 50,000 or more.

The ridge trail traverses old farmland, where overgrown fields and bordering hardwoods provide perfect habitat for a sizable white-tailed deer population. The bluff overlooks Fishers Island Sound, site of the Mystic sailboat races, and Rhode Island's Watch Hill. Below the bluff, the sea has eroded a glacial drumlin; like a giant ripped beanbag, it has spilled a load of erratic boulders onto the beach. To the west Bluff Point Beach, a narrow, half-mile-long tombolo spit largely composed of pea-sized gravel, leads out to **Bushy Point**, another glacial deposit. An extensive sassafras forest with characteristic one-, two-, and three-fingered leaves borders the west side of the park.

Continue east on Route 1 through the historic harbor of Mystic to Stonington, the easternmost of Connecticut's coastal towns. At the end of Palmer Neck Road lies the entrance to **Barn Island Wildlife Management Area❖,** whose 756 acres protect one of the state's largest remaining parcels of salt marshes. Although still full of birds, shellfish, and crabs, the preserve contains only a diminished version of the wildlife that flourished here prior to 1931. At that time the marshes were ditched to control salt-marsh mosquitoes, but the effort failed to eradicate the mosquito and also reduced the marshes' productivity. Since then, the construction of dikes and various experiments have partially restored the marsh's original fecundity.

The trail follows the dikes across the marshes and up into projecting fingers of wooded upland, giving ready access to classic Connecticut salt marshes: small coves of wetland studded with small islands, glacial erratics, and rocky outcroppings. Barn Island's great variety of wetland and upland habitats provides excellent birding opportunities. Nesting and migrant upland species include yellow chats and prairie and blue-winged warblers. Noisy kingfishers, solitary green herons, great blue herons, and snowy egrets catch minnows in the ponds and creeks. Ospreys nest on platforms above the marshes, which are home to seaside and sharp-tailed sparrows and secretive clapper rails. Yellowlegs, spotted sandpipers, and other shorebirds feed in the brackish wetlands, and in the freshwater impoundments coots, gadwalls, Canada geese, and other waterfowl rest during migration.

THE EASTERN UPLANDS AND THE "QUIET CORNER"

The most sizable state forests in Connecticut are in the eastern half of the state, and the largest of these is **Pachaug State Forest❖,** a 24,000-acre

---

OVERLEAF: *Lacy lime-green curtains of spring foliage arch over the one-mile beach trail at Bluff Point in Groton. This "unmanaged" state park attracts seekers of solitude on Connecticut's crowded coast.*

complex that sprawls across six towns. Heavily farmed before the Civil War, the region is covered with second-growth forests full of stone walls and old foundations. Extensive remains of historic mills established along

the rushing streams also abound here. The many areas of natural interest within Pachaug include numerous glacial or kettle-hole ponds. One of the loveliest is the secluded **Green Falls Pond.** From Stonington, take Route 49 north to Voluntown, head east on Route 138, and follow Green Falls Road south to the north shore of the pond. Several rocky islands dot the undisturbed waters, and on the western side a trail circles a pellucid green lagoon lined with granite slabs and thick with stands of mountain laurel blossoms in

ABOVE: *A woodland nester, the hand-some scarlet tanager winters in South America, where the destruction of rain forests has affected it and other migratory songbirds.*

RIGHT: *Sheltered by scarlet-colored blueberry bushes, oak leaves lie like discarded gloves on a granite ridge at the Rock Spring refuge.*

June. At its southern end the pond empties over the Green Falls dam, plummeting into a steep hemlock-filled ravine.

Another part of Pachaug, the **Herman Haupt Management Area** (off Route 49 in Voluntown), is home to an unusual botanical community. The **Rhododendron Sanctuary** combines two species uncommon in the state: the Atlantic white cedar and the great laurel or rosebay rhododendron (*Rhododendron maximum*). A short walk here is particularly impressive in July, when the laurel's large shiny leaves set off its showy pink blossoms to perfection.

Nearby is the **Mount Misery Trail.** Less daunting than its name implies, the path to the 441-foot summit of this mini-monadnock winds through pine woods harboring flocks of wild turkeys and emerges on granite ledges carpeted with a corrugated lichen known as rock tripe. The vista here sweeps east across a broad red-maple swamp, brilliant in early October, to the hills of Arcadia 20 miles away, and south to the Mohegan Hills, the only major east-west range in the state. The ledge trail is also an

excellent place to observe the May warbler migration.

Some two dozen towns in Connecticut's northeastern quadrant call themselves the Quiet Corner, a name that fails to convey its abundance of rich natural sites. Flanked by the granitic Mohegan Hills on the east and the smoother metamorphic Windham Hills to the west, the Quinebaug River flows south through a broad valley known as the Quinebaug lowland. Dotted and threaded with numerous ponds and fishing streams, this scenic area also supports numerous working farms and a full complement of orchards, dairy herds, and horses.

In the town of Scotland, half a mile north of Route 14 on Route 97, is the **Rock Spring Wildlife Refuge❖,** a 445-acre Nature Conservancy preserve in the Little River valley that encompasses abandoned farmland typical of eastern Connecticut. A trail leads down through a mature forest of oaks, sugar maples, and hickories, which form a golden canopy in fall. Beneath the trees a network of stone walls mark the boundaries of former pastures and orchards, creating a strangely evocative landscape where each rock, each boulder, was once moved, hauled, and set in place by long-gone human hands.

The Little River, like many of the lovely streams that meander through this region, contains a sizable beaver dam with an extensive flooded meadow behind it. Here a trail traces the winding ridge of a miniature esker, a snakelike formation created when melting glacial waters carved long caves that subsequently filled with sand and gravel. Unlike the rich alluvial soil of the river bottom, the dry sandy esker supports a fragile vegetative community of bayberry, lichen, and pitch pine.

Continue north on Route 97 about 1.5 miles north of Hampton Center and turn left on Kenyon Road. At the top of a small hill a sign on the left marks the entrance to **Trail Wood❖,** the former home of noted American nature writer Edwin Way Teale and his wife, Nellie. Its 130 acres, now called the **Edwin Way Teale Memorial Sanctuary** and managed by the Connecticut Audubon Society, encompass a remarkable variety of ecosystems—meadows, pastures, wooded brooks, granite ridges, and a large beaver pond. Also evident are such reminders of past human activities as an old colonial road, an abandoned 1830s railroad bed, granite quarries, and a substantial stone wall that mysteriously ends in the middle of the woods.

One of the charms of Trail Wood is that nearly every tree, rock, path, and stream bears a name lovingly bestowed by the Teales during their sojourn here: Seven Springs Swamp, Veery Lane, Pussy Willow Corner, Starfield, Hyla Rill, Wild Plum Tangle, Hellebore Crossover. To the east Trail Wood abuts **Natchaug State Forest❖,** a 13,000-acre preserve that affords extensive opportunities for hiking, horseback riding, and cross-country skiing.

Farther north, Route 44 leads east into Pomfret, a town of picturesque rolling farmland and rocky wooded hills. At the intersection of Routes 44 and 169 is **Mashamoquet Brook State Park❖.** A highlight of this unexpectedly rugged tract of forest is **Wolf Den,** a narrow 20-foot-deep rock cave where in 1742, legend has it, local Revolutionary War hero Israel Putnam shot one of the last wolves in Connecticut, a dubious distinction in this more wildlife-conscious age. The place exudes a powerfully wild atmosphere, especially in June, when white and pink mountain laurel blooms along the dark ravines.

Just off Route 44 in West Ashford, 12 miles west of Mashamoquet, is one of Connecticut's famed specimen trees. Located, appropriately enough, on Giant Oak Lane, the **Ashford Oak Preserve** protects an immense northern red oak that for many years was the largest tree of its kind in the world. Although the 1938 hurricane and subsequent aging have stripped the tree of its title, with a circumference of more than 26 feet, the oak is still one of the largest trees in the state and an impressive presence by any measure.

Boston Hollow❖, in the northern part of Ashford, presents a dramatic example of ancient geologic forces, an unusual tract of northern hardwood forest, and a mecca for local birders. Take Route 89 north to the village of Westford, then go right on Boston Hollow Road, then take the gravel road to the left of the fork. This area is part of a massive 20-mile fault in the underlying metamorphic bedrock, which cracked when the continental plates of North America, Europe, and Asia collided here some 300 million years ago. Glaciers and erosion later carved out the terrain. Down this narrow graded road, once a major thoroughfare from Boston to Hartford, the sides of the abutting hills grow steeper, forming a cold sink that supports a tree community more commonly found in New Hampshire and Vermont: beech, sugar maple, yellow and white birch, hemlock, and white pine.

The northern flora attracts bird species rarely found in eastern Connecticut. In a superb warbler migration in early May, more than 30 species flit through the treetops; also on hand are nesting black-throated blue, black-throated green, Canada, and Blackburnian warblers, as well as wintering pine siskins, grosbeaks, and crossbills.

The hollow adjoins **Yale-Myers Forest❖,** at 7,000 acres the largest nonindustrial privately owned natural area in the state, where the Yale Forestry School conducts management research. A nine-mile section of the **Nipmuck Trail,** open to the public, runs through the forest.

RHODE ISLAND

PART THREE

RHODE ISLAND

Afew years ago, this state's license-plate motto was Discover Rhode Island. Residents and nonresidents alike found it unintentionally humorous, something like Ski Kansas. For those who take the trouble, however, the invitation is anything but a joke. Least but not least, the country's smallest state contains natural assets comparable with those of states many times its size. Although a few attractions are nationally known—the spectacular Cliff Walk at Newport and the isolated beauty of Block Island—most of its landscape remains to be discovered.

Many of Rhode Island's natural areas are small and off the main highways: the sea-carved gorge at Purgatory Chasm, the rare ferns and flowers of Lime Rock, and the soaring granite outcrops, majestic hemlock forests, and spectacular mountain-laurel displays at Ell Pond. Others, such as Prudence Island in Narragansett Bay, look inaccessible at first but turn out to be easy to visit. This most diminutive of states also contains at least two regional superlatives: New England's biggest estuary, Narragansett Bay, and one of its largest freshwater wetlands, the Great Swamp.

The name Rhode Island originally applied only to Aquidneck Island, the largest in Narragansett Bay, which today encompasses the towns of Portsmouth, Middletown, and Newport. Although Paleo-Indians lived there as long as 12,000 years ago, most of the state was occupied by the powerful Narragansett tribe when European settlers arrived in the early seventeenth century. In 1636 the Narragansett sachem Canonicus sold land to Roger Williams, the religious dissenter banished by the Puritans of Massachusetts. Williams was a staunch friend to the Narragansetts, who sided with the colonists during the Pequot War of 1636–37. That same year Williams established Providence as a haven for religious dissenters and later became the first president of the united "plantations" of Rhode Island. (The term, usually applied to estates of the Old South, was ironically appropriate to Rhode Island because this bastion of religious freedom contained more slaves than any other New England state and maintained strong ties to the South.)

PRECEDING PAGES: *A brick sentinel amid shifting sands, North Light stands firm on Sandy Point at Block Island National Wildlife Refuge.*

During the eighteenth century, the fertile lowlands around Narragansett Bay and its deep water harbors helped establish Providence, Bristol, and Newport as centers of commerce and shipping. When relations with England deteriorated in the 1770s, freedom-loving Rhode Islanders were among the first to support independence from the mother country.

Following the American Revolution, they also spearheaded the country's industrial revolution. In 1790 the British expatriate Samuel Slater established America's first successful water-powered textile mill at Pawtucket. By 1814 the Blackstone Valley was filled with mills producing textiles, tools, firearms, and paper. The Blackstone Canal, the first canal system in New England, was completed in 1828, linking the commercial centers of Worcester, Massachusetts, and Providence; only seven years later it was replaced by the Boston and Worcester railroad line, one of the first in the country.

In the decades that followed, the Blackstone Valley became one of the most heavily industrialized areas in the United States, and the Blackstone River earned the nickname "hardest-working river in America." After the Civil War, when many sections of New England entered a period of economic decline, Rhode Island enjoyed its greatest industrial prosperity. Wealthy Rhode Island residents helped to reestablish the town of Newport, destroyed during the Revolutionary War, as a premier seaside resort.

Following World War I, however, Rhode Island's industrial base declined, leaving a legacy of depressed mill towns, polluted rivers, and serious threats to the traditionally rich fisheries of Narragansett Bay. In recent decades, state and federal agencies and private and local organizations have cooperated in substantial efforts to restore and preserve both the human and natural resources of Rhode Island. These projects include the Blackstone River Valley National Heritage Corridor, the Narragansett Bay Research Reserve, and the Nature Conservancy preserves on Block Island. In an environmental version of beating swords into plowshares, decommissioned coastal military bases have been transformed into a series of national wildlife refuges fronting shining barrier beaches and rich salt marshes, and portions of abandoned railroad beds have been incorporated into the state's Trestle Trail system for hikers, linking some of the larger state forests—or management areas, as they are called—in the western part of the state.

From the unique population of American burying beetles on Block Island and the vast wooded stretches of the Great Swamp to the islands of Narragansett Bay and the extraordinary variety of Rhode Island's coastline, both visitors and residents are increasingly discovering and rediscovering the rich natural heritage of the Ocean State.

RHODE ISLAND:
THE OCEAN STATE

J ust as Rhode Island shares many historical roots with the rest of southern New England yet forged its own path, so the state's environment has much in common with that of its neighbors, yet boasts its own distinctive character.

Superficially, Rhode Island's landmass is similar to eastern Connecticut's: low hills of metamorphic rock overlain with thin layers of glacial drift. The highest point in the state, Jerimoth Hill in Foster, is only 812 feet. Much of Rhode Island's western half, however, is underlain by a solid shield of intrusive granite, making it geologically more like Massachusetts's rocky Cape Ann than any nearby area. In many places outcrops of this granite bedrock amid dense forests and numerous small rivers create a surprisingly wild terrain.

Rhode Island's nickname, the Ocean State, is no bantam boast. Although comprising only 1,214 square miles, it contains 420 miles of coastline, which surpasses its larger neighbors' shores in geological variety. Most of the state's coast encompasses the defining natural feature of Rhode Island: Narragansett Bay. Stretching 25 miles north from Point Judith to Pawtucket, it is the largest estuary in New England and one of the richest and most diverse marine habitats on the East Coast.

Rocky eastern Rhode Island, an area of picturesque horse fields and seaside farms, includes some of the region's most dramatic coastline. The

LEFT: *Transported by glaciers and rounded by centuries of wave action, beach cobbles form a bumpy strip between the sandy shoreline and the Cretaceous period deposits at Clay Head on Block Island's eastern shore.*

state's southern shore, on the other hand, is largely a drowned coastal plain, sharing the ancient origins of the Connecticut coast. It differs significantly, however, because it was more recently sculpted by the same glacier that formed the moraines and outwash plains of Cape Cod and the northern shore of Long Island. The Watch Hill (or Charlestown) Moraine stretches from Point Judith to Watch Hill, forming a low mound of glacial till and boulders roughly traced by Route 1. North of the moraine, which acted as a drainage dam, a string of large ponds and swamps formed, including Great Swamp, the largest freshwater swamp in southern New England. Since the retreat of the last glacier, coastal erosion and rising sea levels have formed a nearly continuous series of long barrier beaches, salt ponds, and marshes to the south of this moraine—some of the richest bird refuges in the Northeast.

Beginning at the Massachusetts–Rhode Island line, this itinerary travels down the Blackstone River valley and then explores the state's eastern coast. Next the route turns west, visiting some of the islands of Narragansett Bay and following the southern coast to the Connecticut line. The chapter proceeds to the rugged forested hills of western Rhode Island and concludes with a ferry trip to Block Island, the crown jewel of the state's natural areas.

THE BLACKSTONE RIVER VALLEY

Like most of Rhode Island's notable natural areas, the state's outstanding historical landscape, the Blackstone River valley, is associated with water. Northern Rhode Island encompasses the southern portion of the **Blackstone River Valley National Heritage Corridor❖.** From North Smithfield to Pawtucket, the Blackstone flows through several historic mill towns—Manville, Albion, Ashton, Lonsdale, Valley Falls—containing examples of some of the country's earliest water-powered industrial mills. The heritage corridor was established to restore and interpret the Blackstone River's natural resources, and several outstanding sites can be found in this area. The first—the **Blackstone Gorge,** which straddles the Massachusetts–Rhode Island border in North Smithfield—is described in Chapter Three. Spring is the best time to view this wild stretch of the river, when white-water rapids roar through sheer granite walls in a scene more reminiscent of northern Maine than the second most densely settled state in the nation.

Route 122 leads through Woonsocket (in this tricky urban negotiation, look *carefully* for route signs) into Cumberland. Go east on Route 120, then north on Route 114 to **Diamond Hill Park❖,** which is named for a

Woonsocket

DIAMOND HILL SP
Manville
Cumberland
BLACKSTONE RIVER SP
Albion
Ashton
Valley Falls
LIME ROCK PRESERVE
Lonsdale
Lonsdale Marsh

BLACKSTONE RIVER NAT. HERITAGE CORRIDOR

GEORGE WASHINGTON MANAGEMENT AREA
102
44
Bowdish Reservoir
116
123

x Jerimoth Hill

MASSACHUSETTS

95

SNAKE DEN STATE PARK
295
14
Foster
5
PROVIDENCE
CARATUCK WILDLIFE REFUGE

195

GEORGE B PARKER WOODLAND
116
1
Warren
TOUISSET MARSH WILDLIFE REFUGE

CARBUNCLE POND FISHING AREA
14
Coventry
3

NARRAGANSETT BAY RESEARCH RESERVE
Patience I
Hope I
Prudence Island
Narragansett Bay
24
Tiverton
81
SAPOWET MARSH MGT AREA
EMILIE RUECKER WILDLIFE REFUGE
179

West Greenwich
102

ARCADIA MANAGEMENT AREA
Exeter
138
BAY ISLAND STATE PARK
MARSH MEADOWS WILDLIFE SANCTUARY
DUTCH ISLAND MGT AREA
138
114
FOGLAND MARSH PRESERVE
WEETAMOO WOODS
77
Little Compton

LONG & EEL PONDS NATURAL AREAS
3
138
West Kingston
NORMAN BIRD SANCTUARY
QUICKSAND POND/ GOOSEWING BEACH PRESERVE

Hopkinton
GREAT SWAMP MANAGEMENT AREA
Great Swamp
Worden Pond
138A
Newport
CLIFF WALK
1A
SACHUEST PT NAT WILDLIFE REFUGE
BEAVERTAIL POINT STATE PARK

Patuxet River

Charlestown
1
Westerly
NINIGRET NWR
TRUSTOM POND NWR
Point Judith

Pawtucket
95
1A
Watch Hill
NINIGRET CONSERVATION AREA
QUANOCHONTAUG BREACHWAY

tle rragansett y

Napatree Point

CONNECTICUT
395
95
1A

BLOCK ISLAND NWR
Great Salt Pond
Block Island
THE GREENWAY
FRESH POND/FRESH MARSH PRESERVE
LEWIS-DICKENS FARM NATURE PRESERVE
Mohegan Bluffs

RHODE ISLAND

10   0   10 Miles

10   0   10 Kilometers

geologic oddity, a mile-long bluff of pinkish-white quartz that towers above the surrounding countryside. Because the quartz hill is composed of very resistant rock, it is higher than the surrounding Narragansett basin sediments. Trails ascend to the top of these 150-foot cliffs, which overlook the Diamond Hill Reservoir and the forested hills and villages of the Blackstone River valley.

Return to Route 122 and continue south to Route 116, taking the George Washington Highway bridge west over the Blackstone River. Just below this modern span, on the west side of the river, **Blackstone River State Park❖** contains the best-preserved portion of the **Blackstone Canal** in Rhode Island. Hand-dug by Irish immigrants between 1824 and 1828, the canal from Worcester to Pawtucket opened the Blackstone Valley to worldwide trade and an industrial boom that lasted through the nineteenth century.

A short distance above the bridge is one of the dams that harnessed the river's power. Here the canal parallels the river, and visitors can canoe this section or walk the original towpath some three miles south along the river to the village of Lonsdale, which offers a rich mosaic of historic and natural sights. On the west side of the canal is the Old Ashton Mill House, built about 1810, and across the river to the east the massive brick structure of the Ashton textile mill (1867) is backed by rows of brick millworker housing. Some of the largest sycamores in the state grow along the canal and riverbanks.

Some three miles west of the canal, just west of Route 246 on Wilbur Road, is the **Lime Rock Preserve❖,** an outstanding botanical site named for the area's abundant sedimentary limestone deposits, which were first quarried in the 1660s. One of the largest outcrops of dolomite marble in Rhode Island makes Lime Rock a botanist's and geologist's delight. Here calcareous ledges have created unusually sweet soils that support 30 species of rare plants—including many ferns, trout lilies, yellow lady's slippers, baneberry, and nodding trilliums—several found nowhere else in the state. The main trail follows an old electric train bed, part of the extensive interurban transportation system of the early twentieth century. Late spring and early summer are the best times to observe the flowering plants, and visitors to this generally moist site should wear appropriate footgear and bring plenty of mosquito repellent.

LEFT: *The circa 1825 Blackstone Canal helped to create America's first industrial valley in Rhode Island. The still-sylvan canal declined in importance after rail lines were completed up the valley in 1848.*

215

Head east to Route 126, then south to Lonsdale. Just .2 miles south of the junction of Routes 123 and 122 (Lonsdale Avenue), an unmarked dirt road on the left leads down to **Lonsdale Marsh❖.** Located in the floodplain of the Blackstone River and surrounded by urban sprawl, the freshwater wetlands of Lonsdale Marsh flourish as a haven for wildlife and a vivid reminder of the original natural richness of this industrialized valley.

ABOVE: *Mallards are North America's most abundant and widespread duck. Their ability to hybridize with the closely related black duck is adversely affecting the population of the latter.*

RIGHT: *Drowned tree trunks dominate a winter landscape at Lincoln's Lime Rock Preserve. In spring these wetlands support many rare wildflowers.*

The rounded embayment containing the marsh is a glacial kettle hole, formed by a large chunk of ice that broke off the retreating glacier some 15,000 years ago. Each type of wetland here—including sedge marsh, cattail marsh, shrub swamp, and forested swamp—attracts characteristic wildlife. Cattails provide nesting areas for red-winged blackbirds and material for muskrat lodges. The sedge marsh gives cover to several pairs of nesting Virginia rails, marsh dwellers with long curved bills and rich chestnut plumage; visitors are more likely to hear their clicklike calls and falling *oink* notes than to see these secretive birds. Great blue herons commonly feed during the day, and black-crowned night herons, with their distinctive *quawk* calls, are best seen at dawn and dusk. The shrub swamps are a good place to spot migrating spring warblers in May, and woodcocks, which call in the evening, can occasionally be seen on the moist floor of the forested swamps, probing the soil for earthworms with their long prehensile bills.

By an odd historical circumstance, the next Rhode Island site is actually in Massachusetts. Located on Brown's Avenue in Seekonk, Massachusetts, just east of Providence, the **Caratunk Wildlife Refuge❖** was the country estate of a Pawtucket couple, who bequeathed it to the Audubon Society of Rhode Island. On the site of an old farm, Caratunk's 200 acres boast a rich assortment of habitats, including maple swamps, hemlock and pine

stands, hardwood forests, open fields, ponds, streams, rock ledges, and blocky sequences of glacial erratics known as boulder trains. Coles Brook, a delightfully clear stream, winds through much of the property. Caratunk's diversity of habitat attracts a wide variety of wildlife, particularly birds.

The refuge's symbol is the woodcock, or timberdoodle, a squat upland shorebird with an oversized bill. During the spring months naturalists lead visitors to observe one of the diminutive wonders of the avian world: the evening courtship flight of the woodcock. Shortly after dusk in a field or clearing, the male woodcock begins his characteristic *peenting* calls to attract females. Then, as darkness gathers, he takes off in a wide circling flight, his outer wing feathers producing a whistling sound as he rises in a tightening spiral more than 100 feet in the air. Suddenly he pauses, utters a short twittering song, and plummets silently to earth. During a full moon, this spectacular display can continue for hours.

TIVERTON AND LITTLE COMPTON

From Seekonk, take I-195 east to Exit 3, then Milford Road west into Warren, Rhode Island. On Touisset Road look for the Touisset Fire Company's Engine 6 Station and park in the area to the right, where a gated path leads into the **Touisset Marsh Wildlife Refuge❖.** This little-known Rhode Island Audubon sanctuary fronts the Kickamuit River, a wide brackish tidal river often populated by large concentrations of mergansers, scaup, and other wintering and migrating waterfowl. The paths cross a patchwork of fields and thickets that support a rich variety of songbirds. At the southern end of the refuge, herons and other wading birds commonly feed in a charming little cove. Along the shoreline are specimens of a curious bluish-gray conglomerate rock known as pudding stone, which formed in the sedimentary bedrock of the Narragansett Basin and is found in only a few other areas in New England. Touisset, which can be explored in less than an hour, is a diminutive jewel of Rhode Island's eastern coastline.

Some of Rhode Island's many islands are political, such as its easternmost section, encompassing the towns of Tiverton and Little Compton, which is geographically separated from the rest of Rhode Island by a portion of Massachusetts. Many consider the Tiverton–Little Compton region the most scenic part of the state because its gently rolling countryside is dotted with seaside farms, green fields full of horses, and small New England villages. Bordering the Sakonnet River (a tidal estuary) and Rhode Island Sound, its coastline is a gleaming necklace of barrier beaches, saltwater coves, pristine salt marshes, and picturesque lighthouses.

From Touisset, return to I-195 in Massachusetts and continue east to Exit 8A. Take Route 24 south to Exit 1 in Tiverton, and then follow Route 81 south about eight miles into Little Compton. Here, at the end of South Shore Road in the southeastern corner of Rhode Island, is the access to the **Quicksand Pond/Goosewing Beach Preserve❖.** This superlative site, a large public natural area in exclusive Little Compton, is well worth the parking fee levied during the summer months. The mile-long barrier beach at the eastern tip of the state's shoreline is a major nesting habitat for the least tern and the piping plover (one of only five known nesting sites in the state for this bird federally listed as threatened). Behind the dune line pristine Quicksand Pond is an important feeding area for migrating ducks and shorebirds during the spring and fall. Gray-shingled houses and barns overlooking the beach belong to one of the oldest coastal farms in the state. Throughout the summer, visitors may join nature walks led by the Nature Conservancy's beach manager.

RIGHT: *At Goosewing Beach in Little Compton, deep pink blossoms of* Rosa rugosa, *or beach rose, add a lushness to the dunes in June. The large rose hips of this Asian import are gathered to make jams and jellies.*

On the western shore of Little Compton, **Fogland Marsh Preserve❖** shelters one of the few large undisturbed salt marshes in the state. Take Route 77 north from Little Compton. About 1.5 miles south of Tiverton Four Corners, turn left on Pond Bridge Road, left on Puncatest Neck Road, right on Fogland Road, and left on High Hill Road to the Fogland entrance. The salt marsh here has never been drained or ditched for mosquito control, and its 50 acres of lush Spartina grasses are a rich nursery for clams and fish, which attract great blue herons, snowy egrets, and an occasional mink or northern harrier. Almy Brook, running through the marsh, is the site of a major alewife run. From Pond Bridge Road, just above the refuge, spring visitors can observe these migratory herring as they travel up the brook to spawn above the dam in Nonquit Pond.

At **Weetamoo Woods❖** in Tiverton, a quarter-mile east of Tiverton Four Corners off East Road (Route 179), a 450-acre town-owned "wilderness" abounds with natural and human history. Eight Road Way, a stonewall-flanked road laid out in 1679, leads into the property and still contains patches of the original cobblestones. Other trails—lined with glacial erratics, holly trees, and some giant oaks—pass an impressive early eighteenth-century vertical sawmill site on Borden Brook, stone bridges, and the cellars of old farmhouses and cabins.

At the northern end of a sizable cedar swamp encircled by an Indian trail is **Wildcat Rock,** a large mound of glacial erratics. In an even more imposing formation at the south end of the swamp, the massive granite outcropping of **High Rock,** its base swathed in dark hemlocks, extends several hundred feet and rises 70 feet high. Its western summit affords a commanding view of the Tiverton countryside and the Sakonnet River. The relatively smooth northern slopes of the formation and the sheer, rough southern side are the result of glacial "plucking": The ice mass moving down from the north slid over the northern sides of such outcrops and cracked off the southern ends.

From the junction of Routes 179 and 77, go west on West Road, then north on Sapowet Road. In less than a mile a bridge crosses a tidal creek at **Sapowet Marsh Management Area❖,** a state-owned wildlife preserve that provides one of the few free parking spots in the area. This huge expanse of salt marsh dotted with small marsh islands is an excellent birding spot for shorebirds, herons, and egrets.

North of the preserve, Sapowet Road makes a right turn. A half mile on the left is the entrance to the **Emilie Ruecker Wildlife Refuge❖,** where an old farm and a large salt marsh fronting on the Sakonnet River form a particularly rich birding area. On the 30-acre Audubon refuge alone more than 150 species have been sighted. Well-maintained trails lead to an observation blind on a freshwater wetland where solitary and spotted sandpipers occasionally feed, through old apple orchards and remnants of pasture where woodcocks court and sing in the spring, and through spruce and pine woods laced with old stone walls made from pudding stone. The main attraction of the refuge, though, is two wooded peninsulas jutting into saltwater coves and salt marshes. In summer, along cool, shaded trails, visitors can observe herons, egrets, glossy ibis, plover, sandpipers, yellowlegs, and other shorebirds feeding in the mudflats and marshes at low tide; in the fall thousands of swallows gather here on their migration south.

NARRAGANSETT BAY: MARSHES AND MANSIONS

Narragansett Bay lies within the larger Narragansett Basin, a geologic structure that stretches into southeastern Massachusetts. Like the Boston Basin, the Narragansett is filled with softer sedimentary Cretaceous deposits; it also contains impressive outcrops of an uncommon geologic conglomerate known as pudding stone. In the late nineteenth century, the bay's exquisite beaches, temperate summer climate, and magnificent views made it a prime resort for the country's millionaires, who built the famous seaside mansions, or "cottages," of Newport. Deep, sheltered harbors enabled Providence and other ports to become important shipping centers. Newport became home to a major naval base.

First and foremost, Narragansett Bay is an estuary, its character formed by the mixing of salt water from the sea and freshwater runoff from the surrounding land. Seven large rivers and numerous tributaries empty into Narragansett Bay. The watershed of the Blackstone River alone, reaching into central Massachusetts, drains an area as large as Rhode Island, and the entire watershed of Narragansett Bay is twice the size of the state. Once an incredibly rich nursery for marine life, Narragansett Bay, like many estuaries in industrialized regions, has suffered from pollution, overfishing, and the degradation of natural coastal processes. Although impoverished and polluted in many places, it still supports a significant shellfish industry, including 10 percent of the national quahog, or hard-shell clam, crop.

Among significant efforts to reclaim and restore large portions of the bay was the establishment in 1980 of the federal **Narragansett Bay Research Reserve❖,** the first such sanctuary in the Northeast. The reserve encompasses more than 2,500 acres of the bay's islands and shallow waters, including **Hope Island, Patience Island,** and most of **Prudence Is-**

ABOVE: *An almost surreal light suffuses this dramatic depiction of Rhode Island's rugged eastern shoreline in a detail from* **Approaching Storm:**

land. A major nesting area for egrets, herons, and ibis, Hope Island is off limits to visitors during the nesting season; Patience Island can be reached only by private boat. The largest of the three, Prudence Island, is readily accessible by private ferry from the old shipping port of Bristol.

Snake-shaped and some five miles long, Prudence is a low, flat wooded island originally inhabited by the Narragansett, who left copious shell middens. After it was purchased from them in 1637 by Roger Williams and Massachusetts governor John Winthrop, Prudence became one of Rhode Island's first "plantations." Although usually applied to the southern states, the term is appropriate because Rhode Island had more slaves than any other New England state and strong ties to the South. At one time the island supported 200 people, and until the early part of this century it supplied vegetables and dairy products to many Narragansett Bay communities. Today its farms and numerous stone walls are smothered in a tangle of vines and shrubs, giving it almost a tropical air in summer. About a hundred year-round residents live in the small community of Homestead, which has no public accommodations or restaurants. Amid a busy New England estuary, Prudence Island offers solitude in abundance.

Also in abundance are white-tailed deer—the densest population in

Beach Near Newport *(1860). This painting is considered the masterpiece of Martin Johnson Heade, a noted nineteenth-century American luminist.*

New England—which have made the island the deer tick capital of the region. Deer ticks are carriers of Lyme disease, a widespread, potentially debilitating infection that assumed epidemic proportions in the late 1980s in many parts of the Northeast. Visitors are strongly urged to wear protective clothing and to see their physician if they develop the characteristic rash and flulike symptoms. The disease is readily curable if treated early. So prevalent is Lyme disease on Prudence that the state has canceled its public ferry service and closed the campground at **Bay Island State Park❖,** at the southern end of the island. A former World War II naval base, the park is still open for hiking and swimming, and deer can often be seen strolling among the abandoned ammunition bunkers. (The park is about 3 miles south of Homestead via driveable roads.)

The northern end of the island, part of the research reserve, features broad mown walking paths, stunning saltwater coves, and a shoreline strewn with thick windrows of blue mussels and pink slipper shells. A trail winds past an abandoned mansion and North End Farm, an 1840 historical archaeological site. In summer Potter and Coggeshall coves are often crowded with pleasure boats; in early fall, however, Potter Cove is a gathering place for thousands of swallows, and Pine Knoll, above Cogge-

ABOVE: *Of the three pudding-stone ridges at the Norman Bird Sanctuary, Hanging Rock is the most dramatic. Here, wreathed in crimson blueberry bushes, enormous gray rock fingers project above the ocean.*

shall Cove, provides welcome shade and an excellent vantage spot for observing herons and egrets feeding in the marsh below.

From Bristol, Route 114 leads south across the Mount Hope Bridge onto Aquidneck Island, the original "Rhode Island." In Middletown, in the southeastern corner of the island, the **Norman Bird Sanctuary**❖ and nearby **Sachuest Point National Wildlife Refuge**❖ constitute an extremely rich birding area. The Norman Bird Sanctuary, a 450-acre private preserve, is unlike any other coastal bird sanctuary in the region. Instead of broad, low barrier beaches and salt marshes, Norman boasts dramatic terrain. Three enormous rock ridges jut south from the sanctuary headquarters, providing commanding views of two large reservoirs, Nelson and Gardner, that attract numerous waterfowl.

These ridges are perhaps the most impressive examples of pudding stone, a sedimentary rock common only in the Narragansett and Boston basins. Pudding stone is named for its peculiar appearance: Small cobbles and stones are embedded in a matrix like the raisins and currants in plum pudding, an early New England dessert. Its geologic story began millions of

ABOVE: *The lime green "slime" outlining the shore of this small pond at the Norman Bird Sanctuary is actually a surface coating of duckweed, a minute floating plant that provides food for fish and waterfowl.*

years ago, when enormous amounts of sand, gravel, and stones were deposited at the mouths of rivers in Narragansett Basin, an ancient glacial river valley. These deposits were covered with hundreds of feet of sediment, which pressed them deep into the earth. There pressure and heat transformed, or lithified, the mixture into a hard, erosion-resistant conglomerate. Subsequent uplifts raised the formations above sea level, and recent erosion has scoured away the softer sedimentary layers, leaving the ridges exposed and separated. Pudding-stone ledges resemble distorted cobbled streets in which individual rocks are elongated in a north-south direction. Between the ridges are isolated wet valleys full of blooming swamp roses.

Southeast of these ridges are the low, shrubby knolls of the Sachuest Point refuge, a 250-acre peninsula stretching into Rhode Island Sound. Its rocky shoreline, in places composed of huge granite slabs, is a fine place to observe migrating ducks, hawks, and shorebirds in fall and spring. A visitor center provides information about the more than 200 species seen here. Formerly a U.S. Navy rifle range, the upland is now covered with shrubs and vines crisscrossed with broad grassy swaths that form "bunny

LEFT: *A shy bird of marshes and reedy ponds, the American bittern has heavily streaked plumage that provides superb camouflage.*
RIGHT: *Tall seed stalks of beach grass and the fluffy seed heads of goldenrod form a bright border above a cobble beach at Sachuest Point.*

alleys" full of darting rabbits. The small mammals attract red-tailed hawks and northern harriers, as well as the rare diurnal short-eared owl. Sachuest is also the best place on the East Coast to see wintering flocks of harlequin ducks. Three wooden observation decks provide excellent birding vantage points.

From Sachuest, drive west on the shore road and then left on Tuckerman Avenue to a small parking lot and the entrance to **Purgatory Chasm❖.** Only a few yards wide, this 150-foot-long crack was carved through a narrow pudding-stone ridge in a fracture of the bedrock crust formed hundreds of millions of years ago. Although the gorge was primarily chiseled out by glacial action, pounding ocean waves continue to widen and roar through it today. A small wooden footbridge over the chasm affords a safe and close view of these ongoing processes.

To undertake one of the most unusual and impressive walks along the American shoreline, continue west on Route 138A into Newport. On the left, at the end of Newport Beach, is parking for the **Cliff Walk❖.** About three miles long, this unique National Recreation Trail offers unparalleled views of the ocean on one side, and on the other, glimpses of some of the country's most elaborate and famous mansions, including Rosecliff and the Vanderbilts' "cottage" the Breakers. The trail winds along a dramatic stretch of rocky shoreline where steep ravines border formal rose gardens and Oriental teahouses perched on granite outcrops. In few other spots does conspicuous opulence rub so closely against untrammeled wildness.

Across the Newport Bridge, at the southernmost tip of Conanicut Island, is **Beavertail Point State Park❖,** a remote, windswept stretch of coast that includes the oldest lighthouse site in Rhode Island. The striking blue-gray, pale pink, and ocher rock formations sloping into the water are outcrops of hard schists and slates that resisted the glacial erosion that scooped out Narragansett Bay. Beavertail is a splendid place to

ABOVE: *Awkward and ungainly on land, harbor seals are graceful swimmers and highly efficient predators in the ocean. Mainly fish eaters, they can dive to 300 feet and stay submerged for half an hour.*

observe migrating hawks in the fall, and its rocky shores are a favorite haul-out spot for harbor seals in winter. Like so many coastal refuges, Beavertail is a former military installation, dotted with remnants of gun emplacements, communication centers, and bunkers.

Beavertail's eastern shore may be the most dramatic and geologically varied rocky coast south of Cape Ann. At its northern end are striking blue-gray slate formations streaked with ribbonlike orange intrusions. Its honeycombed rocks shot with quartz and feldspar, **Lion's Head Gorge** is a natural chasm that becomes a boiling and thunderous cauldron during northeasters. Farther south along the beach, in a curious juxtaposition of natural and artificial formations, bedrock outcrops and glacial erratics are interspersed with a dozen large granite and marble blocks, some of them shaped into pediments or carved with floral designs. The ship carrying a cargo of stone for a public building in Virginia sank at Shipwreck Rock more than a hundred years ago, and the artifacts were thrown onto these ledges by the 1938 hurricane.

ABOVE: *Shown here clockwise from top left are three coastal breeding birds found in Rhode Island: a laughing gull, a common moorhen, and a roseate tern, which has caught a sand eel, its main source of food.*

North Road toward the Jamestown bridge crosses Great Creek at **Marsh Meadows Wildlife Sanctuary❖,** an excellent spot to view snowy egrets in the salt marsh framed by the towering span of the Newport Bridge to the east. Directly west is the **Dutch Island Management Area❖,** accessible by private boat. Part of the Bay Islands State Park system, Dutch Island has an intense legacy of human use. A seventeenth-century Dutch colony, eighteenth-century smallpox quarantine colony, and Civil War fort are only the beginning. The landscape is littered with the remains of Fort Greble, a massive installation of bunkers, barracks, tunnels, gun emplacements, and other military structures that was manned primarily between the world wars. Despite its somewhat grim and unnatural history, the island is today an appealingly solitary place to

OVERLEAF: *Fall clusters of high-tide bush edge the salt waters of Ninigret Pond near Charlestown. Once part of a naval air base, Ninigret is one of a string of waterfowl refuges along Rhode Island's south coast.*

229

stroll in lower Narragansett Bay, and in June its gun batteries are smothered in mounds of wild rose blossoms.

From Jamestown, follow Route 138 across the Jamestown Bridge and
west into West Kingston. Turn west onto Liberty Lane to the railroad
tracks, then bear left again on a gravel road for about a mile to the parking area at a barred gate. This is the entrance to the **Great Swamp
Wildlife Management Area❖,** a premier natural preserve whose dirt
roads and raised dikes provide rare access to a large swamp's interior.
Occupying a basin scooped out by the Wisconsin glacier, the preserve's
more than 3,000 acres encompass Rhode Island's largest freshwater wetland and largest natural body of water, 1,000-acre **Worden Pond.**

Great Swamp is probably best visited in spring, when the flowering dog-
woods are in bloom and the mosquitoes and blackflies of summer have not
yet appeared. Its tupelos and red maples are especially lovely in autumn,
but hunters are numerous then. The forested swamps, open marshes, and
upland peninsulas support a floral richness unsurpassed in the state. A highlight is large stands of native American holly, a southern tree that nears its
northern limit in southern New England. As in many of the region's natural
areas, the hand of man, past and present, is evident in the swamp's interior.
Visitors walking through its wooded corridors may be surprised by the loud
whistle and thunder of a train, because an Amtrak line cuts through the middle of the area. Great Swamp also boasts Rhode Island's largest colony of
nesting ospreys, which can be viewed from the road circling the diked impoundment. Biologists have erected nesting poles for these handsome fish
hawks, whose numbers have recovered dramatically over the past few
decades from the effects of pesticides. Ironically, the birds commonly
choose to build their large nests of sticks on the tall towers supporting utility
lines that cross the marsh.

THE SOUTHERN SHORE:
POINT JUDITH TO WATCH HILL

In South Kingstown, **Trustom Pond National Wildlife Refuge❖** is one of
a magnificent series of eight coastal ponds—separated from the ocean by
long sandy barrier beaches—strung along Rhode Island's western coast.
The refuge, on Matunuck Schoolhouse Road south of Route 1 near Green
Hill, is the site of an old seaside farm. Its broad, well-maintained trails
wander through pastures, young forest, and maple swamps; past old
windmills, stone walls, and sheep sheds; and out to two peninsulas of land
that jut into the pond. A large population of mute swans rule this pond. In-

troduced from Europe as decorative park waterfowl more than a century ago, the swans have become naturalized and multiplied on hundreds of ponds and lakes throughout the Northeast. Although their large, graceful white bodies are an impressive sight, these aggressive birds often drive native species from the ponds they inhabit. Despite their presence, Trustom Pond hosts large numbers of mergansers, black ducks, Canada geese, buffleheads, goldeneyes, and other waterfowl during spring and fall migration. In summer ospreys nest on small islands in the pond, and Moonstone beach, the fragile, dynamic arm of sand between the pond and the sea, is home to an important protected piping plover and least tern colony.

After returning to Route 1 and continuing west into Charlestown, take the exit for Ninigret Park on Old Post Road. Ninigret Park is a municipal recreational area at the eastern entrance to **Ninigret National Wildlife Refuge❖,** where extensive marshes, grassy fields, and a barrier beach (not accessible from the refuge) enclose Ninigret Pond, the state's largest coastal lagoon. Ninigret's 400 acres are the site of a World War II naval air station, where today herring gulls open clams by dropping them on abandoned runways. Where fighters once taxied, the forms of marsh hawks now glide and swoop. Beside the runways, half smothered by the encroaching tangle of viburnum, Virginia creeper, and multiflora roses, large landing-strip numbers seem like overgrown nature-trail signs. The songs of yellowthroats, wood thrushes, and mockingbirds now drift along the grassy paths, and the distant roar of pleasure boats in Ninigret Pond sounds like the ghosts of planes.

To gain access to Ninigret's barrier beach, continue west on Route 1 to East Beach Road and follow it south to the state beach at **Ninigret Conservation Area❖,** where bordering salt marshes provide an important natural nursery for shellfish and fish species. Just west is the **Quonochontaug Breachway❖,** a state-owned boat-launching area. Considered one of the best birding areas in southern New England, the large salt marsh here attracts such wading birds as snowy egrets, energetically stalking the shallows for fish, and glossy ibis, unmistakable bronze-plumaged birds with long down-curved bills.

The next coastal area to the west is **Quonochontaug Beach Conservation Area❖,** at the end of Ninigret Avenue in Westerly. Quonochontaug—a private two-mile beach open for walking, birding, and fishing—is composed of nearly pure sand and subject to massive starfish strandings in the spring. On its north side, projecting into Quonochontaug Pond, is a forested knoll, a clump of glacial till dropped millennia ago by the retreating ice and subsequently connected to the mainland by the growth of this barrier beach.

233

Continuing west, rejoin Route 1A and follow it to Watch Hill, a picturesque old resort town atop a large glacial mound where the Pawcatuck River enters Little Narragansett Bay, separating Rhode Island from Connecticut. Stretching west from Watch Hill is **Napatree Point❖**, an unusual tombolo beach that forms the shifting southwestern tip of Rhode Island. Napatree, one of the most dynamic beach systems along this coast, is a good example of a highly developed shoreline that was returned to its natural state when the 1938 hurricane swept 35 summer cottages from the spit. At the end of the beach, atop a large mound covered with shrubs and vines, the surroundings seem like the hidden remains of some extensive ancient temple—actually the walls, turrets, and batteries of turn-of-the-century Fort Mansfield. From mid-September to mid-October, the old fort is the best site on the Rhode Island coast for watching migrating sharp-shinned and Cooper's hawks, American kestrels, and occasionally peregrine falcons. Visible to the west, Sandy Point, an island once connected to Napatree and separated by the hurricane, now lies partially in Connecticut.

WESTERN RHODE ISLAND: FORESTS AND FALLS, LEDGES AND LEGENDS

From Watch Hill the route heads north, out of the world of barrier beaches, coastal ponds, and salt marshes into a very different terrain characterized by extensive woodlands, slow meandering rivers, and the thick granite shield that underlies western Rhode Island. The most dramatic examples of this landscape and particularly rich botanical areas are the **Long and Ell Ponds Natural Areas❖**. From Westerly, take Route 3 north to the village of Hopkinton, then turn north on West Rockville Road to the small parking area on the right. For Rhode Island, the terrain here is extremely rugged, and good hiking shoes are advised.

Established in 1974 as the first and only National Natural Landmark in the state, this area comprises a mile-long granite gorge that actually rises above the surrounding landscape some 70 feet. Cupped within the gorge, the larger Long Pond is a rare preglacial body of water, and smaller Ell Pond was scraped out by the glacial mass that also sculpted the deep clefts and sheer drop-offs in these granite ridges. The two ponds, connected by a narrow wetland dense with tall white cedars, border superb examples of a

---

RIGHT: *At Quonochontaug Beach, strong sea winds and salt spray have sculpted the marsh shrubs growing on this glacial-till island into a sleek aerodynamic shape that resembles an airplane wing.*

floating sphagnum, or "quaking," bog. Visitors clambering up and down the trails pass through an unusual "forest" of giant rosebay rhododendrons, 15 to 20 feet high, with 6-inch-long leathery leaves. In July their pink-white blossoms create a colorful display against the gray granite outcrops and huge glacial erratics.

On the south side of Long Pond is an impressive grove of hemlocks known as the **Cathedral,** one of the few old-growth hemlock stands in the state. Some of these venerable conifers are more than 200 years old and extend three feet in diameter. Unfortunately, these towering monarchs are threatened with destruction by a tiny aphidlike insect called the woolly adelgid. Scientists believe that the adelgid, an alien species introduced in the South, was blown into Connecticut by Hurricane Gloria in 1985 and spread into Rhode Island a few years ago. Already a large portion of the Cathedral hemlocks show the characteristic white moldlike colonies of adelgids on the undersides of their needles, and more and more trees have become lacy black skeletons. The adelgids have no natural predator here, and sylviculturists have found no practical control for the pest. It seems small comfort that the death of these magnificent trees is opening views of the ponds and the cliffs to the north.

North of Ell Pond stretches the vast, sprawling complex of natural regions known as the **Arcadia Management Area❖.** Covering portions of West Greenwich, Exeter, Hopkinton, and Richmond, its 14,000 acres constitute Rhode Island's largest state forest. It abuts Connecticut's 14,000-acre Pachaug State Forest, making it part of one of the largest contiguous preserved areas in the region. A showcase of western Rhode Island's varied terrain and biota, Arcadia contains several large ponds; mountain laurel that explodes into pinkish blossoms each June; old-growth hemlocks; the state's most extensive

Above: *Like bright yellow parachutes, black-eyed Susans dominate this floral composite that also includes the daisylike white mayweed and tiny wild magenta pinks.*

Left: *A lone pitch pine stands vigil atop a massive granite outcrop overlooking Long Pond. A grove of ancient hemlocks known as the Cathedral occupies the far shore.*

Overleaf: *A group of white pine, southern New England's dominant conifer, is mirrored in Browning Mill Pond in the Arcadia Management Area.*

beech forests (which provide a food source for wild turkeys); meandering forest streams with natural and man-made falls; expanses of open field habitat; and immense granite outcroppings that challenge the image of a tame Rhode Island landscape.

One of the more interesting areas in this vast maze of dirt roads and streams, **Falls River** provides a fine example of the rocky waterways of the Eastern Highlands of Rhode Island and Connecticut. From Route 165, two miles east of the Connecticut line, take Escoheag Road north for about a mile, and at an old state forest cabin, turn east onto Austin Farm Road. After two miles the dirt road crosses Falls River, a clear, swift stream running across a granite bed. Park here and follow the river north along the **Ben Utter Trail,** a particularly lovely walk in the fall, when the overarching beech trees turn honey gold and cast a magical light on the needle-covered forest floor. Along the stream are the remains of an old gristmill and sawmill. At the north end of the trail, where it crosses another dirt road, **Stepstone Falls**—a white fury in the spring and a braided cascade when the water is lower—pours over a series of broad natural granite ledges.

From Arcadia, head north on Route 102 into Coventry. The gently hilly terrain of western Rhode Island contains less active farmland than the Eastern Highlands of Connecticut just to the west, and the second-growth forests here are comparatively scrubby. The hard granite bedrock underlying most of this area and the sandy overlay of glacial deposits combine to produce a comparatively unfertile soil for farms and forests.

Throughout the state, Rhode Island's Division of Fish and Wildlife has established dozens of designated public fishing areas that provide access to stocked ponds and rivers. Many of these sites are in western towns, and several attract visitors who are not avid anglers. Along Route 14 in Coventry, near the Connecticut line, the **Carbuncle Pond Fishing Area❖** centers on a deep, clear pond reclaimed from intense human use not by conservationists, but by nature's engineers. Formerly, the southern end of the pond was a popular swimming beach, but several years ago beavers dammed the outlet stream, raising the pond water level and inundating the access road. Visitors can still walk to the broad sandy beach, however, which is usually deserted, even on a hot August day. To see the beaver's handiwork, continue south of the pond onto an old raised railroad bed. North of the bed is a marshy area blanketed with a spectacular bloom of white water lilies in summer. To the south is a small pond created by a large beaver dam at its southern end. The railroad bed is part of the state's **Trestle Trail❖,** which runs seven miles from the Connecticut line to

Although it looks uneasy, the snowshoe hare (above)—whose coat becomes white in winter—is too large to be prey for the 14-inch-tall barn owl (left), distinguished by its heart-shaped face.

Coventry Center. The 50-foot trestle that gives the trail its name affords a panoramic view of the Moosup River, a wide meandering trout stream with bordering marshes.

East off 102, Maple Valley Road leads to the **George B. Parker Woodland❖,** a fine example of historical archaeology that illustrates how the present "natural" landscape has been affected by past human activity and how that activity was shaped and influenced by the local environment. Trails pass a number of interpretative excavation sites, including two large circular mounds where charcoal was produced in the eighteenth and nineteenth centuries; a hundred mysterious beehive-shaped stone cairns, whose origin and purpose have not been explained; and the **Vaughan Farm Site,** an extremely well built and preserved farmhouse foundation with outbuildings. The archaeological sites are set in a hilly woodland that encompasses several long granite ledges, two house-sized glacial erratics with sculpted overhangs, and a boardwalk through a maple swamp. Along the rocky banks of Turkey Meadow Brook in late summer, the brilliant scarlet stalks of cardinal flowers appear among the ruins of a sawmill. Although seemingly healthy, the tall American chestnut saplings here are doomed by the same fungus that killed their magnificent ancestors earlier in this century. The disappearance of the native chestnuts has left a gaping hole in the Northeast woodlands. Before the blight they constituted 30 to 35 percent of the southern hardwood forest, producing wood valued for construction and furniture and an abundant nut crop that sustained turkeys, grouse, bears, and other wildlife. Today a few of their ancient hollow hulks can still be found here.

On Route 44 in Glocester, some ten miles to the northwest, is the **Bowdish Reservoir❖,** originally a small pond and sphagnum, or "quak-

241

ing," bog, a northern wetland uncommon in southern New England. When the bog was flooded to create the reservoir, large portions of the sphagnum mat broke off and became floating islands. The mats support carnivorous plants such as pitcher plants and sundews, whose bristly hairs and sticky stems trap small insects that they digest for nourishment in this highly acidic, nutrient-poor environment. Other more solid islands in the reservation contain stands of black spruce, another northern wetland species uncommon in Rhode Island, and spreading across their branches is the rare dwarf mistletoe, a small semiparasitic evergreen plant. Although Bowdish is adjacent to a busy highway, on an early fall morning its mist-laden, spruce-bordered waters resemble lakes far to the north. Adjacent to the reservoir, the 3,500-plus acres of the **George Washington Management Area❖** offer extensive hemlock stands, opportunities to view nesting wood ducks on Peck Pond, and hiking along the Walkabout Trail, an eight-mile system created by Australian sailors in 1965 while their ship was dry-docked at Newport.

Follow Route 44 east toward Providence; shortly before it intersects I-295, take Route 5 south, and then bear right onto Brown Avenue. On the left is **Snake Den State Park❖,** a largely undeveloped preserve named for the massive granite ledges just off the road, which may once have supported a rattlesnake population, although the reptiles' presence has never been proven. Farther along the road on the left is the entrance to eighteenth-century **Dame Farm,** a part of the state park leased to and still run by the Dame family. Here, on the outskirts of the Providence metropolitan area, a traditional agricultural landscape persists: hay meadows and cornfields, apple orchards, truck farms, and duck ponds. In one of the upper pastures, which no longer support cattle and have reverted to woodland, the blasted hulk of a 300-year-old oak that no doubt provided shade for the vanished cows slowly molders back into the earth.

BLOCK ISLAND

The Nature Conservancy calls Block Island one of the Last Great Places in the Western Hemisphere. Although the claim is arguable, Block Island is the most environmentally significant area in Rhode Island and one of the truly special places in southern New England. Its 11 square miles provide refuge for some 40 rare species in the state, including the federally endan-

RIGHT: *Named for one of the original Native American tribes of eastern Connecticut and western Rhode Island, Mohegan Bluffs features clay cliffs laid down millions of years ago during the age of dinosaurs.*

gered American burying beetle, a fascinating insect that buries the carcasses of small birds and mammals for a food supply. In addition, the island contains extensive stretches of morainal grasslands, a very uncommon habitat, and some of the best migratory birding sites in New England. Beyond these ecological credentials, it is simply one of the most beautiful islands anywhere, and thanks to the efforts of private agencies such as the Nature Conservancy, the Block Island Conservancy Association, and the Block Island Land Trust, more than 20 percent of its 6,400 acres have been preserved for posterity's enjoyment.

Although formed by the same broad glacial processes as Martha's Vineyard, Nantucket, and other offshore islands of southern New England, Block Island has a unique geologic history that is largely responsible for its distinctive character. Generally speaking, it is a glacial stepping-stone in the long Wisconsin moraine that stretches from the west along the southern coast of Long Island, dips beneath the ocean at Montauk, surfaces at Block Island, submerges again, and reappears at Martha's Vineyard. More specifically, Block Island is the product of two overlapping recessional moraines—one formed some 40,000 years ago, the other some 24,000 years ago—creating the southern and northern parts of the island respectively.

As the glacier retreated and sea level rose, the two halves of the island were separated; but erosion and the subsequent formation of barrier beaches have reconnected them with a double tombolo encircling Great Salt Pond. The island's glacial deposits are largely till that contains heavy clay, resulting in the dramatic cliff formations on its eastern and southern coasts and also in the hundreds of small "perched ponds," bodies of water with impermeable clay bottoms elevated above the general aquifer. Another outstanding feature of the island's topography is the nearly 400 miles of rock walls made from its abundant glacial erratics. According to local legend, during the seventeenth and eighteenth centuries slaves and indentured servants could earn their freedom by constructing a wall across the island—and a few actually succeeded. Compared to the mainland, Block Island supports few animal species: only two indigenous mammals, three amphibians, and five reptiles. On the other hand, its lack of mammalian predators and presence of unusual habitats give it an extraordinarily high percentage of rare animals and plants.

LEFT: *Flowering shadbushes glisten like white fountains above stands of feathery reeds at New Meadow Hill Swamp. Shadbush blossoms at about the time that its namesake fish begin their annual spring runs.*

LEFT: *The population of the double-crested cormorant has increased dramatically along the coast of southern New England. These highly adaptive birds are distinguished by their orange throat patches.*
RIGHT: *The shoreline below Mohegan Bluffs is a mixture of clay boulders and glacial till. Block Island is part of an archipelago of terminal moraines that trace the coastline from Long Island to Nantucket.*

Since the late-nineteenth century, Block Island has been an important summer resort and the site of some of New England's major boating regattas. Although there is enough open space to enjoy at all seasons, the optimum times to visit are probably mid-May, June, September, and October, when wildlife activity is at its height. Block Island can be reached by air or from one of four ferry terminals; the most convenient and only year-round ferry leaves from Point Judith. A one-hour voyage takes visitors past the low scarred, honeycombed hills of Clay Head to Old Harbor, the commercial and tourist center of the island, which shelters a fleet of old and often elegant seaside hotels.

Drive or better yet rent a bicycle and pedal north on Corn Neck Road. On the left by **Great Salt Pond** is the long flat hill of Indian Head Neck, the largest of several glacial drumlins in this area. Four miles north, past seaside farms and fields ablaze with wildflowers, the road ends at Settler's Rock, a monument to the arrival of the first European settlers in 1661. Into the distance stretches a wide curving neck of barrier beach and low dunes known as Sandy Point, which contains the **Block Island National Wildlife Refuge❖**. This postglacial point of land was formed by material eroded from the clay cliffs to the south and carried north by longshore currents. Thus, as its southern and eastern portions are whittled away at about three to six feet a year, the island is elongating northward, although not at the same rate.

The large brackish coastal pond to the left is Sachem Pond, an excel-

lent place to view cormorants, Canada geese, yellowlegs, and other waterfowl and shorebirds. A sandy road leads out to the imposing granite
structure of North Light, an 1867 lighthouse that has been converted into
a maritime museum open Memorial Day through Columbus Day. In June
the dunes are alive with a blaze of color and sound: the showy white and
magenta blossoms of beach roses, the diminutive yellow flowers of
poverty grass, and the raucous cries of the largest gull colony in Rhode Island—up to 2,000 pairs of herring and great black-backed gulls with their
fluffy speckled chicks.

Off Corn Neck Road a small dirt road marks the beginning of the **Clay
Head Trail❖,** a fascinating walk that winds for nearly two miles along 100-
foot cliffs. Clay Head is considered one of the best spots in New England to
observe the fall migration of birds. From late September through October,
large numbers of avian migrants converge on the mainland and head out
over the ocean or are blown out to sea by storms, making their first landfall
at Clay Head. Here visitors can see flocks of warblers, vireos, sparrows,
cedar waxwings, kinglets, geese, ducks, and solitary peregrine falcons.

Clay Head boasts superlative attractions at other seasons as well. A
large active colony of bank swallows nest in small burrows that they ex-
cavate in the clay cliffs just below the crest. Barn owls nest in the cliff as
well. The cliffs contain unusual geologic formations, conglomerates of
iron oxide formed by a leaching process known as water piping. The hol-

247

low rods and globular clumps thus produced superficially resemble geodes and sometimes contain loose pebbles and stones that rattle inside them. Along the bluffs are several of the island's small perched ponds, which occasionally erode out to the edge of the cliff and drain in a sudden, brief waterfall down to the beach. The 11 miles of largely unmarked trails west of the cliff path are accurately designated the Maze.

Return to Old Harbor and follow Spring Street south as it ascends to the highest part of the coast. On the right the road passes Southeast Lighthouse, a massive brick tower built in 1873 and once threatened by erosion. In 1994, in an incredible feat of engineering, the lighthouse was moved in one piece 245 feet back from the bluffs. Just west lies the entrance to **Mohegan Bluffs❖,** the most dramatic of Block Island's coastal cliffs. Here glacial clay is mixed with whiter lenses of Cretaceous clay, sediments formed 135 million years ago and pushed up by the ice mass. After the glacier retreated, a long sloping outwash plain stretched south; but erosion and a rise in sea level have caused these colorful clay layers to loom 150 feet above the beach in jagged and sculpted formations reminiscent of those formed by water in caves.

Continue west on the shore road until it turns north at Painted Rock, becoming Lakeside Drive. Half a mile farther on the left is marshy **Peckham Pond,** a breeding site of the American bittern, a large marsh bird with a long, pointed bill and richly streaked brown plumage whose characteristic *oonk-a-lunk* call has earned it the local name of "thunderpumper." Just north of this pond, the **Fresh Pond/Fresh Marsh Preserve❖** encompasses two of the island's largest and most scenic wetlands.

Follow the road north, past the Indian Cemetery on the right, for half a mile. On the left, opposite the airport runway, is an entrance to **The Greenway❖,** a network of foot trails through the island's interior linking more than 600 acres of conservation land. One path wanders through a drumlin field of kame hills and kettle holes reminiscent of an overgrown English garden and leads into the Enchanted Forest, a labyrinthine grove of planted Norway spruce and red pine partially blown down in 1991 by Hurricane Bob. The trail continues past an old windmill foundation and a nineteenth-century cemetery.

One Greenway trail runs south to **Rodman's Hollow❖** (south of

---

LEFT: *The slit pads and white blossoms of fragrant water lilies blanket the surface of Fresh Marsh. Most of Block Island's numerous small ponds are eutrophic—shallow, nutrient rich, and thickly vegetated.*

LEFT: *Extirpated from the East Coast by DDT poisoning in the 1960s, peregrine falcons have made a modest comeback. Swift and powerful flyers, peregrines tend to migrate along coastlines.* **RIGHT:** *Footprints mark the ubiquitous presence of humans at Sandy Point. Vastly increased use of the beach has made even once-innocent behavior, such as walking, a threat to the stability of this fragile dune ecosystem.*

Cooneymus Road), an exceptionally deep and long outwash valley created by the meltwaters of the retreating glacier 25,000 years ago. Unlike most other deep kettle holes and hollows on Block Island, Rodman's is dry because its floor is formed by porous sandy drift. Along its densely vegetated slopes visitors often glimpse the broad dark wings and characteristic white tail patch of the northern harrier (formerly called the marsh hawk) as it swoops and twists through the hollow hunting for rodents. A rare species in the state, the harrier nests only on Block Island.

At the western end of Cooneymus Road is the **Lewis-Dickens Farm Nature Preserve✥,** owned and managed by the Nature Conservancy and the Audubon Society of Rhode Island. Because of the property's sensitive nature, entrance is restricted to summer guided tours led by the Nature Conservancy. The tours are well worth the effort, however, for this preserve is one of the most unusual natural areas in the state.

The preserve's flora and fauna are a virtual who's who of the island's rare species. It is the premier habitat for the unique and globally endangered American burying beetle. Through the grass weave the tunnels of the Block Island meadow vole, considered a distinct subspecies of the common vole and one of the island's two indigenous mammals. These meadows provide habitat for such open-field nesters and hunters as the barn owl, upland sandpiper, grasshopper sparrow, and northern harrier—all threatened species—as well as several rare plants, such as the bushy rockrose, northern blazing star, and Maryland golden aster. Visually stunning, Lewis-Dickens encompasses some 200 acres of seaside farm fields crisscrossed with rock walls. A magnificent ocean of grass, showing complex patterns of sea light and wind movement, undulates down to the edge of high clay bluffs in a scene that resembles the downs of southern England.

FURTHER READING ABOUT SOUTHERN NEW ENGLAND

BELL, MICHAEL. *The Face of Connecticut: People, Geology, and the Land.* Hartford: Connecticut Geological and Natural History Survey, 1985. A beautifully illustrated and highly readable human and natural history of the landscape and geology of Connecticut.

BESTON, HENRY. *The Outermost House: A Year of Life on the Great Beach of Cape Cod.* New York: Henry Holt, 1992. A lyrical and profoundly meditative account of a year spent in a small beach cottage on the Atlantic beach of Cape Cod.

Connecticut Walk Book. Middletown: Connecticut Forest and Park Association, 1987. A complete guide, with fold-out maps, to Connecticut's famous Blue-Blazed Hiking Trail System.

CRONON, WILLIAM. *Changes in the Land: Indians, Colonists, and the Ecology of New England.* New York: Hill and Wang, 1983. A groundbreaking and illuminating chronicle of the impact of Native American and early European settlers on the New England landscape.

DWELLEY, MARILYN J. *Trees and Shrubs of New England.* Camden, ME: Down East Books, 1980. A comprehensive guide to the woody plants of New England, illustrated with fine color drawings.

FINCH, ROBERT. *Cape Cod.* Washington, D.C.: National Park Service, 1994. The official guidebook to the Cape Cod National Seashore, with illustrations, covering both its natural and cultural history.

GODIN, ALFRED J. *Wild Mammals of New England.* Baltimore: Johns Hopkins University Press, 1977. The definitive guide to the region's mammals, with range maps, drawings, and descriptions.

JORGENSEN, NEIL. *A Sierra Club Naturalist's Guide: Southern New England.* San Francisco: Sierra Club Books, 1978. An indispensable field guide and history of the region's major forest types and the animal and plant communities that inhabit them. Excellent color plates and maps.

LAUBACH, RENE. *A Guide to Natural Places in the Berkshire Hills.* Stockbridge, MA: Berkshire House, 1992. A site-oriented guide to Massachusetts's rugged Berkshire County, containing a wealth of information on the natural history of the area.

PATTON, PETER C., AND JAMES M. KENT. *A Moveable Shore: The Fate of the Connecticut Coast.* Durham: Duke University Press, 1992. A profusely illustrated general user's guide to Connecticut's 254 miles of shoreline, including discussions of the climatic and geological forces that have shaped it and suggested field trips.

RAYMO, CHET, AND MAUREEN E. RAYMO. *Written in Stone: A Geological History of the Northeastern United States.* Old Saybrook, CT: Globe Pequot Press, 1989. An updated, comprehensive, and concise account of more than four billion years of geological history in this region.

STERLING, DOROTHY. *The Outer Lands: A Natural History Guide to Cape Cod, Martha's Vineyard, Nantucket, Block Island, and Long Island.* New York: Norton, 1978. An informative account of the glacial formations and major ecosystems of Cape Cod and the Islands, with beautiful illustrations by Winifred Lubbell.

STILGOE, JOHN R. *Alongshore.* New Haven: Yale University Press, 1994. Using the South Shore of Massachusetts as an example, this fascinating socio-environmental history explores our constantly changing relationship to the shoreline.

THOREAU, HENRY DAVID. *Walden; or, Life in the Woods.* Boston: Ticknor and Fields, 1854. Reprinted 1971, Princeton University Press. The world-famous chronicle of Thoreau's experiment in independent living also contains evocative descriptions of Concord's ponds, woods, fields, and wildlife.

WEBER, KEN. *Canoeing Massachusetts, Rhode Island, and Connecticut.* Woodstock, VT: Backcountry Publications, 1988. A practical guide to 25 canoeing trips in Southern New England. With detailed maps and information.

ABOVE: *About 1890 an unknown amateur photographer immortalized this pair of intrepid Berkshire bicyclists traveling the road to Willilamstown.*

253

GLOSSARY

archipelago group of neighboring islands in any large body of water

barrier island narrow island of sediment—sand, silt, and gravel—that protects the coast from direct battering by storm waves and wind

bog wetland, formed in glacial kettle holes, common to cool climates of North America, Europe, and Asia; its acidic nature produces large quantities of peat moss

boreal relating to the northern biotic area characterized especially by dominance of coniferous trees

cirque large, bowl-shaped depression in a mountain, hollowed out by glacial movement

crust rocky outermost layer of the earth that includes the continents and the ocean basins

dike vertical sheet of rock formed when molten rock cools on its way to the earth's surface and is exposed when surrounding rock erodes

drumlin hill of glacial debris smoothed by overriding ice into the shape of an overturned spoon

escarpment cliff or steep rock face, formed by faulting or fracturing of the earth's crust, that separates two comparatively level land surfaces

esker long, winding rise of gravel and sand that marks the trail where a stream once flowed beneath a glacier

estuary region of interaction between ocean water and the end of a river, where tidal action and river flow mix fresh and salt water

fjord narrow inlet of the sea between cliffs or steep slopes

glacial erratic rock or boulder transported by a glacier

glacial till unsorted rock debris, usually of a wide range of sizes, deposited directly from the ice without reworking by streams

igneous referring to rock formed by cooled and hardened lava or magma

kettle hole glacial depression that, when fed by groundwater and precipitation, often evolves into a bog or pond

magma molten rock material within the earth that becomes igneous rock when it cools

massif zone of the earth's crust raised or depressed by plate movement and bounded by faults

metamorphic referring to a rock that has been changed into its present state after being subjected to heat, pressure, or chemical change

midden refuse heap; prehistoric middens are often studied by archaeologists to learn about the culture that left the refuse

monadnock height of land containing more erosion-resistant rock than the surrounding area

oxbow lake that forms where a meandering river overflows and creates a crescent-shaped body of water; called an oxbow because its curved shape looks like the U-shaped harness frame that fits around an ox's neck

plates thick slabs of rock that make up the earth's outer shell, including the ocean floor and the continental land masses; movement and interaction of the plates is known as plate tectonics

rift valley narrow valley with steep sides and flat floor that forms where the earth's crust is spreading or splitting apart; movement is caused by the action of plate tectonics

scarp line of steep cliffs formed by erosion

schist metamorphic rock with a layered appearance; composed of often flaky parallel layers of minerals

sedimentary rocks formed from deposits of small eroded debris such as gravel, sand, mud, silt, or peat

slough swampy, backwater area; inlet on a river; or creek in a marsh or tidal flat

sphagnum moss that grows in wet, acidic areas; decomposes and compacts to form peat

talus accumulated rock debris at the base of a cliff

tectonic referring to the deformation of the earth's crust, the forces involved, and the resulting formations

terminal moraine final deposit of rock and debris that has formed at a glacier's farthest leading edge and is left behind as the glacier retreats

tombolo sandbar connecting an island to the mainland or to another island

ABOVE: *Day-trippers on Martha's Vineyard board a paddlewheeler at Oak Bluffs for a bracing excursion to Gay Head or Nantucket about 1900.*

LAND MANAGEMENT RESOURCES

The following public and private organizations are among the important administrators of the preserved and protected areas described in this volume. Brief explanations of the various legal and legislative designations of these areas follow.

MANAGING ORGANIZATIONS

Connecticut State Parks Division

Manages 91 state parks, including shoreline and undeveloped natural areas and 104 boat launchs. Part of the Department of Environmental Protection.

Connecticut Wildlife Division

Conserves state wildlife and fisheries. Administers approximately 100 wildlife management areas and regulates hunting and fishing licenses. Part of the Department of Environmental Protection.

Massachusetts Division of Fisheries and Wildlife

Manages 109,000 acres in 87 wildlife management areas; regulates hunting and fishing licenses. Part of the Executive Office of Environmental Affairs.

Massachusetts Division of Forests and Parks

Manages 125 state parks and forests, 6 state beaches, and some 125 smaller wilderness areas. Part of the Executive Office of Environmental Affairs.

National Audubon Society (NAS) Private Organization

International nonprofit conservation, lobbying, and educational organization. Owns a private network of wildlife sanctuaries. Strives to protect natural ecosystems through grassroots organization and education.

National Oceanic and Atmospheric Administration (NOAA)
Department of Commerce

Federal program that oversees U.S. Ocean Service, U.S. Weather Service, marine fisheries, satellite service, and atmospheric research programs.

National Park Service (NPS) Department of the Interior

Regulates the use of national parks, monuments and preserves. Resources are managed to protect landscape, natural and historic artifacts, and wildlife. Administers historic and national landmarks, national seashores, wild and scenic rivers, and the national trail system.

The Nature Conservancy (TNC) Private organization

International nonprofit organization that owns the largest private system of nature sanctuaries in the world, some 1,300 preserves. Aims to preserve significant and diverse plants, animals, and natural communities.

Rhode Island Division of Fish and Wildlife

Manages 46,000 acres in 17 wildlife management areas. Regulates hunting and fishing licenses. Part of the Department of Environmental Management.

Rhode Island Division of Parks and Recreation

Manages five state parks and all state beach areas for public access and recreation. Part of the Department of Environmental Management.

The Trustees of Reservations

Private nonprofit land trust organization in Massachusetts that preserves natural and historic lands for public enjoyment and recreation throughout the state. Administers 76 reservations and 12 historic houses.

U.S. Fish and Wildlife Service (USFWS) Department of the Interior
Principal federal agency responsible for conserving, protecting, and enhancing the country's fish and wildlife and their habitats. Manages national wildlife refuges, fish hatcheries, and programs for migratory birds and endangered and threatened species.

LAND DESIGNATIONS

Conservation Area
Area set aside to protect specific environments. May be used for recreation, research, or other specific purposes. Managed by individual states.

National Heritage Corridor
Congressionally designated area where natural, cultural, historic, and recreational resources combine to form a cohesive landscape representing a certain aspect of the national experience. Managed by the NPS.

National Marine Sanctuary
Coastal waters protected for their natural, cultural, or historic resources. Restricted fishing, boating, and diving allowed. Managed by the NOAA.

National Seashore
Area of pristine undeveloped seashore designated to protect its natural value and provide public recreation. Camping and ORVs allowed with restrictions. Managed by the NPS.

National Wildlife Refuge
Public lands set aside for wild animals; protects migratory waterfowl, endangered and threatened species, and native plants. Managed by the USFWS.

Recreation Area
Natural area for recreation; hunting, fishing, camping, powerboats, dirt and mountain bikes, and ORVs allowed with restrictions. Managed by the NPS.

Research Reserve
Area of unique natural features and/or rare and endangered plants and animals; protected for conservation and, in some areas, for day-use recreation. Managed by individual states.

State Forest
Large acreage managed for the use of forests, watersheds, wildlife, and recreation. Managed by individual state forestry divisions.

Wilderness Area
Area with particular ecological, geological, or scientific, scenic, or historical value that has been set aside in its natural condition as wild land. Limited recreational use is permitted. Managed by individual states.

Wildlife Management Area
Natural area owned, protected, and maintained for recreation; hunting, fishing, trapping, and cross-country skiing permitted. Managed by individual states.

NATURE TRAVEL

The following is a selection of national and local organizations that sponsor nature-related travel activities or can provide specialized regional travel information.

NATIONAL

National Audubon Society
700 Broadway
New York, NY 10003
(212) 979-3000
Offers a wide range of ecological field studies, tours, and cruises throughout the United States

National Wildlife Federation
1400 16th St. NW
Washington D.C. 20036
(703) 790-4363
Offers training in environmental education for all ages, wildlife camp and teen adventures, conservation summits involving nature walks, field trips, and classes

The Nature Conservancy
1815 North Lynn Street
Arlington, VA 22209
(703) 841-5300
Offers a variety of excursions based out of regional and state offices. May include hiking, backpacking, canoeing, horseback riding. Contact above number to locate state offices

Sierra Club Outings
730 Polk Street
San Francisco, CA 94109
(415) 923-5630
Offers tours of different lengths for all ages throughout the United States. Outings may include backpacking, hiking, biking, skiing, and water excursions

Smithsonian Study Tours and Seminars
1100 Jefferson Dr. SW
MRC 702
Washington, D.C. 20560
(202) 357-4700
Offers extended tours, cruises, research expeditions, and seminars throughout the United States

REGIONAL

Appalachian Mountain Club
5 Joy Street, Boston, MA 02108
(617) 523-0636
Organizes hikes, backpacking trips, and nature travel workshops throughout the Northeast. Publishes hiking guides to the trails of Connecticut and Massachusetts

Audubon Society of Rhode Island
12 Sanderson Rd.
Smithfield, RI 02917
(401) 949-5454
Nonprofit organization leads nature walks and hikes through its refuges and other natural areas throughout southern New England, including Block Island, Connecticut's lakes, and the birding regions of Massachusetts

Connecticut Department of Economic Development
Tourism Division
865 Brook St., Rocky Hill, CT 06067
(800) CT BOUND (282-6863) for vacation guide and accommodations
(860) 258-4355
Provides travel guides, answers specific questions on sites and travel, and furnishes site phone numbers

Massachusetts Office of Travel and Tourism
100 Cambridge St., 13th Fl.
Boston, MA 02202
(800) 447-MASS (6277) for travel guides
(800) 227-MASS (6277) fall foliage hotline and seasonal events calendar
Call for vacation planning guides and specific travel and recreation queries

Rhode Island Division of Tourism
7 Jackson Walkway
Providence, RI 02903
(800) 556-2484
Vacation guides available. Answers specific travel and recreation questions

How to Use This Site Guide

The following site information guide will assist you in planning your tour of the natural areas of Massachusetts, Connecticut, and Rhode Island. Sites set in boldface and followed by the symbol ❖ in the text are here organized alphabetically by state. Each entry is followed by the mailing address (sometimes different from the street address) and phone number of the immediate managing office, plus brief notes and a list of facilities and activities available. (A key appears on each page.)

Information on hours of operation, seasonal closings, and fees is often not listed, as these vary from season to season and year to year. Please bear in mind that responsibility for the management of some sites may change. Call well in advance to obtain maps, brochures, and pertinent, up-to-date information that will help you plan your adventures in Southern New England.

Each site entry in the guide includes the address and phone number of its immediate managing agency. Many of these sites are under the stewardship of a forest or park ranger or supervised from a small nearby office. Hence, in many cases, those sites will be difficult to contact directly, and it is preferable to call the managing agency.

The following umbrella organizations can provide general information for individual natural sites, as well as the area as a whole:

CONNECTICUT

Connecticut State Parks Division
79 Elm St.
Hartford, CT 06106
(860) 424-3200

Connecticut Wildlife Division
79 Elm St.
Hartford, CT 06106
(203) 424-3011

National Audubon Society
613 Riversville Rd.
Greenwich, CT 06831
(203) 869-5272

The Nature Conservancy
55 High St.
Middletown, CT 06457
(860) 344-0716

MASSACHUSETTS

Massachusetts Audubon Society
208 South Great Rd.
Lincoln, MA 01773
(617) 259-9500

Massachusetts Division of Forests and Parks
100 Cambridge St., 19th Fl.
Boston, MA 02202
(617) 727-3180

National Park Service
North Atlantic Office
15 State Street
Boston, MA 02109
(617) 223-5001

Trustees of Reservations
572 Essex St.
Beverly, MA 01915
(508) 921-1944

RHODE ISLAND

Audubon Society of Rhode Island
12 Sanderson Rd.
Smithfield, RI 02917
(401) 949-5454

The Nature Conservancy
45 S. Angell St.
Smithfield, RI 02906
(401) 331-7100

Rhode Island Division of Fish and Wildlife
4808 Tower Hill Rd.
Wakefield, RI 02879
(401) 789-3094

Rhode Island Div. of Parks and Recreation
2321 Hartford Ave.
Johnston, RI 02919
(401) 277-2632

259

CONNECTICUT

APPALACHIAN TRAIL CORRIDOR
Appalachian Trail Conference
PO Box 807, Harpers Ferry, WV 25425
(304) 535-6331 **BW, H, MT, RC**

AUDUBON CENTER IN GREENWICH
National Audubon Society
613 Riversville Rd.
Greenwich, CT 06831
(203) 869-5272 **BW, GS, H, I, MT, T, TG**

AUDUBON FAIRCHILD GARDEN
National Audubon Society
613 Riversville Rd.
Greenwich, CT 06831
(203) 869-5272 **BW, H, MT, T**

BARN ISLAND WILDLIFE MANAGEMENT AREA
Connecticut Wildlife Div.
79 Elm St., Hartford, CT 06106
(860) 424-3011 **BT, BW, F, H, MB, T**

BEAR MOUNTAIN
Connecticut State Parks Div.
79 Elm St., Hartford, CT 06106-5127
(860) 424-3200 **BW, H, MT**

BLUFF HEAD
South Central Regional
Water Authority
90 Sargent Dr.
New Haven, CT 06511
(203) 624-6671
Very limited parking; recreation permit
required (fee) **BW, H, MT**

BLUFF POINT STATE PARK
Connecticut State Parks Div.
79 Elm St., Hartford, CT 06106-5127
(860) 445-1729; (860) 424-3200
Must walk or bike to headlands (beach
area) **BT, BW, F, H**

BOSTON HOLLOW
Yale School of Forestry
and Environmental Studies
c/o School Forests
360 Prospect St., New Haven, CT 06511
(203) 432-5100
Includes blue-blazed Nipmuck Trail; road
often impassable in winter and spring
BW, H

BULL'S BRIDGE RECREATION AREA
Connecticut Light and Power
41 Park Lane Rd.
New Milford, CT 06776
(860) 354-8840
Canoeing above the dam and below the
power plant **BW, C, H**

CAMPBELL FALLS STATE PARK
Connecticut State Parks Div.
79 Elm St.
Hartford, CT 06106-5127
(860) 482-1817; (860) 424-3200 **BW, F, H**

CATHEDRAL PINES
The Nature Conservancy
55 High St.
Middletown, CT 06457
(860) 344-0716 **H**

CHAPMAN POND
The Nature Conservancy
55 High St.
Middletown, CT 06457
(860) 344-0716 **CK**

CONNECTICUT COLLEGE ARBORETUM
PO Box 5201
New London, CT 06320
(860) 439-5020 **BW**

DEVIL'S DEN PRESERVE
The Nature Conservancy
PO Box 1162, Weston, CT 06883
(203) 226-4991
Call in advance for tour information
BW, H, I, MT, TG, XC

DEVIL'S HOPYARD STATE PARK
Connecticut State Parks Div.
79 Elm St.
Hartford, CT 06106-5127
(860) 345-8521; (860) 424-3200
Pit toilets **BW, C, F, H, MT, PA, T**

DINOSAUR STATE PARK
Connecticut State Parks Div.
79 Elm St., Hartford, CT 06106-5127
(860) 529-8423 (machine information)
(860) 529-5816 (office)
BW, GS, H, MT, PA, RA, T, TG

GIFFORD PINCHOT SYCAMORE PARK
Simsbury Parks and Recreation Dept.
PO Box 495, Simsbury, CT 06070
(860) 658-3255 **PA**

BT Bike Trails
BW Bird-watching
C Camping
CK Canoeing, Kayaking
DS Downhill Skiing
F Fishing
GS Gift Shop
H Hiking
HR Horseback Riding
I Information Center

GILLETTE CASTLE STATE PARK
Connecticut State Parks Div.
79 Elm St.
Hartford, CT 06106-5127
(860) 526-2336; (860) 424-3200
  Castle open Memorial Day weekend
  through Columbus Day and weekends
  from Columbus Day to mid-December
                    H, MT, PA, T, TG

GREAT ISLAND MARSH PRESERVE
The Nature Conservancy
55 High St.
Middletown, CT 06457
(860) 344-0716   **BW, CK**

HAMMONASSET BEACH STATE PARK
Connecticut State Parks Div.
79 Elm St.
Hartford, CT 06106-5127
(203) 245-2785; (860) 424-3200
  Includes a nature center
              BT, BW, C, F, PA, RA, S, T

HOUSATONIC MEADOWS STATE PARK
Connecticut State Parks Div.
79 Elm St.
Hartford, CT 06106-5127
(860) 927-3238; (860) 424-3200
  Fly-fishing only
            BW, C, CK, F, H, MT, PA, T

HUBBARD PARK
Meriden Dept. of Parks and Recreation
460 Liberty St.
Meriden, CT 06450
(203) 630-4259
  Includes East Peak/West Peak and
  Castle Craig Tower; road to tower open
  April through October 10 AM to 5 PM;
  swimming for ages under 15 only
            BW, F, H, MB, MT, PA, S

HURD STATE PARK
Connecticut State Parks Div.
79 Elm St.
Hartford, CT 06106-5127
(860) 526-2336; (860) 424-3200
  Pit toilets
                  BW, F, H, MT, PA, T

KENT FALLS STATE PARK
Connecticut State Parks Div.
79 Elm St., Hartford, CT 06106-5127
(860) 927-3238; (860) 424-3200
                        F, H, PA, T

MASHAMOQUET BROOK STATE PARK
Connecticut State Parks Div.
79 Elm St.
Hartford, CT 06106-5127
(860) 928-6121; (860) 424-3200
                BW, C, F, H, MT, PA, S, T

McCLEAN GAME REFUGE
75 Great Pond Rd.
Simsbury, CT 06070
(860) 653-7869
  Outhouses   **BW, H, MT, XC**

MILFORD POINT
Connecticut Audubon Coastal Center
1 Milford Point Road
Milford, CT 06460
(203) 878-7440
  Includes Smith-Hubbell Wildlife
  Sanctuary and Charles E. Wheeler
  Wildlife Refuge (a state property)
                    BW, I, RA, T, TG

MOHAWK MOUNTAIN STATE PARK AND STATE FOREST
Connecticut State Parks Div.
79 Elm St., Hartford, CT 06106-5127
(860) 927-3238; (860) 424-3200
                  BW, DS, F, H, MB, MT

MOUNT HIGBY
The Nature Conservancy
55 High St.
Middletown, CT 06457
(860) 344-0716   **H**

NATCHAUG STATE FOREST
Connecticut State Parks Div., 79 Elm St.
Hartford, CT 06106-5127
(860) 928-6121; (860) 424-3200
  Pit toilets
                  F, H, HR, MT, PA, T, XC

NORTHWEST PARK
Town of Windsor
145 Lang Rd., Windsor, CT 06095
(860) 285-1886
  Includes Luddy/Taylor Connecticut
  Valley Tobacco Museum
            BW, GS, H, I, MT, PA, RA, T, XC

NORWALK ISLANDS
U.S. Fish and Wildlife Service
PO Box 1030, Westbrook, CT 06498
(860) 399-2513
  Acccess only to portions of islands, call
  office   **BW, CK, H**

L	Lodging	**PA**	Picnic Areas	**RC** Rock Climbing	**TG** Tours, Guides
MB	Mountain Biking	**RA**	Ranger-led Activities	**S** Swimming	**XC** Cross-country Skiing
MT	Marked Trails			**T** Toilets	

PACHAUG STATE FOREST
Connecticut State Parks Div., 79 Elm St.
Hartford, CT 06106-5127
(860) 376-4075; (860) 424-3200
Pit toilets **C, F, H, MT, PA, S, T**

ROBBINS SWAMP WILDLIFE MANAGEMENT AREA
Connecticut Wildlife Div.
79 Elm St., 6th Fl.
Hartford, CT 06106
(860) 424-3942
Day use only; area prone to flooding;
parking lot on Rte. 126
BW, CK, F, H, MB, XC

ROCK SPRING WILDLIFE REFUGE
The Nature Conservancy
55 High St., Middletown, CT 06457
(860) 344-0716 **H**

ROCKY NECK STATE PARK
Connecticut State Parks Div.
79 Elm St., Hartford, CT 06106-5127
(860) 739-5471; (860) 424-3200
Includes a nature center
BW, C, F, H, MT, PA, RA, S, T

SAUGATUCK RESERVOIR
Bridgeport Hydraulic Co.
714 Black Rock Rd.
Easton, CT 06612-1146
(203) 336-7788
Fishing permit (fee) required from BHC
as well as state permit; hiking permit
(free) also required **F, H, MT, T, XC**

SELDEN NECK STATE PARK
Connecticut State Parks Div.
79 Elm St., Hartford, CT 06106-5127
(860) 526-2336; (860) 424-3200
Access by boat only; advance reservations required for camping **BW, C, F**

SHARON AUDUBON CENTER
National Audubon Society
325 Cornwall Bridge Rd.
Sharon, CT 06069
(860) 364-0520 **BW, GS, H, I, MT,
RA, T, TG, XC**

SLEEPING GIANT STATE PARK
Connecticut State Parks Div., 79 Elm St.
Hartford, CT 06106-5127
(203) 789-7498; (860) 424-3200
BW, F, H, MT, PA, T

STEWART B. McKINNEY NATIONAL WILDLIFE REFUGE
U.S. Fish and Wildlife Service
PO Box 1030
Westbrook, CT 06498
(860) 399-2513 **BW, H, MT, XC**

TALCOTT MOUNTAIN STATE PARK
Connecticut State Parks Div.
79 Elm St.
Hartford, CT 06106-5127
(860) 424-3200
Walk in only (1.5 miles); tower open
Thurs.–Sun. from mid-April–August and
daily September–October
H, MT, PA, T

TRAIL WOOD
The Edwin Way Teale Memorial Sanctuary
Connecticut Audubon Society
118 Oak St.
Hartford, CT 06106
(860) 455-0759 **BW, I, MT**

TURTLE CREEK PRESERVE
The Nature Conservancy
55 High St.
Middletown, CT 06457
(860) 344-0716 **H**

WADSWORTH FALLS STATE PARK
Connecticut State Parks Div.
79 Elm St.
Hartford, CT 06106-5127
(860) 663-2030; (860) 424-3200
BW, F, H, MT, PA, S, T

WESTWOODS
Guilford Land Trust
Guilford Town Hall, Park St.
Guilford, CT 06437
(203) 453-8001
Maps available
BT, BW, H, HR, MB, MT, XC

WEST ROCK RIDGE STATE PARK
Connecticut State Parks Div.
79 Elm St.
Hartford, CT 06106-5127
(203) 789-7498; (860) 424-3200 **BW, H**

WHITE MEMORIAL FOUNDATION
PO Box 368
Litchfield, CT 06759
(860) 567-0857
**BT, BW, C, CK, F, GS, H,
HR, I, MT, PA, T, TG, XC**

BT	Bike Trails	**CK**	Canoeing, Kayaking	**F**	Fishing
BW	Bird-watching			**GS**	Gift Shop
C	Camping	**DS**	Downhill Skiing	**H**	Hiking

HR Horseback Riding
I Information Center

WINDSOR LOCKS
Connecticut Tourism Div.
865 Brook St., Rocky Hill, CT 06067-4355
(860) 258-4355

BT, BW, F, H, MB

YALE-MYERS FOREST
Yale School of Forestry
and Environmental Studies
c/o School Forests
360 Prospect St., New Haven, CT 06511
(203) 432-5100

BW, CK, F, H, HR, MB, MT, XC

MASSACHUSETTS

ALBERT F. NORRIS RESERVATION
The Trustees of Reservations, 572 Essex St.
Beverly, MA 01915
(617) 821-2977   BW, CK, F, H, PA

ASHBURNHAM STATE FOREST
Massachusetts Div. of Forests and Parks
86 Winchendon Rd.
Baldwinville, MA 01436
(508) 939-8962   BW, H, HR, MB, XC

ATLANTIC WHITE CEDAR SWAMP
Cape Cod National Seashore
PO Box 250, South Wellfleet, MA 02663
(508) 349-3785   BW, H, MT, RA

BARTHOLOMEW'S COBBLE
The Trustees of Reservations
PO Box 792, Stockbridge, MA 01262
(413) 229-8600
  Noted for hawk migrations in the fall

BW, CK, H, I, MT, RA, T, TG, XC

**BARTON COVE NATURE
AND CAMPING AREA**
Northeast Utilities/Northfield Mountain
99 Millers Falls Rd.
Northfield, MA 01360
(413) 863-9300, seasonal
(800) 859-2960, (Northfield Mt. Visitor
Center, Nature trail)

BW, C, CK, F, GS, H, PA, T

BASH BISH FALLS STATE PARK
Massachusetts Div. of Forests and Parks
East St., Mt. Washington, MA 01258
(413) 528-0330
  Day use only   BW, F, H, MT, T

BEARTOWN STATE FOREST
PO Box 97
Monterey, MA 01245
(413) 528-0904
  Parking fee   BT, BW, C, DS, F, H, HR, I, MB, MT, PA, S, T, XC

BELLE ISLE MARSH RESERVATION
Metropolitan District Commission
c/o Reservations
20 Somerset St.
Boston, MA 02108
(617) 727-5250
  Day use only; keep pets on leashes

BT, BW, CK, F, MT, PA, RA, TG

BLACK POND RESERVATION
The Nature Conservancy
79 Milk St., Suite 300
Boston, MA 02109
(617) 423-2545   BW, H, MT

**BLACKSTONE GORGE
STATE PARK**
Massachusetts Div. of Forests and Parks
c/o Blackstone State Forest
Hartford Ave., Northbridge, MA 01534
(508) 278-6486

BT, BW, F, H, MT, PA, RA, TG

**BLACKSTONE RIVER AND CANAL
HERITAGE STATE PARK**
Massachusetts Div. of Forests and Parks
366 E. Hartford Ave.
Uxbridge, MA 01569
(508) 278-6486
  Includes River Bend Farm Visitor Center

BW, CK, H, I, MB, PA, RA, T, TG, XC

**BLACKSTONE RIVER VALLEY NATIONAL
HERITAGE CORRIDOR**
National Park Service
1 Depot Square
Woonsocket, RI 02895
(401) 762-0440

BT, BW, C, CK, F, H, HR, I, L, MT, PA, RA, RC, S, T, TG, XC

BLUE HILLS RESERVATION
Metropolitan District Commission
Hillside St.
Milton, MA 02186
(617) 698-1802

BT, BW, CK, DS, F, H, HR, MB, MT, PA, RA, RC, S, T, TG, XC

L	Lodging	**PA** Picnic Areas	**RC** Rock Climbing	**TG** Tours, Guides
MB	Mountain Biking	**RA** Ranger-led Activities	**S** Swimming	**XC** Cross-country Skiing
MT	Marked Trails		**T** Toilets	

BOSTON HARBOR ISLANDS STATE PARK
Massachusetts Div. of Forests and Parks
349 Lincoln St., Bldg. #45
Hingham, MA 02043
(617) 740-1605
Includes Webb Memorial State Park (day use); primitive camping, permits required; no camping on Gallops; large group picnics by permit only
**BW, C, CK, F, GS, H, I,
MT, PA, RA, S, T, TG**

BOXFORD STATE FOREST
Massachusetts Div. of Forests and Parks
PO Box 829
Carlisle, MA 01741
(508) 369-3350; (508) 686-3391
BW, H, MB

BROADMOOR WILDLIFE SANCTUARY
Massachusetts Audubon Society
280 Eliot St.
South Natick, MA 01760-5513
(508) 655-2296; (617) 235-3929
Closed Mondays **BW, H, I, MT, T**

CANOE MEADOWS WILDLIFE SANCTUARY
Massachusetts Audubon Society
472 West Mountain Rd.
Lenox, MA 01240
(413) 637-0320 **BW, H, MT, RA, XC**

CAPE COD NATIONAL SEASHORE
National Park Service
PO Box 250, Marconi Station
South Wellfleet, MA 02663
(508) 349-3785
BT, BW, CK, F, H, I, MT, PA, RA, S, T

CAPE POGE WILDLIFE REFUGE
The Trustees of Reservations
572 Essex St.
Beverly, MA 01915-1530
(508) 627-7689; (508) 627-3599 (seasonal)
**BW, CK, F, H, HR,
MT, PA, RA, S, T, TG**

CHARLES W. WARD RESERVATION
The Trustees of Reservations
PO Box 563, Ipswich, MA 01935
(508) 356-4351 **BW, H, MT, XC**

CHESTERFIELD GORGE RESERVATION
The Trustees of Reservations
PO Box 792, Stockbridge, MA 01262
(413) 298-3239 **BW, F, H, PA, T**

COLD RIVER OLD GROWTH FOREST
c/o Savoy Mountain State Forest
260 Central Shaft Rd., Florida, MA 01247
(413) 663-8469
**BT, BW, C, CK, F, H, HR, I,
MB, MT, PA, RA, S, T, XC**

**CORNELIUS AND MINÉ S. CRANE
WILDLIFE REFUGE**
The Trustees of Reservations
PO Box 563, Ipswich, MA 01935
(508) 356-4351 **BW, F, I, T**

**COSKATA-COATUE, GREAT POINT
WILDLIFE REFUGE SYSTEM**
The Trustees of Reservations
PO Box 172
Nantucket, MA 02554
(508) 228-0006 **BW, F, H, MT, S, T, TG**

CUTTYHUNK ISLAND
Town of Gosnold
Cuttyhunk, MA 02713
(508) 990-7408 **BW**

DANIEL WEBSTER WILDLIFE SANCTUARY
Massachusetts Audubon Society
2000 Main St.
Marshfield, MA 02050
(617) 837-9400 **BW, I, MT, TG**

DEMAREST LLOYD STATE PARK
Massachusetts Div. of Forests and Parks
c/o Horseneck Beach State Reservation
PO Box 328, Westport Point, MA 02791
(508) 636-8816
Day use only **BW, F, H, PA, S, T**

DINOSAUR FOOTPRINTS RESERVATION
The Trustees of Reservations
PO Box 792, Stockbridge, MA 01262
(413) 298-3259 **BW, MT**

DOANE'S FALLS RESERVATION
The Trustees of Reservations
325 Lindell Ave., Leominster, MA 01453
(508) 840-4446; (508) 921-1944
BW, F, H, MT, S, XC

DUXBURY BEACH
Duxbury Beach Reservation, Inc.
PO Box 2593, Duxbury, MA 02331
(617) 934-2866
4WD allowed with permit; public parking at west end, east for residents only
BW, F, S

BT Bike Trails	**CK** Canoeing, Kayaking	**F** Fishing	**HR** Horseback Riding
BW Bird-watching	**DS** Downhill Skiing	**GS** Gift Shop	**I** Information Center
C Camping		**H** Hiking	

EEL POINT
Nantucket Conservation Foundation
PO Box 13
Nantucket, MA 02554
(508) 228-2884
Unguarded swimming   **BW, F, S**

ELLISVILLE STATE PARK
Massachusetts Div. of Forests and Parks
PO Box 66
South Carver, MA 02366
(508) 866-2580
Day use only   **BW, H**

EUGENE D. MORAN WILDLIFE MANAGEMENT AREA
Massachusetts Div. of
Fisheries and Wildlife
400 Hubbard Ave.
Pittsfield, MA 01201
(413) 447-9789
No motorized vehicles; no fires
BW, H, HR

FELIX NECK WILDLIFE SANCTUARY
Massachusetts Audubon Society
PO Box 494
Vineyard Haven, MA 02568
(508) 627-4850   **BW, GS, H, I, MT, RA, T, TG**

FLINT'S POND
Lincoln Conservation Commission
PO Box 6353
Lincoln, MA 01773
(617) 259-8850   **BW, H, MT, XC**

FORT HILL AREA
National Park Service
PO Box 250
South Wellfleet, MA 02663
(508) 349-3785   **BW, H, MT, RA**

FRENCH KING GORGE
Massachusetts Div. of Forests and Parks
136 Damon Rd.
Northhampton, MA 01060
(413) 586-8706   **BW, CK, F**

GAY HEAD CLAY CLIFFS
Martha's Vineyard Land Bank Commission
PO Box 2057
Edgartown, MA 02539
(508) 627-7141
Day use only; summer parking fee; no
climbing on cliffs; no collecting or use
of clay   **BW, F, H, S, T**

GLENDALE FALLS RESERVATION
The Trustees of Reservations
PO Box 792
Stockbridge, MA 01262
(413) 298-3239   **BW, H, PA**

GREAT BLUE HILL
Metropolitan District Commission
Hillside, MA 02186
(617) 698-1802   **BT, BW, DS, GS, H, HR, I, MB, MT, PA, RA, T, TG, XC**

GREAT MEADOWS NATIONAL WILDLIFE REFUGE
U.S. Fish and Wildlife Service
Weir Hill Rd.
Sudbury, MA 01776
(508) 443-4661
Canoeing and fishing in rivers only, not
ponds or bays; ranger-led activities on
weekends in May and October
BW, CK, F, GS, H, I, MT, RA, XC

HALIBUT POINT RESERVATION
The Trustees of Reservations
PO Box 563, Ipswich, MA 01935
(508) 356-4351   **BW, F, H, T**

HALIBUT POINT STATE PARK
Massachusetts Div. of Forests and Parks
PO Box 829, Carlisle, MA 01741
(508) 546-2297; (508) 369-3350
Day use only; pets on leashes
BW, F, H, MT, T

HARVARD FOREST
Harvard University
PO Box 68, Petersham, MA 01366-0068
(508) 724-3302
Includes Fisher Museum of Forestry
BW, GS, H, I, MB, MT, T, XC

HARWICH CONSERVATION LANDS
Harwich Conservation Commission
732 Main St., Harwich, MA 02645
(508) 430-7506
BW, CK, H

HEMLOCK GORGE RESERVATION
Metropolitan District Commission
695 Hillside St.
Milton, MA 02186
(617) 698-1802
Day use only; canoeing upriver from
here; occasional ranger-led hikes
BW, CK, F, H, RA

L	Lodging	**PA**	Picnic Areas	**RC**	Rock Climbing	**TG** Tours, Guides
MB	Mountain Biking	**RA**	Ranger-led Activities	**S**	Swimming	**XC** Cross-country Skiing
MT	Marked Trails			**T**	Toilets	

Site Guide

HIGH LEDGES WILDLIFE SANCTUARY
Massachusetts Audubon Society
Property Mgr. for Eastern Sanctuaries
293 Moose Hill St.
Sharon, MA 02067
(617) 784-5691 (Sharon)
(617) 259-9500 (Lincoln)
Day use only; inaccessible to vehicles
late fall to spring; advisable to call before visiting   **BW, H, I, MT**

HOLYOKE RANGE STATE PARK
c/o Skinner State Park
PO Box 91, Hadley, MA 01035
(413) 586-0350   **BW, H, I, MT, PA,
RA, T, TG, XC**

HORSENECK BEACH STATE RESERVATION
Massachusetts Div. of Forests and Parks
PO Box 328, Westport Point, MA 02791
(508) 636-881   **BW, C, F, H,
PA, RA, S, T**

ICE GLEN
Town of Stockbridge
PO Box 417, Stockbridge, MA 01262-0417
(413) 298-4714   **BW, H, MT, RC**

IPSWICH RIVER WILDLIFE SANCTUARY
Massachusetts Audubon Society
87 Perkins Row
Topsfield, MA 01983
(508) 887-9264
Closed Mondays except holidays; admission fee for nonmembers; camping and
canoeing for members only
BW, GS, H, I, MT, T, XC

LAKE DENNISON RECREATION AREA
Massachusetts Div. of Forests and Parks
86 Winchendon Rd.
Baldwinville, MA 01436
(508) 939-8962   **BW, C, CK, F, H,
HR, PA, S, T, XC**

**LLOYD CENTER FOR
ENVIRONMENTAL STUDIES**
PO Box 87037
South Dartmouth, MA 02748
(508) 990-0505   **BW, H, I, MT, T**

LONG POINT WILDLIFE REFUGE
The Trustees of Reservations
PO Box 631, Chilmark, MA 02535
(508) 693-3678
BW, F, H, I, MT, S, T, TG

LOWELL HOLLY RESERVATION
The Trustees of Reservations
2468 B Washington St.
Canton, MA 02021
(617) 821-2977
Admission fee Memorial Day to
Columbus Day   **BW, CK, F, H, PA, S**

LYNN WOODS RESERVATION
Lynn Dept. of Public Works, City Hall
Pennybrook Rd.
Lynn, MA 01901
(617) 598-4000
(617) 477-7123   **BT, BW, H, HR,
MB, RA, TG, XC**

MASSACHUSETTS AUDUBON AT ARCADIA
Massachusetts Audubon Society
127 Combs Rd.
Easthampton, MA 01027
(413) 584-3009
BW, CK, H, MT, PA, T, XC

MENEMSHA HILLS RESERVATION
The Trustees of Reservations
PO Box 631
Chilmark, MA 02535
(508) 693-3678
No pets   **BW, F, H, MT, T, TG**

MIDDLE MOORS
Nantucket Conservation Foundation
PO Box 13, Nantucket, MA 02554
(508) 228-2884   **BT, BW, H, MB**

MIDDLESEX FELLS RESERVATION
Middlesex District Commission
1 Woodland Rd.
Stoneham, MA 02180
(617) 662-5230
Ranger activities daily during summer,
weekends rest of year
**BT, BW, F, H, HR, I, MB,
MT, PA, RA, RC, XC**

MILESTONE BOG
Nantucket Conservation Foundation
PO Box 13
Nantucket, MA 02554
(508) 228-2884   **BT, BW, H, MB**

MOHAWK TRAIL STATE FOREST
Massachusetts Div. of Forests and Parks
PO Box 7, Charlemont, MA 01339-0007
(413) 339-5504
BW, C, CK, F, H, MT, PA, RA, S, T, XC

BT Bike Trails	**CK** Canoeing, Kayaking	**F** Fishing	**HR** Horseback Riding
BW Bird-watching	**DS** Downhill Skiing	**GS** Gift Shop	**I** Information Center
C Camping		**H** Hiking	

266

MONOMOY ISLAND WILDERNESS AREA
U.S. Fish and Wildlife Service
Morris Island
Chatham, MA 02633
(508) 945-0594
(508) 443-4661   **BW, F, H, MT**

MONOMOY NATIONAL WILDLIFE REFUGE
U.S. Fish and Wildlife Service
Morris Island
Chatham, MA 02633
(508) 945-0594; (508) 443-4661
                    BW, F, GS, H, I, MT

MONUMENT MOUNTAIN RESERVATION
The Trustees of Reservations
PO Box 792
Stockbridge, MA 01262
(413) 298-3239   **BW, H, MT, PA**

MOUNT EVERETT STATE RESERVATION
Massachusetts Div. of Forests and Parks
East St., Mt. Washington, MA 01258
(413) 528-0330
    Day use only   **BW, CK, F,**
                         H, MB, MT, PA, T

MOUNT GREYLOCK STATE RESERVATION
Massachusetts Div. of Forests and Parks
PO Box 138
Lanesborough, MA 01237
(413) 499-4262   **BW, C, GS, H, I, L, MB,**
                   MT, PA, RA, T, TG, XC

MOUNT MISERY
Lincoln Conservation Commission
PO Box 6353, Lincoln, MA 01773
(617) 259-8850
         BW, CK, F, H, HR, MT, XC

MOUNT SUGARLOAF STATE RESERVATION
Massachusetts Div. of Forests and Parks
PO Box 484, Amherst, MA 01004
(413) 545-5993 (regional office)
(413) 665-2828 (site)
(413) 586-8706 (information)
    No jet skis   **BT, BW, C, CK, F, GS, H,**
                     I, MT, PA, RA, S, T, TG

MOUNT TOBY RESERVATION
Massachusetts Div. of Forests and Parks
136 Damon Rd.
Northampton, MA 01060
(413) 586-8706
    No motorized vehicles
         BW, H, HR, I, MB, MT, XC

MOUNT TOM RESERVATION
Massachusetts Div. of Forests and Parks
PO Box 985
Northampton, MA 01061
(413) 527-4805; (413) 545-5993
    Day use only   **BW, CK, F, H,**
                       MT, PA, RC, T, XC

MYLES STANDISH STATE FOREST
Massachusetts Div. of Forests and Parks
PO Box 66
South Carver, MA 02366
(508) 866-2526   **BT, BW, C, CK, F, GS, H,**
                   HR, I, MB, MT, PA, RA, S, T, XC

NATURAL BRIDGE STATE PARK
Massachusetts Div. of Forests and Parks
PO Box 1757
North Adams, MA 01247
(413) 663-6312, year-round
(413) 663-6392, seasonal
         BW, F, H, MT, PA, RA, T, TG

NOANET WOODLANDS
The Trustees of Reservations, 572 Essex St.
Beverly, MA 01915
(617) 821-2977
    Permits required for horseback riding
    and mountain biking; information center
    open on weekends
         BT, BW, F, H, HR, I, MB, MT, XC

**NORTHFIELD MOUNTAIN RECREATION
AND ENVIRONMENTAL CENTER**
Northeast Utilities
99 Millers Falls Rd.
Northfield, MA 01360
(800) 859-2960
         BT, BW, C, CK, F, GS, H, HR, I,
         MB, MT, PA, RA, RC, T, TG, XC

**NORTH HILL MARSH WILDLIFE
SANCTUARY**
Massachusetts Audubon Society
2000 Main St.
Marshfield, MA 02050
(617) 837-9400   **BW, H, MT**

NORTH RIVER WATERSHED
North and South Rivers Watershed Assoc.
PO Box 43
Norwell, MA 02061
(617) 659-8168
    Check tides before boating
         BW, C, CK, F, H, HR,
         I, MB, MT, PA, S, XC

L	Lodging	**PA**	Picnic Areas	**RC**	Rock Climbing	**TG** Tours, Guides
MB	Mountain Biking	**RA**	Ranger-led Activities	**S**	Swimming	**XC** Cross-country Skiing
MT	Marked Trails			**T**	Toilets	

NORTH RIVER WILDLIFE SANCTUARY
Massachusetts Audubon Society
2000 Main St., Marshfield, MA 02050
(617) 837-9400   **BW, GS, I, MT, T**

NOTCHVIEW RESERVATION
The Trustees of Reservations
PO Box 792, Stockbridge, MA 01262
(413) 684-0418   **BW, H, I, PA, T, XC**

OCTOBER MOUNTAIN STATE FOREST
Massachusetts Div. of Forests and Parks
317 Woodland Road
Lee, MA 01238
(413) 243-1778
Seasonal camping through
Columbus Day   **BW, C, CK, F, H,**
                      HR, MB, MT, T, XC

ONOTA LAKE
Pittsfield Parks Commission
874 North St., Pittsfield, MA 01201
(413) 499-9343   **F, PA, S**

OTTER RIVER STATE FOREST
Massachusetts Div. of Forests and Parks
86 Winchendon Rd.
Baldwinville, MA 01436
(508) 939-8962
          BW, C, F, H, MT, PA, S, T, XC

OXBOW NATIONAL WILDLIFE REFUGE
c/o Great Meadows
National Wildlife Refuge
Weir Hill Rd.
Sudbury, MA 01776
(508) 443-4661   **BW, CK, H, MT**

PARKER RIVER NATIONAL WILDLIFE REFUGE
U.S. Fish and Wildlife Service
Northern Blvd., Plum Island
Newburyport, MA 01950
(508) 465-5753
Day use only; handicapped accessible;
beach closed during nesting season;
tours available occasionally
          BW, F, H, I, MT, RA, S, T, TG, XC

PILGRIM MEMORIAL STATE PARK
Massachusetts Div. of Forests and Parks
PO Box 66, South Carver, MA 02366
(508) 866-2580
Includes Plymouth Rock, Cole Hill
Observatory, and *Mayflower* replica
          I, RA, T

PLEASANT VALLEY WILDLIFE SANCTUARY
Massachusetts Audubon Society
472 West Mountain Rd.
Lenox, MA 01240
(413) 637-0320   **BW, GS, H, I,**
                        MT, RA, T, XC

PLYMOUTH BEACH
Town of Plymouth
11 Lincoln St.
Plymouth, MA 02360
(508) 830-4095
Cars of nonresidents not allowed beyond main parking lot
          BW, CK, F, H, PA, S, T

PROVINCE LANDS BEECH FOREST
Cape Cod National Seashore
PO Box 250
South Wellfleet, MA 02663
(508) 349-3785
          BT, BW, H, MT, PA, RA, T

PROVINCE LANDS VISITOR CENTER
Cape Cod National Seashore
PO Box 250, South Wellfleet, MA 02663
(508) 349-3785
          BT, BW, GS, H, I, MT, RA, T

PUNKHORN PARKLANDS
Brewster Conservation Commission
2198 Main St., Brewster, MA 02631
(508) 896-3701; (508) 896-5454
          BW, CK, F, H, HR, MT, PA, S, T, XC

PURGATORY CHASM STATE RESERVATION
Massachusetts Div. of Forests and Parks
Purgatory Rd., Sutton, MA 01590
(508) 234-3733   **H, MT, PA, T**

QUABBIN RESERVOIR
Metropolitan District Commission
Div. of Watershed Management
PO Box 628, Belchertown, MA 01007
(413) 323-7221
No pets   **BW, F, H, I, MT, PA, T**

QUABOAG WILDLIFE MANAGEMENT AREA
Massachusetts Div.
of Fisheries and Wildlife
Central Wildlife District
211 Temple St.
West Boylston, MA 01583
(508) 835-3607
No motorized vehicles; use caution during hunting season
          BW, CK, F, H, HR, MB, S

268	Bike Trails	**CK**	Canoeing,	**F**	Fishing	**HR**	Horseback
	Bird-watching		Kayaking	**GS**	Gift Shop		Riding
	Camping	**DS**	Downhill	**H**	Hiking	**I**	Information
			Skiing				Center

Ram Pasture
Nantucket Conservation Foundation
PO Box 13
Nantucket, MA 02554
(508) 228-2884
Includes Sanford Farm
BT, BW, H, MB, MT

Ravenswood Park
The Trustees of Reservations
PO Box 563
Ipswich, MA 01935
(508) 356-4351 **BW, H, MT, XC**

Reed Brook Preserve
The Nature Conservancy
79 Milk St., Ste. 300
Boston, MA 02109
(617) 423-2545 **BW, H**

Richard T. Crane, Jr., Memorial Reservation
The Trustees of Reservations,
PO Box 563
Ipswich, MA 01935
(508) 356-4351 **BW, F, H, HR, MT, PA, S, T, XC**

Rock House Reservation
c/o Doyle Reservation
325 Lindell Ave.
Leominster, MA 01452
(508) 840-4446
Day use only **BW, H, I, MT, PA, RA, XC**

Rocky Woods Reservation
The Trustees of Reservations
572 Essex St.
Beverly, MA 01915
(617) 821-2977
Admission fee on weekends; info. ctr. open weekends; permit required for horseback riding
BT, BW, F, H, HR, I, MB, MT, PA, T, XC

Roland C. Nickerson State Park
Massachusetts Div. of
Forests and Parks
3488 Main St.
Brewster, MA 02631-1521
(508) 896-3491
(508) 896-4615 (reservations)
BT, BW, C, CK, F, H, I, MB, MT, PA, RA, S, T, XC

Royalston Falls Reservation
The Trustees of Reservations
325 Lindell Ave.
Leominster, MA 01453
(508) 840-4446; (508) 921-1944
BW, H, MB, MT, XC

Sage's Ravine
Appalachian Mountain Club
PO Box 1800
Lanesborough, MA 01237
(413) 443-0011
Primitive camping **BW, C, H, MT**

Salmon Falls Glacial Potholes
Town Hall
Shelburne Falls, MA 01370
(413) 625-0301
Access limited; recreational activities prohibited

Salt Pond Visitor Center
Cape Cod National Seashore
PO Box 250
South Wellfleet, MA 02663
(508) 349-3785 **BT, BW, CK, GS, H, I, MT, RA, T**

Sandy Neck Reservation
Town of Barnstable
141 Bassett Lane, Hyannis, MA 02601
(508) 362-8306; (508) 790-6350
BW, C, CK, F, H, HR, I, MT, T, XC

Sandy Point State Reservation
c/o Salisbury Beach State Reservation
PO Box 5303
Salisbury, MA 01952
(508) 462-4481; (508) 369-3350
Unguarded swimming **BW, F, H, S, T**

Skinner State Park
Massachusetts Div. of Forests and Parks
Rte. 47, PO Box 91
Hadley, MA 01035
(413) 586-0350
Car entrance fee
BW, H, I, MT, PA, RA, T, TG, XC

South Cape Beach State Park
Waquoit Bay National
Estuarine Research Reserve
PO Box 3092, Waquoit, MA 02536
(508) 457-0495
BW, CK, F, H, MT, RA, S, T, TG

L Lodging	**PA** Picnic Areas	**RC** Rock Climbing	**TG** Tours, Guides
MB Mountain Biking	**RA** Ranger-led Activities	**S** Swimming	**XC** Cross-country Skiing
MT Marked Trails		**T** Toilets	

SOUTH RIVER STATE FOREST
c/o Mohawk Trail State Forest
PO Box 7, Charlemont, MA 01339-0007
(413) 339-5504
    Day use only   **BW, CK, F, H, HR, XC**

STELLWAGEN BANK
NATIONAL MARINE SANCTUARY
National Oceanic and
Atmospheric Administration
14 Union St., Plymouth, MA 02360
(508) 747-1691   **BW, F**

STONY BROOK MILL SITES
Mill Sites Committee / Conservation
Commission
Town of Brewster
2198 Main St.
Brewster, MA 02631
(508) 896-3701   **BW**

TYRINGHAM COBBLE
The Trustees of Reservations
PO Box 792
Stockbridge, MA 01262
(413) 298-3239   **BW, H, MT, XC**

UPPER GOOSE POND
Appalachian Mountain Club
PO Box 1800, Lanesborough, MA 01237
(413) 443-0011
    Tent camping in designated areas; rustic
    cabin available   **BW, C, H, L, MT**

WACHUSETT MEADOW WILDLIFE
SANCTUARY
Massachusetts Audubon Society
113 Goodnow Rd.
Princeton, MA 01541
(508) 464-2712

                    BW, H, MT, PA, T

WACHUSETT MOUNTAIN STATE
RESERVATION
Massachusetts Div. of Forests and Parks
PO Box 248,
Princeton, MA 01541
(508) 464-2987
                    BW, DS, H, I, MT, PA, T, XC

WACONAH FALLS STATE PARK
Massachusetts Div.
of Forests and Parks
PO Box 1433
Pittsfield, MA 01202
(413) 442-8928   **BT, BW, F, H**

WALDEN POND STATE RESERVATION
Massachusetts Div. of Forests and Parks
Rte. 126, Concord, MA 01742
(508) 369-3254
    Day use only; no pets; parking fee
                    BW, CK, F, GS,
                    H, RA, S, T, TG, XC

WAQUOIT BAY NATIONAL
ESTUARINE RESEARCH RESERVE
National Oceanic and
Atmospheric Administration
Massachusetts Dept.
of Environmental Management
PO Box 3092, Waquoit, MA 02536
(508) 457-0495
        BW, CK, F, H, I, MT, RA, S, T, TG

WASHBURN ISLAND
Waquoit Bay National
Estuarine Research Reserve
PO Box 3092, Waquoit, MA 02536
(508) 457-0495
    Pit toilets   **BW, C, CK, F, H,**
                    MT, RA, S, T, TG

WASQUE RESERVATION
The Trustees of Reservations
572 Essex St.
Beverly, MA 01915-1530
(508) 627-7689; (508) 627-3599 (seasonal)
    BW, CK, F, H, HR, MT, PA, RA, S, T, TG

WATATIC MOUNTAIN
WILDLIFE SANCTUARY
Massachusetts Div. of
Fisheries and Wildlife
211 Temple St.
West Boylston, MA 01583
(508) 835-3607   **BW, H**

WELLFLEET BAY
WILDLIFE SANCTUARY
Massachusetts Audubon Society
PO Box 236, South Wellfleet. MA 02663
(508) 349-2615
    Camping for members only; guided
    walks, cruises, and workshops year-
    round   **BW, CK, GS, H,**
                    I, MT, PA, RA, T, TG

WINDSOR STATE FOREST
Massachusetts Div. of Forests and Parks
c/o Post Office, Windsor, MA 01270
(413) 684-0948   **BT, BW, C, F, H, HR, MB,**
                    MT, PA, S, T, XC

270	Bike Trails	**CK**	Canoeing, Kayaking	**F**	Fishing	**HR**	Horseback Riding
	Bird-watching			**GS**	Gift Shop		
	Camping	**DS**	Downhill Skiing	**H**	Hiking	**I**	Information Center

WING ISLAND
Cape Cod Museum of Natural History
Town of Brewster
PO Box 1710
Brewster, MA 02631
   Includes South Trail
(508) 896-3867   BW, CK, GS, H, I,
                                      MT, PA, RA, S, T, TG

WORLD'S END RESERVATION
The Trustees of Reservations
572 Essex St.
Beverly, MA 01915
(617) 821-2977; (617) 749-8956
   Admission fee; permit required for
   horseback riding
                    BW, F, H, HR, I, MT, T, XC

RHODE ISLAND

ARCADIA MANAGEMENT AREA
Rhode Island Divs. of Forest
Environment and Fish and Wildlife
1037 Hartford Pike
North Scituate, RI 02857
(401) 539-2356; (401) 789-3094
                    BT, BW, C, CK, F, H,
                    HR, I, MB, MT, PA, S, T

BAY ISLAND STATE PARK
Rhode Island Div. of Fish and Wildlife
4808 Tower Hill Rd.
Wakefield, RI 02879
(401) 789-3094   BW, F, H, S

BEAVERTAIL POINT STATE PARK
Rhode Island Div. of Parks and Recreation
2321 Hartford Ave.
Johnston, RI 02919
(401) 884-2010   BW, F, T

BLACKSTONE RIVER STATE PARK
Rhode Island Div. of
Planning and Development
83 Park St., Providence, RI 02903
(401) 277-2776
   Undeveloped

BLACKSTONE RIVER VALLEY NATIONAL HERITAGE CORRIDOR
National Park Service
1 Depot Sq.
Woonsocket, RI 02895
(401) 762-0440
          BT, BW, C, CK, F, H, HR, I, L,
          MT, PA, RA, RC, S, T, TG, XC

BLOCK ISLAND NATIONAL WILDLIFE REFUGE
U.S. Fish and Wildlife Service
PO Box 307
Charlestown, RI 02813
(401) 364-9124
                    BW, CK, F, H, MT, TG

BOWDISH RESERVOIR
Rhode Island Div. of Fish and Wildlife
4808 Tower Hill Rd.
Wakefield, RI 02879
(401) 568-2013
                    BW, C, F, H, I, MT,
                    PA, S, T, XC

CARATUNK WILDLIFE REFUGE
Audubon Society of Rhode Island
12 Sanderson Rd.
Smithfield, RI 02917
(508) 761-8230 (site)
(401) 949-5454 (headquarters)
                    BW, GS, H, I, MT,
                    RA, T, TG, XC

CARBUNCLE POND FISHING AREA
Rhode Island Div. of Fish and Wildlife
4808 Tower Hill Rd.
Wakefield, RI 02879
(401) 789-3094
   Day use only
                    BW, F, H

CLAY HEAD TRAIL
The Nature Conservancy
PO Box 1287
Block Island, RI 02807
(401) 466-2129
   Mostly private property; unguarded
   swimming
                    BW, H, MT, PA, RA, S, TG

CLIFF WALK
Newport Convention
and Visitors Bureau
23 America's Cup Ave.
Newport, RI 02840
(800) 326-6030   BW, H, MT

DIAMOND HILL PARK
Town of Cumberland
45 Broad St.
Cumberland, RI 02864
(401) 728-2400 ext. 28
   Day use only; no climbing on rocks;
   stay on trail   BW, H, PA, T

L Lodging	**PA** Picnic Areas	**RC** Rock Climbing	**TG** Tours, Guides
MB Mountain Biking	**RA** Ranger-led Activities	**S** Swimming	**XC** Cross-country Skiing
MT Marked Trails		**T** Toilets	

DUTCH ISLAND MANAGEMENT AREA
Rhode Island Div. of Fish and Wildlife
4808 Tower Hill Rd.
Wakefield, RI 02879
(401) 789-3094
Accessible by private boat only;
limited camping

BW, C, F, H, PA, S

EMILIE RUECKER WILDLIFE REFUGE
Audubon Society of Rhode Island
12 Sanderson Rd.
Smithfield, RI 02917
(401) 949-5454   **BW, H, MT, RA, TG**

FOGLAND MARSH PRESERVE
The Nature Conservancy
45 S. Angell St.
Providence, RI 02906
(401) 331-7110   **BW**

FRESH POND/FRESH MARSH PRESERVE
The Nature Conservancy
PO Box 1287
Block Island, RI 02807
(401) 466-2129   **BW, MT, RA, TG**

GEORGE B. PARKER WOODLAND
Audubon Society of Rhode Island
12 Sanderson Rd.
Smithfield, RI 02917
(401) 949-5454   **BW, H, MT, RA, TG, XC**

**GEORGE WASHINGTON
MANAGEMENT AREA**
Rhode Island Div.
of Forest Environment
1037 Hartford Pike
North Scituate, RI 02857
(401) 568-2013   **BT, BW, C, F,
HR, MT, PA, S, T, XC**

**GREAT SWAMP WILDLIFE
MANAGEMENT AREA**
Rhode Island Div.
of Fish and Wildlife
4808 Tower Hill Rd.
Wakefield, RI 02879
(401) 789-3094   **BW, CK, F, H, I, MT, XC**

THE GREENWAY
The Nature Conservancy
PO Box 1287
Block Island, RI 02807
(401) 466-2129   **BW, H, MT, PA, RA, TG**

**LEWIS-DICKENS
FARM NATURE PRESERVE**
The Nature Conservancy
PO Box 1287, Block Island, RI 02807
(401) 466-2129
Call for permission to visit   **BW, RA, TG**

LIME ROCK PRESERVE
The Nature Conservancy
45 S. Angell St., Providence, RI 02906
(401) 331-7110   **H**

LONG AND ELL PONDS NATURAL AREAS
The Nature Conservancy
45 S. Angell St., Providence, RI 02906
(401) 331-7110   **BW, H**

LONSDALE MARSH
Rhode Island Div. of Planning
and Development
83 Park St., Providence, RI 02903
(401) 277-2776   **BW, F**

MARSH MEADOWS WILDLIFE SANCTUARY
Audubon Society of Rhode Island
12 Sanderson Rd.
Smithfield, RI 02917-2600
(401) 949-5454   **BW**

MOHEGAN BLUFFS
The Nature Conservancy
PO Box 1287, Block Island, RI 02807
(401) 466-2129
Overlook area; unguarded swimming
BW, F, MT, S

NAPATREE POINT
Watch Hill Fire District
PO Box 326, Westerly, RI 02891
No vehicle access; no pets   **BW, H**

**NARRAGANSETT BAY
RESEARCH RESERVE**
Rhode Island Dept. of
Environmental Management
Asst. Director, Natural Resource Protection
22 Hayes St.,Providence, RI 02908
(401) 277-6605   **BW, CK, F, H, MT**

NINIGRET CONSERVATION AREA
Rhode Island Div. of Parks and Recreation
2321 Hartford Ave.
Johnston, RI 02917
(401) 277-2632
Windsurfing   **BW, C, F, S, T**

272 Bike Trails	**CK** Canoeing,	**F** Fishing	**HR** Horseback
Bird-watching	Kayaking	**GS** Gift Shop	Riding
Camping	**DS** Downhill	**H** Hiking	**I** Information
	Skiing		Center

NINIGRET NATIONAL WILDLIFE REFUGE
U.S. Fish and Wildlife Service
PO Box 307
Charlestown, RI 02813
(401) 364-9124 **BW, CK, F, H,**
MT, RA, T, TG, XC

NORMAN BIRD SANCTUARY
Friends of the Norman
Bird Sanctuary
583 Third Beach Rd.
Middletown, RI 02842
(401) 846-2577 **BW, GS, H, I, MT,**
RA, T, TG, XC

PURGATORY CHASM
Rhode Island Div. of Parks and Recreation
2321 Hartford Ave.
Johnston, RI 02919
(401) 277-2632
Scenic overlook

QUICKSAND POND/GOOSEWING
BEACH PRESERVE
The Nature Conservancy
45 S. Angell St.
Providence, RI 02906
(401) 331-7110
Toilets at adjacent town beach
during season **BW, S, T, TG**

QUONOCHONTAUG BEACH
CONSERVATION AREA
Quonochontaug Beach
Conservation Commission
4 Wawaloam Dr.
Weekapaug, RI 02891
(401) 322-1450 (Weekapaug Fire District)
Mostly private property; no parking
available; foot access only; best time to
visit is fall **BW, F, H**

QUONOCHONTAUG BREACHWAY
Rhode Island Div. of Fish and Wildlife
4808 Tower Hill Rd.
Wakefield, RI 02879
(401) 789-3094 **BW, CK, F, H, S**

RODMAN'S HOLLOW
The Nature Conservancy
PO Box 1287, Block Island, RI 02807
(401) 466-2129
Mountain biking on Black Rock Rd.
only; unguarded swimming
BW, F, H, MB, MT, RA, S, TG

SACHUEST POINT NATIONAL
WILDLIFE REFUGE
U.S. Fish and Wildlife Service
739 Sachuest Point Rd.
Middletown, RI 02842
(401) 847-5571
Visitor center hours vary by season, call
office **BW, CK, F, H, I,**
MT, RA, T, TG, XC

SAPOWET MARSH MANAGEMENT AREA
Rhode Island Div. of Fish and Wildlife
4808 Tower Hill Rd.
Wakefield, RI 02879
(401) 789-3094 **BW, CK, F**

SNAKE DEN STATE PARK
Rhode Island Div. of Parks and Recreation
2321 Hartford Ave.
Johnston, RI 02919
(401) 277-2632
Undeveloped; active farm on property
BW, H

TOUISSET MARSH WILDLIFE REFUGE
Audubon Society of Rhode Island
12 Sanderson Rd.
Smithfield, RI 02917
(401) 949-5454 **BW, H, MT, RA, TG, XC**

TRESTLE TRAIL
Rhode Island Div. of Fish and Wildlife
4808 Tower Hill Rd.
Wakefield, RI 02879
(401) 789-3094 **BT, BW, HR**

TRUSTOM POND NATIONAL
WILDLIFE REFUGE
U.S. Fish and Wildlife Service
PO Box 307, Charlestown, RI 02813
(401) 364-9124 **BW, H, MT,**
RA, T, TG, XC

WEETAMOO WOODS
Open Space and Land
Preservation Commission
Town Hall
Tiverton, RI 02878
(401) 625-6700
Tours by prearrangement
BW, H, MT, TG

L	Lodging	**PA**	Picnic Areas	**RC**	Rock Climbing	**TG** Tours, Guides
MB	Mountain Biking	**RA**	Ranger-led Activities	**S**	Swimming	**XC** Cross-country Skiing
MT	Marked Trails			**T**	Toilets	

INDEX

Numbers in **bold** indicate illustrations; numbers in ***bold italics*** indicate maps.

Albert F. Norris Reservation, 69, 263
alder, 86
alewives, 32, 47, 192, 220
Ames Pond, 57
Andromeda Ponds, 77
Appalachian Trail Corridor, 124, **125**, 161, 164, 260
Approaching Storm: Beach Near Newport (Heade), 222–23, **222–23**
arbutus, trailing, 81–82, 97
Arcadia Management Area, 237, **238–39**, 240, 271
arrowhead, tidewater, xvii, 192
ash, 192
Ashburnham State Forest, 94, 263
Ashford Oak Preserve, 205
Assabet-Sudbury-Concord River System, 72, 75–76
aster
  Maryland golden, 250
  New England, 144
Atlantic White Cedar Swamp, 38, 39, **39**, 263
Audubon Center in Greenwich, 167, 260
Audubon Fairchild Garden, 168–69, 260
azalea
  mountain, 124
  swamp, 167

Bachelor's buttons, **170–71**, 171
baneberry, 215
Bar Head, 86
Barndoor Hills, 183
Barn Island Wildlife Management Area, 199, 260
Bartholomew's Cobble, 143–44, **145**, 263
Barton Cove Nature and Camping Area, 97, 263
Bash Bish Falls, 140, **141,**

143
Bash Bish Falls State Park, 142, 263
bass, 107
  striped, 10
basswood, 78
bats, 76
  big brown, 165
  brown, 139
  eastern pipistrelle, 165
  Keen's, 165
  little brown, 165
bayberry, 58, 204
Bay Island State Park, 223, 271
beach grass, 46, **50**, 51, 226, **227**
  American, 22, **24–25**, 83, **84–85**
beach plum, 172
bearberry, 51, 180
Bear Mountain, 155, 260
bears, 13, 127
  black, 113, 123, 127, **127,** 139
Beartown State Forest, 138, **138–39**, 139, 263
beavers, 13, 78, 86, 94, 105, 107, 113, 127, 129, 132, 138, **138**, 139, 140, 155, 193, 204, 240
Beavertail Point State Park, 226, 228, 271
beeches, 10, **16–17**, 18, 31, 32, 42, 47, 48, 57, 77, 89, 94, 133, 154, 167, 177, 205, 240
beetle
  American burying, xiii, 209, 245, 250
  tiger, 54
beetlebungs, 54, **55**
Belle Isle Marsh Reservation, 70, 263
Benedict Pond, 139
Ben Utter Trail, 240
Berkshire Mountains, **iv,** vi
  central, 129–33
  northern, 121–24
  southern, 133–45
Berkshire plateau, 124–29
Beston, Henry (writer), xvii, 36, 46
birches, **16–17**, 18, 72, 78,

86, **88**, 89, 94, 129, 177
  black, 10, 47, 149, 154, 167, 183, 191
  paper, 97, **112,** 113
  river, 82
  white, 10, **112**, 113, 123, 205
  yellow, 121, 123, 124, 133, **166**, 167, 193, 205
bitterns, American, 107, 132, 226, **226**, 249
blackberries, 191
blackbirds, red-winged, 81, 216
black-eyed Susans, 144, 237, **237**
black gum, 47
blackpolls, 81
Black Pond Reservation, 69, 263
Black Spruce Bog, 158, **159**
Blackstone Canal (RI), **214,** 215
Blackstone Gorge (MA and RI), 212
Blackstone Gorge State Park (MA), 109, 263
Blackstone River and Canal Heritage State Park (MA), 109, 263
Blackstone River State Park (RI), 215, 271
Blackstone River Valley National Heritage Corridor (MA and RI), 109, 212, 263, 271
bladderwort, Goose Pond, xii, 133
blazing star
  New England, 53
  northern, 250
Block, Adriaen, xii
Block Island, **x–xi,** xii, xiii, 14, **15**, **210**, 211, 242, **243, 244,** 245–47, **247, 248,** 249–50, **251**
Block Island National Wildlife Refuge, 14, **15**, **206–07**, 208, 246–47, 271
bloodroot, 144
bluebells, 144
blueberries, 51, 52, 191, 202, **203**, 224, **224**
bluebirds, 36

eastern, 4, **4**
Blue Hills Reservation, **68,**
69, 70, 71, **71,** 263
Bluff Head, 177–78, 260
Bluff Point State Park,
198–99, **200–01,** 260
bobcats, 13, 76, 105, 113,
123, 139
bobolinks, 92, 129, 134, 144
Bolleswood Natural Area,
198
Boston Harbor Islands State
Park, 70, 264
Boston Hollow, 205, 260
Bowdish Reservoir, 241–42,
271
Boxford State Forest, 78, 264
Bradford, William (Pilgrim),
2
brant, 198
Broadmoor Wildlife Sanctuary, 72, **73,** 74, 264
Browning Mill Pond, 237,
238–39
buffleheads, 233
Bull's Bridge Recreation
Area, 164, 260
bulrushes, Torrey's, xvii, 192
Bunker Meadows, **60,** 61
buntings
indigo, 36, 124, **124**
snow, 52
Burroughs, John (naturalist),
14
Bushy Point, 199
buteos
see hawks
butter-and-eggs, 144
butterflies, 54, 90, 129
black swallowtail, 93, **93**
monarch, 66, **66**
pipevine, 93
skipper, 102
sulphur, 102
swallowtail, 102
tiger swallowtail, 93, **93**
buttonbush, 78

*C*allinectes sapidus, 198
Campbell Falls State
Park, 154, 260
Canoe Meadows Wildlife
Sanctuary, 129, 132, 264
Canonicus (sachem), 108

canvasbacks, 129
Cape Cod (Thoreau), 38
Cape Cod Museum of Natur-
al History, 31
Cape Cod National Seashore,
32, **33–34,** 36–38, **38,** 264
Cape Poge Wildlife Refuge,
53, 264
Caratunk Wildlife Refuge,
216–17, 271
Carbuncle Pond Fishing
Area, 240, 271
cardinal flowers, 105, **105,**
241
cardinals, 13
Castle Craig, 181
Castle Hill, 83
catawba, 47
catfish, 107
Cathedral, the, **236,** 237
Cathedral Pines, 157, 260
Catlin Woods, 158
cattails, 76, 107, 134,
136–37, 216
cedars, 10, 18, 165, 173, 183,
220
Atlantic white, 202
northern white, 155
white, 32, 37, 38, 39, **39,**
69, 191, 234
Cedar Tree Nick, 57
Champlain, Samuel de (ex-
plorer), 36, 38
Changes in the Land
(Cronon), xiii, 3
Chapman Falls, 192, **193,**
193
Chapman Pond, 192, 260
Charles E. Wheeler Wildlife
Refuge, 172
Charles River, 72, 74–75
Charles W. Ward Reserva-
tion, 78, 264
chats, yellow, 199
Chesterfield Gorge Reservation, **126,** 127, 128, 264
chestnut, American, 241
chickadees
black-capped, 127
boreal, 127
chipmunk, 158, **158**
Church, Frederic Edwin,
176
cinquefoils, 144

Clamshell, 165
Clay Head, **210,** 211
Clay Head Trail, 247, 249,
271
Cliff Walk, 226, 271
clintonia, 1213
cod, 10, 13
Cold River, xiii, **xiv–xv**
Cold River Old Growth Forest, 121, 264
Cole, Thomas (painter), 98,
102
columbine, 31
compass grass, **50,** 51
Concord Impoundments, 76
Connecticut, *iii, xviii–xix*
eastern, 184–86, **187,**
188–209
western, 151–52, *153,*
154–83
Connecticut Beautiful (Nutting), 13
Connecticut College Arboretum, 198, 260
Conuel, Tom (writer), 89
coots, 118, 199
cordgrass, 30
cormorants, 13, 247
double-crested, 246, **246**
Cornelius and Mine S. Crane
Wildlife Refuge, 82, **84–85,**
264
Coskata-Coatue, Great Point
Wildlife Refuge System, 51,
264
cottonwoods, 144, 192
coyotes, 13, 105, 106, 123
eastern, 102, **102**
crabs, 199
blue, 10, 198
fiddler, 42
hermit, 81
cranberries, 18, 21, 31, 39,
48–49, 49, 52, 82
*Cranberry Harvest, Nantuck-
et Island, The* (Johnson),
48–49, **48–49**
Crane's Beach, 83, **84–85**
Crepidula, xii
Crocker Maple, 92
Cronon, Willian (historian),
xiii, 3
crossbills, 205
red, 127

white-winged, 127
Cuttyhunk Island, 57–58, 264

Daisies, oxeye, 144
Dame Farm, 242
Daniel Webster Wildlife
Sanctuary, 66, 264
deer, 31, 45, 46, 51, 58, 82,
105, 106, 139
white-tailed, 13, 76, 123,
132, **133, 170–71,** 171,
194, 198, 222–23
Demarest Lloyd State Park,
22, **24–25,** 58, **59,** 264
Devil's Den Preserve, 165,
167, 168, **168–69,** 260
Devil's Hopyard State Park,
192–93, **193,** 260
devil's paintbrush, 144
Diamond Hill Park, 212, 215,
271
Dinosaur Footprints Reservation, 103, 264
Dinosaur State Park, 191,
260
Doane Rock, 36
Doane's Falls Reservation,
96, 264
dogwood, 10, 149, 173, 232
dragonflies, 57, 90
drumlins, xii, 7, 18, 62, 69,
70, 76, 83, 86, 199, 246,
249, 254
ducks, 11, 45, 53, 161, 177,
225, 247
American black, 86
black, 36, 76, 173, 192, 216,
233
harlequin, 81, 226
ring-necked, 76
ruddy, 129
sea, 53
winter, 51, 171
wood, xiii, 74, 76, 81, 103,
109, 118, 129, 144, 155,
167, 191, 242
see also buffleheads; canvasbacks; gadwalls; gold-
eneyes; mallard; mer-
gansers; old-squaws;
scaup; scoters; shovelers,
northern; teal; wigeon
duckweed, 225, **225**
Dungeon Rock, 72

dunlins, 171
Dunwiddie, Peter (plant
ecologist), 51
Durand, Asher (painter), 114
Dutch Island Management
Area, 229, 232, 272
Dutchman's-breeches, 144
Duxbury Beach, 66, 264

Eagles, 93
bald, 13, 36, 66, 97,
105–06, **108,** 109, 190, 192,
194
East Peak/West Peak, 181
Edwin Way Teale Memorial
Sanctuary, 204
Eel Point, 52, 265
eels, sand, 229, **229**
egrets, 194, 197, 220, 221,
222, 224
cattle, 58
great, 81, 177
snowy, 47, **47,** 81, 171,
172, 173, 177, 199, 220,
229, 233
Ellisville State Park, 26,
26–27, 30, 265
Emerson Rocks, 86
Emerson's Cliff, 77
Emilie Ruecker Wildlife Refuge, 220–21, 272
Enfield Lookout, 106
Enfield Rapids, 190
eskers, 7, 62, 78, 183, 204, 254
Eugene D. Moran Wildlife
Management Area, 127,
265

Falcons, 86, 93
peregrine, 45, 66, 81,
139, 183, 234, 247, 250,
250
Falls River, 240
Felix Neck Wildlife Sanctuary, 52–53, 265
ferns, xiii, 39, **39,** 78, 94, 97,
112, 113, 128, 140, 143,
143, 144, 208, 215
bulbet, 122
Christmas, 134
cinnamon, 102
maidenhair, 134
ostrich, 102
royal, 102

fir, 114
balsam, 47, 123
fire pink, **142,** 143
fishers, 105, 107, 113, 123
Flint's Pond, 77, 265
flounder
winter, 10
yellowtail, 13
flycatchers
Acadian, 193
great crested, 81
Fogland Marsh Preserve,
220, 272
Fort Hill Area, 36, 38, **38,** 39,
40–41, 265
Fountain Pond, 134, **136–37**
foxes, 74, 167
red, 168, **168**
French King Gorge, 97, 265
Fresh Pond/Fresh Marsh Preserve, **248,** 249, 272
frogs, 13
Fuertes, Louis Agassiz
(artist), 128

Gadwalls, 76, 86, 199
Gay Head Clay Cliffs,
54, **56,** 57, 265
geese, 45, 53, 247
Canada, 76, 86, **86,** 103,
144, 155, 198, 199, 233,
247
snow, 86
gentian, Plymouth, 30, 32,
32
George B. Parker Woodland,
241, 272
George Washington Man-
agement Area, 242, 272
geranium, wild, 180, **180**
gerardia, sandplain, 48
Giant Laurel, 178
Gifford Pinchot Sycamore
Park, 182, 260
Gillette Castle State Park,
185, 193, 261
ginger, wild, 123
glacial boulders
see glacial erratics
glacial erratics, xii, 7, 22, 27,
36, 39, **40–41,** 106,
110–11, 124, 199, 212,
217, 220, 228, 237, 241,
245, 254

glacial till, 21, 22, 57, 70,
152, 182, 197, 212, 233,
234, 245, 246, **247,** 254
glasswort, **12,** 13
Glendale Falls Reservation,
129, 265
Godfrey Pond, 167
godwits, Hudsonian, 45
goldeneyes, 81, 233
goldenrod, **xx–1,** 2, 144,
226, **227**
seaside, 22, **24–25,** 58, **59,**
66, **66**
Gooseberry Island, 58
goshawks, 78, 183
Gosnold, Bartholomew (settler), 58
Grand Allee, 83
grapes, wild, 191
grasshoppers, sand, 39
Graves, Arthur Harmount,
xiii
Great Barrington State Park,
134, **136–37**
Great Blue Hill, **68,** 69, 70,
265
Great Hemlock, 177
Great Island, 42, **43**
Great Island Marsh Preserve,
196–97, 261
Great Island Trail, 42, **43**
great laurel, 202
Great Ledge, 165
Great Marshes, 28, **29,** 30–31
Great Meadows National
Wildlife Refuge, 76, 265
Great Salt Pond, 246
Great Swamp Wildlife Man-
agement Area, 232, 272
grebes, 129, 197
Green Falls Pond, 202
Greenway, The, 249, 272
Greenwich Point Park, 169,
171
Griswold Point, 196–97
grosbeaks, 154, 205
evening, 124, **124,** 127, 183
pine, 127
grouse, 139
ruffed, 123, 127
Guilder Pond, 140
gulls, 51
black-backed, 31, 47, **47**
great black-backed, 247

herring, 31, 233, 247
laughing, 47, **47,** 229, **229**

Haddock, 13
Hadlyme ferry, **184,**
185
Halibut Point Reservation,
81, 265
Halibut Point State Park, **80,**
81, 265
Hammonasset Beach State
Park, 194, 261
Hammonasset Natural Area,
194, 196, **196–97**
Hanging Rock, 224, **224**
Hank's Picnic Place, 107,
107
hares, snowshoe, 123, 127,
241, **241**
harriers, 53, 54, 66, 86
northern, 52, 220, 226, 250
Harvard Forest, 96, 265
Harwich Conservation
Lands, 47, 265
hawks, 11, 53, 74, 93, 94, 98,
138, 140, 152, 155, 161,
225, 228
broad-winged, 78, 93, 98,
144, 183
buteo, 93
Cooper's, 234
marsh, 233
red-shouldered, 78
red-tailed, 81, 94, 226
red-winged, 144
sharp-shinned, 234
Hawthorne, Nathaniel
(writer), 114
Hay, John (writer), 32
Heade, Martin Johnson
(painter), 223
heath hen, xiii
Hellcat Swamp, 82, **82–83,**
86
Hemlock Gorge Reservation,
74, 265
hemlocks, xvii, 10, 14, 47,
66, 71, 72, **73,** 74, 81, 92,
94, 96, 97, 98, 109, 118,
121, 124, 127, 128, 133,
134, 140, 154, 157, 158,
164, 165, **166,** 167, 177,
178, 180, **180–81,** 183,
191, 193, 198, 202, 205,

208, 217, 220, **236,** 237,
242
hepatica, **142,** 143
Herman Haupt Management
Area, 202
herons, 66, 70, 107, 118, 191,
218, 220, 221, 222, 224
black-crowned night, 216
great blue, 28, **28,** 103,
106, 129, 194, 199, 216,
220
green, 103, 199
tricolored, 196, **196**
herrings, 32, 47, 220
Heublein Tower, 183
hickories, 10, 31, 89, 98, 103,
149, 183, 194, 204
shagbark, 167, 178
Hidden Valley, 164
High Head, 38
High Ledges Wildlife Sanctuary, 118, 266
High Rock, 220
hobblebush, 123
holly trees, 47, 58, 220
American, 232
Holyoke Range State Park,
98, 266
honeysuckle, 129
Hope Island, 221–22
hop hornbeam, eastern, 134
Hopper, the, 123
Horseneck Beach State
Reservation, 58, 266
horsetail, dwarf, 122
Housatonic Meadows State
Park, 156, 261
Housatonic River, **150,** 151,
154, **154,** 155, **155**
Hubbard Park, 181, 261
huckleberry, 51
hummingbirds, 105
Hurd State Park, 186,
188–89, 191, 261
Hutchinsoniella, xii

Ibis, 222
glossy, 58, 70, 171, 173,
173, 221, 233
Ice Glen, 134, 266
Ipswich River Wildlife Sanctuary, **60,** 61, 78, **79,** 81,
266
irises, wild, 169

ironwood, 134

Jack-in-the-pulpits, 123
  jackrabbits, 52
    black-tailed, 49
Jeremy Point, 42
John C. Phillips Wildlife
  Sanctuary, 78
Johnson, Eastman (artist), 48
Judge's Hill, 127
Jug End Trail, 94, **95**

Kent Falls, **160**, 161
  Kent Falls State Park,
    160, 161, 261
kestrels, American, 234
kettle holes, 18, 21, 22, 28,
  30, 36, 58, 69, 76, 202,
  216, 249, 250, 254
kingbirds, 81
kingfishers, 57, 103, 199
kinglets, 165, 247

Lady's slippers
  pink, 81, 118, 194
    showy, 72, 194
    white, 118
    yellow, xvii, 118, 215
Lake Dennison Recreation
  Area, 93–94, 266
larch, 78
leatherleaf, 158
Ledges, the, 139
Lenox Mountain, 132
Lewis-Dickens Farm Nature
  Preserve, 250, 272
lichens, 178, **179**, 204
  foliose, 96
  old-man's beard, 38
  rock tripe, 202
  toadskin, 72
Lime Rock Preserve, 215,
  216, **217**, 272
Lion's Head Gorge, 228
Litchfield Hills, 156–57,
  156–57
little bluestem, 52
Lloyd Center for Environ-
  mental Studies, 58, 266
lobelia, great blue, 144
Long and Ell Ponds Natural
  Areas, 234, 272
Long Point Wildlife Refuge,
  53, 266

longspurs, Lapland, 52
Lonsdale Marsh, 216, 272
loons, 129, 197
loosestrife, purple, 107, 78,
  79, 154, 154
Lost Lake, 177
Lowell Holly Reservation,
  47–48, 266
Luddy/Taylor Connecticut
  Valley Tobacco Museum,
  190
Lynn Woods Reservation, 72,
  266

MacMillan Wharf, 42
  Magnolia Swamp, 82
mallard, 76, 192, 216, **216**
Mamacoke Natural Area, 198
maples, 10, **16–17**, 18, 72,
  82, 83, **88**, 89, 92, 94, 107,
  107, 129, 155, **166**, 167,
  216, 232, 241
  mountain, 154, 182
  red, 10, 36, 69, 76, 94, **95,**
    106, **106**, 149, 165, 191,
    192, 202, 232
  silver, 81, 192
  sugar, 10, 78, 90, 121, 133,
    154, 177, 183, **184**, 185,
    191, 204, 205
Marconi Site, 38
marshmallows, 225
marsh marigolds, 168
Marsh Meadows Wildlife
  Sanctuary, 229, 272
marsh samphire, **12**, 13
Martha's Vineyard, xiii,
  52–54, **55, 56**, 57, 255,
  255
Mashamoquet Brook State
  Park, 205, 261
Massachusetts, *iii*, *xviii–xix*
  central, 88–90, **91**, 92–111
  eastern, 60–62, **63**, 64–87
  southeastern, 20–22, *23,*
    24–59
  western, 112–14, *115,*
    116–45
Massachusetts Audubon at
  Arcadia, 102–03, 266
Massachusetts Beautiful
  (Nutting), 13
mayapples, 168
mayflower

see arbutus, trailing
mayweed, 237, **237**
McClean Game Refuge, 183,
  261
meadow beauty, Maryland,
  30
meadowlarks, 36, 54, 144
Melville, Herman (writer),
  49, 114, 122
Menemsha Hills Reservation,
  54, 266
mergansers, 86, 144, 192,
  218, 233
  hooded, 128, **128**, 155
Metacomet (sachem), 152
mice, jumping, 76
Middle Moors, 51, 266
Middlesex Fells Reservatiion,
  70–71, 266
Milestone Bog, 52, 266
Milford Point, 172, 261
milkweed, **xx–1**, 2, 93, **93**,
  129, 144
Mill Falls, 72, **73**
Mine Hill Preserve, 165, **166,**
  167
mink, 105, 127, 192, 220
minnows, 199
mistletoe, dwarf, 242
Moby Dick (Melville), 49
mockingbirds, 233
Mohawk Mountain State Park
  and State Forest, 157–58,
  261
Mohawk Trail State Forest,
  xiv–xv, xiii, 121, 266
Mohegan Bluffs, **x–xi**, xii,
  242, **243**, 246, **247**, 249,
  272
mollusk, xii
monadnocks, 18, 92, 94, 202,
  254
Money Brook Falls, 123–24
Money Brook Trail, 123–24
Monomoy Island Wilderness
  Area, **44**, 45–46, 267
Monomoy National Wildlife
  Refuge, **44**, 45–46, 267
Monomoy Point Lighthouse,
  44, 45, 46
Monument Mountain, 114,
  116–17, 134, **135, 137,**
  138
Monument Mountain Reser-

vation, 138–39, 267

moorhen, common, 140, 229, **229**

moss, 13, 39, **39,** 72, **120,** 121, 128, 140, 143, 169, 198

  sphagnum, 10, 18, 69, 92, **92,** 158, **159,** 191, 198, 237, 241–42, 255

moths, 54

mountain ash, northern, 123

mountain laurel, 47, 97, 108, 140, 158, 161, **161,** 167, 173, 176, 177, 178, 193, 194, 198, 202, 205, 237

mountain lions, 105

Mount Everett, 140, 143, **143**

Mount Everett State Reservation, 140, 267

Mount Greylock, 122, 124, 134, **135**

Mount Greylock State Reservation, 122–24, **122,** 267

Mount Greylock Visitor Center, **xx–1,** 2

Mount Higby, 178, 261

Mount Holyoke, 98

Mount Misery, 77, 267

Mount Misery Trail, 202, 204

Mount Sugarloaf State Reservation, 98, 267

Mount Toby, 97

Mount Toby Reservation, 97, 267

Mount Tom Reservation, 103, 267

muskrat, 53, 103, 107, 139, 192, 216

mussels, 86

  blue, 10

Myles Standish State Forest, 28, 30, 267

Nantucket Island, 48–49, **48–49,** 52

Napatree Point, 234, 272

Narragansett Bay Research Reserve, 221–24, 272

Natchaug State Forest, 205, 261

Natural Bridge State Park, 121–22, 267

Newcomb Hollow Beach, 32, **33–34**

New Meadow Hill Swamp, **244,** 245

Ninigret Conservation Area, 233, 272

Ninigret National Wildlife Refuge, 233, 273

Ninigret Pond, 229, **230–31**

Nipmuck Trail, 205

Noanet Peak, 74

Noanet Woodlands, 74, 267

Norman Bird Sanctuary, 224–26, **224, 225,** 273

North Beach, 45

Northfield Mountain Recreation and Environmental Center, 94, **95,** 96–97, 267

North Hill Marsh Wildlife Sanctuary, 66, 267

North Light, **207,** 208

North River Watershed, 66, 69, 267

North River Wildlife Sanctuary, 69, 268

Northwest Park, 190–91, 261

Norwalk Islands, 171, 261

Notchview Reservation, 127, 268

Nutting, Wallace (writer), 13

Oaks, 10, 30, 31, 36, 57, 61, 71, 76, 77, **77,** 89, 98, 127, **127,** 149, 158, 167, 183, **184,** 185, 204, 220, 242

  black, 118, 186, **188–89**

  bur, 155

  chestnut, 178, 192

  English, 7, **8–9,** 69

  red, 93, 205

  scrub, 10, 21, 173

  white, 168, 178, **179**

October Mountain State Forest, **16–17,** 18, 129, **130–31,** 132, 268

old-squaws, 86, 129

Olmsted, Frederick Law, 62, 69, 70

Onota Lake, 129, 268

opossums, 13

Opuntia, xii

orchids, 69

  see also lady's slippers; white-fringed orchis

orioles, 81

ospreys, xvii, 13, 53, 54, **54,** 58, 74, 93, 177, 194, 197, 199, 232, 233

Otter River State Forest, 94, 268

otters, 53, 105

  river, 74, **74,** 76, 192

Outermost House, The (Beston), xvii, 36

owls

  barn, 241, **241,** 247, 250

  barred, 78, 123

  short-eared, 45, 52, 53, 69, **69,** 70, 226

  snowy, 70

Oxbow Lake, 102

Oxbow National Wildlife Refuge, 90, 268

oxbows, **100–01,** 102, 254

oystercatchers, American, 45, 47, **47,** 51

Pachaug State Forest, 199, 202, 262

panfish, 107

Parker River National Wildlife Refuge, 83, **82–83,** 86, **87,** 268

Parker River Preserve, **12,** 13

Patience Island, 221–22

pear trees, 165

Peckham Pond, 249

peepers, 118

peregrines

  see falcons, peregrine

periwinkles, 81, 86

Perkins Island, 81

Peterson, Roger Tory, xvii

phlox, 129

phragmites reeds, 138, **138–39**

pike, 107

Pike's Pond, 132

Pilgrim Memorial State Park, 27, 268

Pinchot, Gifford, xvii

Pine Knob Loop, 156

pines, 36, 42, 76, 76, 77, **77,** 96, 106, 164, 202, 217, 221

  pitch, 10, 18, 21, 30, 51, 61, 82, 134, **135,** 138, 183, **236,** 237, 204

  red, 32, **33,** 249

  white, xvii, 10, 36, 47, 61,

66, 77, 81, **88,** 89, 98, 132, 133, 134, 154, 157, 158, 165, 183, 205, 237, **238–39**
pine siskins, 154, 205
pinks, 237, **237**
pitcher plants, 69, 92, **92,** 198, 242
Pleasant Bay, 45
Pleasant Valley Wildlife Sanctuary, 132, 268
plover, 66, 86, 172, 221
golden, 45
piping, 13, 28, 31, **31,**37, 52, 53, 58, 66, 82, 86, 172–73, 197, 218, 233
Plum Island, **12,** 13, 82, **82–83,** 83, 86
Plymouth Beach, 27–28, 268
Plymouth Rock, 27
Ponkapoag Pond, 71, **71**
poplar, 86
porcupines, 113, 123, 127
Potter Mountain, **xx–1,** 2
poverty grass, 247
prickly pear cactus, xii, 51
Prospect Hill, 54
Province Lands, 39
Province Lands Beech Forest, 39, 42, 268
Province Lands Visitor Center, 39, 268
Prudence Island, 221–24
Punkhorn Parklands, 32, 268
Purgatory Chasm, 226, 273
Purgatory Chasm State Reservation, 107, 109, 268

Quabbin Hill Lookout Tower, 106
Quabbin Reservoir, **88,** 89, **104,** 105–06, **106, 107,** 109, 268
Quaboag Wildlife Management Area, 107, 268
quahogs, 47, **47,** 221
Queen Anne's lace, 7, **8–9, 170–71,** 171
Quicksand Pond/Goosewing Beach, 218, **219,** 273
Quonochontaug Beach Conservation Area, 233, 234, **235,** 273
Quonochontaug Breachway, 233, 273

Rabbits, 31, 226
  see also hares, snow shoe; jackrabbits
raccoon, 192, **192**
rails
clapper, 199
sora, 132
Virginia, 132, 216
Ram Pasture, 52, 269
ravens, 103, 118, 123, 139
Ravenswood Park, 81, 269
redcedars, 36, 178
eastern, 26, **26–27**
redstarts, 144, 161
redwings, 118
Reed Brook, **120,** 121
Reed Brook Preserve, 121, 269
reeds, **244,** 245
see also phragmites reeds
Rhode Island, *iii, xviii–xix,* 206–12, **213,** 214–51
rhododendrons, 47, 178, **179,** 198, 202
Rhododendron maximum, 202
rosebay, 237
Rhododendron Sanctuary, 202
rhodora, 132, **132**
Rice City Pond Natural Area, 109
Richard T. Crane, Jr., Memorial Reservation, 82, **84–85,** 269
Robbins Swamp Wildlife Management Area, 154–55, 262
Rock House, 106
Rock House Reservation, 106, 109, **110–11,** 269
Rock Spring Wildlife Refuge, 202, **203,** 204, 262
rockrose, bushy, 250
rock tripe, 202
Rockwell, Norman (painter), 134
Rocky Neck State Park, 197–98, 262
Rocky Woods Reservation, 75, 269
Rodman's Hollow, 249–50, 273
Roland C. Nickerson State Park, 32, **33,** 36, 269

rosebay, 47, 202
Rose Ledges Trail, 96–97
rose mallow, swamp, 62, **64–65**
roses
beach, 39, **40–41,** 218, **219,** 247
multiflora, 233
Rosa rugosa, 39, **40–41,** 218, **219**
wild, 232
Royalston Falls Reservation, 94, 269

Sachuest Point National Wildlife Refuge, 224–26, **227,** 273
Sage's Ravine, 140, 269
Saggitaria montevidensis, 192
Saint Johns Ledges, 161, **162–63,** 164
salamanders, 13, 76, 132
four-toed, 133
Jefferson's, 133
spotted, 58, 133
salmon, Atlantic, xvii, 13, 96
Salmon Falls Glacial Potholes, 118, 269
salt hay, 30
saltmarsh fleabane, **44,** 45
Salt Pond Visitor Center, 36, 269
sand dollars, 86
sanderlings, 46, **46,** 171
sandpipers, xiii, 66, 86, 172, 221
solitary, 221
spotted, 199, 221
upland, 250
see also dunlins
Sandy Neck Reservation, 28, **29,** 30–31, 269
Sandy Point (RI), **206–07,** 208, 250, **251**
Sandy Point State Reservation (MA), 86, 269
Sapowet Marsh Management Area, 220, 273
sassafras, 194, 199
Saugatuck Falls Natural Area, 165
Saugatuck Reservoir, 165, 262

Saugatuck Valley Trails, 165
scarps, 37
scaup, 129, 192, 198, 218, 255
Scirpus torreyi, 192
scoters, 129, 197
seals, 45–46
    gray, 46
    harbor, 37, 42, 228, **228**
sedge, 216
Selden Creek, **146–47,** 148
Selden Neck State Park, 193, 194, **195,** 262
shad, 190
shadbush, 37, **37, 244,** 245
Sharon Audubon Center, 155–56, 262
sheep laurel, 158
shovelers, northern, 86
skimmers, 45
Skinner State Park, 98, 269
skunk, striped, 74, **75**
skunk cabbage, 169
Slater, Samuel (British expatriot), 209
Sleeping Giant State Park, 173, 176, 262
Smith-Hubbell Wildlife Sanctuary, 172
Snake Den State Park, 6, **6,** 242, 273
snakes
    copperhead, 98, 176, 178, **178**
    red-bellied, 54
    timber rattlesnake, 13, 70, 98, 139, 143, 178
    water, 76
South Cape Beach State Park, 48, 269
South River State Forest, 118, 270
South Trail, 31–32
sparrows, 247
    English, 4
    grasshopper, 250
    seaside, 199
    sharp-tailed, 199
    swamp, 81
Spartina grasses, 220
sphagnum
    see moss, sphagnum
spider, orb weaver, 171
spleenworts, 78

maidenhair, 121, 122
Split Rock Trail, 191
Spot Pond Brook Archaeological District, 71
spring beauties, 123, **142,** 143
spruce, 10, 83, 92, 114, 127, 128, 221
    black 78, 158, 242
    Norway, 249
    red, 123, 124
Squaw Peak, 138
squirrels, flying, 76
starfish, 81, 233
starlings, 4
Steep Hill, 83
Steep Rock, 164
Steep Rock Cliff, 164
Steep Rock Reservation, 164
Stellwagen Bank National Marine Sanctuary, 42, 270
Stepstone Falls, 240
Stewart B. McKinney National Wildlife Refuge, 171, 262
Stony Brook Mill Sites, 32, 270
Stony Ledge Trail, 123
sundews, 69, 78, 198, 242
swallows, 53, 86, 221, 223
    bank, 144, 247
    barn, 92
    tree, 66, 92, 144
swans, 45, 53
    mute, 192, 232–33
sweet bay magnolia, 82
sweet pepperbush, 78
sycamores, 182, 215

Talcott Mountain, 182–83
    Talcott Mountain State Park, 182, 262
Tall Spruces, 124
tamarack
    see larch
tanager, scarlet, 202, **202**
Tariffville Gorge, 183
teal, 109, 129, 192
    blue-winged, 76, 86
    green-winged, 76, 86
Teale, Edwin Way (writer), xvii, 204
terminal moraines, xii, 21, 49, 212, 245, 246, 255
terns

common, 28, 45, 51, 53, 54, 57, **57,** 86
    Forster's, 53
    least, 31, 37, 66, 82, **82,** 172, 197, 218, 233
    roseate, 229, **229**
terrapins, diamondback, 21, 30–31, **30**
Thoreau, Henry David (naturalist), xvii, 14, 21, 36, 38, 62, 72, 76, 77
thrushes, 123, 144
    Swainson's, 94
    wood, 13, 81, 233
timberdoodle
    see woodcocks
toads, Fowler's, 39
tombolos, 42, 199, 234, 245, 255
Touisset Marsh Wildlife Refuge, 218, 273
towhees, 13
Trail Wood, 204, 262
Trestle Trail, 240–41, 273
trillium, 31
    nodding, 215
    painted, 123, **142,** 143
    red, 123, 144
trout, 241
trout lilies, 81, 123, **142,** 143, 144, 215
Trustom Pond National Wildlife Refuge, 232–33, 273
Try Island, 42
tulip trees, 168
tuna, 10
tupelos, 54, **55,** 232
turkeys, wild, **i,** vi, xvii, 13, 26, **26,** 30, 105, 106, 113, 123, 127, 139, 140, 151, 193, 202, 240
Turtle Creek Preserve, 194, 262
turtles, 57, 118
    box, 178
    painted, 107, 129
    Plymouth redbelly, xvii, 30
    snapping, 76
    spotted, 58
Twain, Mark (writer), 149
Tyning, Tom (naturalist), 138
Tyringham Cobble, 133–34, 270

Under Mountain Feeder Trail, 155
Upper Goose Pond, 133, 270
Usnea, 38

Vaughan Farm Site, 241
veeries, 81
viburnum, 233
View from Mount Holyoke, Northampton, Massachusetts, after a Thunderstorm (The Oxbow) (Cole), 98, **100–01**
violets, 81
bird's-foot, 168
Canadian, 123
purple, 167
smooth yellow, 123
white, 167
vireos, 247
Virginia creeper, 233
vole, Block Island meadow, xiii, 250
vultures
black, 144
turkey, 144, 164

Wachusett Meadow Wildlife Sanctuary, 90, 92, 270
Wachusett Mountain State Reservation, 92, 270
Waconah Falls State Park, 124, 270
Wadsworth Falls, 180, **180–81**
Wadsworth Falls State Park, 178, 262
Walden Pond State Reservation, 76–77, **77,** 270
Waquoit Bay National Estuarine Research Reserve, 48, 270
warblers, 11, 13, 53, 161,

194, 204, 216, 247
black-and-white, 173
Blackburnian, 167, **167,** 205
blackpoll, 123
black-throated blue, 161, 205
black-throated green, 81, 205
blue-winged, 199
Brewster's, 90
Canada, 205
golden-winged, 161
northern parula, 37, **37,** 38
pine, 183
prairie, 31, 37, **37,** 173, 199
worm-eating, 90, 143, 161
yellow, 81, 107, 173
Washburn Island, 48, 270
Wasque Reservation, 53, 270
Watatic Mountain Wildlife Sanctuary, 94, 270
water fleas, 133
water lilies, 134, **136–37,** 240, **248,** 249
waterthrushes
Louisiana, 78, 140, 167
northern, 154
waxwings, cedar, 247
Weetamoo Woods, 220, 273
Weir Hill, 76
Wellfleet Bay Wildlife Sanctuary, **20,** 21, 42, 270
West Rock, 173, 176, **176**
West Rock Ridge State Park, 173, **174–75,** 262
Westwoods, 176–77, 178, **179,** 262
Whale Rock, 75
whales
fin, 42
humpback, 42
northern right, 42
whimbrels, 45

white-fringed orchis, **142,** 143
White Memorial Foundation, **xvi,** xvii, 158, 262
wigeon, American, 76, 86, **86,** 129
Wildcat Rock, 220
wild rice, 193
willets, 45
Williams, Roger (religious dissenter), 208, 222
Windsor Jambs, 128
Windsor Locks, 190, 263
Windsor State Forest, 127–28, 270
Wing Island, 31, 271
winterberry, 86
Winthrop, John (Massachusetts governor), 222
witchgrass, 58
witch hazel, 144
Wolf Den, 205
Wolf Pine, 132
woodcocks, 216, 217, 221
woodpeckers, pileated, 76, **76,** 78, 105, 123, 167
Worden Pond, 232
World's End Reservation, 7, **8–9,** 62, **64–65,** 66, **67,** 69, 271
wrens, 165
marsh, 81
winter, 139

Yale-Myers Forest, 205, 263
yellow corydalis, 180
yellowlegs, 199, 221, 247
greater, 45, **45**
yellow poplars, 10, 144, 149
yellowthroats, 81, 233
yew, 134
American, 182